# A Hypersexual Society

# A HYPERSEXUAL SOCIETY

## SEXUAL DISCOURSE, EROTICA, AND PORNOGRAPHY IN AMERICA TODAY

Kenneth C. W. Kammeyer

A HYPERSEXUAL SOCIETY

First published in 2008 by PALGRAVE MACMILLAN® in the US—a
division of St. Martin's Press LLC, 175 Fifth Avenue, New York, NY 10010.

Where this book is distributed in the UK, Europe and the rest of the world,
this is by Palgrave Macmillan, a division of Macmillan Publishers Limited,
registered in England, company number 785998, of Houndmills,
Basingstoke, Hampshire RG21 6XS.

Palgrave Macmillan is the global academic imprint of the above companies
and has companies and representatives throughout the world.

Palgrave® and Macmillan® are registered trademarks in the United States,
the United Kingdom, Europe and other countries.

ISBN-13: 978-0-230-60942-6
ISBN-10: 0-230-60942-2

Library of Congress Cataloging-in-Publication Data is available from the
Library of Congress.

A catalogue record of the book is available from the British Library.

Design by Scribe Inc.

First edition: November 2008

10 9 8 7 6 5 4 3 2 1

Printed in the United States of America.

# Contents

# PREFACE

The origins of this book started quite casually at a Baltimore Orioles baseball game. I was with my longtime friend and colleague George Ritzer. George had just agreed to edit a series about social issues in American society and he asked if I would be interested in writing a book about pornography in American society. The subject of pornography was one that I had previously written about, and since I had no other pressing obligations I replied, "Sure."

As I drove home from the game that night, I was thinking about sex and pornography in American society when the concept of "sexual saturation" jumped into my mind. It seemed to be a good working title for a book. I had recently written an essay about pornography in which I argued that sexual materials, including erotica and pornography, were pervasive in American society.

The "sexual saturation" title did not make the final cut, but the term will still appear at various times in this book because others have described American society as sexually saturated.

As I was working on various renditions of this book, I had a number of conversations with Ritzer and it was on one of these occasions that he suggested I consider "hypersexuality" as a title for the book. This concept is a derivative of Jean Baudrillard's overarching concept of "hyperreality," and though I was not initially drawn to his meaning of the term, I did eventually find parts of his view consistent with my original notion of sexual saturation. A conceptual analysis of the book's title will be discussed further in Chapter 1.

A second conceptual and theoretical foundation of this book is the work of the French social historian Michel Foucault. Again, it was Ritzer, my theory advisor of choice, who sensitized me to Foucault's work. While some of my interpretations of Foucault's writing may not be completely faithful to what he was saying, his work has been extremely useful to my understanding of the hypersexuality of American society. Foucault's importance will be discussed in greater detail in Chapter 2.

This book has been written over a number of years—many more than I had originally anticipated. Some of the delays were the result of personal events in my life, some were the result of my own procrastination, and others were caused by the capricious nature of the book publishing world. But the considerable amount of time it has taken to write this book does have some positive aspects. In the years when this book was "in progress" it was never far from my mind. I may not have been actively writing, but I was keeping my eyes and ears open for relevant material. Every time I read a newspaper, magazine, or book, or watched a television show or movie, or surfed the Internet, I found new and important information relating to the book. I sincerely believe the book is better for the several years it has taken to reach the point of publication.

But, of course, you the reader will make the final judgment about the usefulness of this book. You alone can decide if the book is understandable, convincing, and important.

# ACKNOWLEDGMENTS

I have already described some of the contributions of George Ritzer, but there is much more to add. He has diligently read several versions of the manuscript. His observations and suggestions have been many. Even if I didn't follow all of his suggestions, I considered all of them seriously. How lucky for me that I have had George Ritzer as an editor, colleague, and friend.

A second person who has contributed greatly to this book is Professor Joseph Slade in the College of Communication at Ohio University. Joe has read and reviewed two versions of the manuscript and done so with close attention that reflects his copious knowledge of the field. His contributions have ranged from specific corrections and suggestions to overall assessments of the book. Joe has also made a contribution to the book by his own publications in the realm of sexual representations and pornography. His work on this topic has been my most trustworthy source of information. His three volume *Pornography and Sexual Representation: A Reference Guide* is without equal as a reference in this field. I want to take this opportunity to thank him for his contributions and support.

I also want to thank Professor Meike Loe of Colgate University for giving her attention to my manuscript. I became aware of Meike because of her prize-winning essay that analyzed her work experience in a restaurant chain she called "Bazooms" (perhaps a pseudonym for a well-known restaurant chain that also uses a slang name for women's breasts). She has also written a monograph on Viagra (*The Rise of Viagra: How a Little Blue Pill Changed Sex in America*), which connected with Chapter 6 of my book. Meike gave me support and encouragement at a time when I needed it, and I do wish her the best in her sociology career.

Several other people spent varying amounts of time working on and trying to improve earlier versions of the manuscript. I will not be identifying them by name because most were employees of a previous potential publisher (editors, developmental editors, and so forth). Another was an outside reader who, coyly or overcautiously, chose to remain anonymous. I believe all of these people were sincerely interested in improving my book, even though most wanted me to write a different book. Yet all did make contributions: sometimes correcting grammatical and substantive errors, sometimes providing new sources and suggesting new directions, and very often causing me to rethink what I had written. To these unnamed people I want to give my thanks for their many hours of work.

For this now-to-be published book I am grateful for the efforts of several key people at Palgrave Macmillan. In particular I want to thank editor Luba Ostashevsky, who quickly saw the possibilities for my manuscript and recommended publication. Her assistant at the time was Joanna Mericle, who was an excellent facilitator, and I wish her the best in her new career. Finally, Matt Robison handled the production process, and he (along with Dale Rohrbaugh at Scribe) was very understanding about my inexperience with the "tracking" system of copyediting. The resulting copyediting was excellent and gave me complete confidence as I went through the final version of the manuscript. Thanks to all.

Another set of people, while not generally in the scholarly world, has continued to show an interest in this project. Their interest has usually been expressed with some version of the question, "How is the book coming along Ken?" This question, while revealing their interest, has also acted as a spur to keep me moving along. I will name a few here, hoping I have not forgotten anyone. Two of my college friends Don Briggs and Ed Dansdill often ask about the book and both have promised to read it. We'll see. Our Florida friends Oli and Systa Jonsson, Don and Sharon Smith White, and Rita Tabish continue to express their interest in the book whenever we see them. Our wonderful friends Richard Pollack and Susan Roberts never fail to ask about the book and promote it to their friends. David Meyers, from Kansas has maintained an interest, as has George Nielson, my favorite PhD student of many years ago. Tom and Helen Daugherty, our southern Maryland friends, and our neighbor friends Bob and Susan Fischell also occasionally inquire about how the book is going. My golfing buddy, Bob Elwell, and his wife, Christine, have also kept up with the progress of the book (or sometimes the lack of progress).

Our special friend Ritva Ross, who divides her time between Finland and England, gets a special acknowledgment here because when I brought up the name Bob Guccione (creator of *Penthouse* magazine—see Chapter 4) in a recent phone conversation, she casually replied, "Oh I knew him when was starting the magazine in London. He asked me to pose for the first centerfold." It is typical of Ritva that she should mention this about four decades after it happened. Oh how I wish she had appeared in the premier issue *Penthouse*.

Sonia's children, Siobhan and Sean (and his wife Sherry), as well as my children, Leslie (and her husband Scott) and Robert, often ask what I am doing and then listen attentively when I detail what has been happening with the book. I'm sure they are all waiting with bated breath to read the final product.

My wife, Sonia, has had enough time to have had many reactions to this book. She has been excited, hopeful, encouraging, distracted, attentive, supportive, and most of all, tolerant of my ongoing interest in the subject matter of this book. Not only tolerant, but always keeping her eye out for anything that she thinks may be of interest to me. We have discussed many aspects of the book because when I wanted to talk things over she was always interested. I have been very lucky to have had Sonia with me, supporting me with this and all else in my life.

# SEXUAL MATERIALS AND PORNOGRAPHY IN TODAY'S SOCIETY

Americans today are avid consumers (Ritzer 2005) who desire an ever-larger number of products, from video cell phones and plasma-screen television sets to multiple vehicles and mansion-size homes. The appetite of Americans for consumption has been heightened by recent developments in the *means of consumption*—the various venues and environments in which consumers are enticed to consume more and more things (Ritzer 2005, 2). A brief examination of the consumption patterns of Americans—and the environments in which they purchase things—will provide a quick glimpse into how much contemporary American culture is saturated with sexual discourse, erotica, and pornography.

The means of consumption in the United States are many. Among the most prominent and showy are theme parks, gambling casinos and their accompanying hotels, tourist resorts, and cruise ships. While these are the showplaces of consumption, most American consumers shop and spend their money in the very familiar shopping malls, followed by big-box stores, home-shopping television networks, and online shopping Web sites. Shopping malls offer American consumers nearly everything and anything they might want and are constantly being enhanced to provide an ever-more enticing shopping environment (Ritzer 2005).[1]

Our exploration of sexual discourse, erotica, and pornography in today's society will begin with the examination of a standard American shopping mall.

## A TOUR THROUGH AN AMERICAN SHOPPING MALL

Shopping malls of the *enclosed* type first came into existence a little more than a half century ago (Gladwell 2004; Ritzer 2005).[2] Enclosed shopping malls may differ in some ways, but they all have essentially the same basic structure. The Bal Harbor mall in Miami Beach is decidedly more upscale, for example, than the Crossroads Center in Waterloo, Iowa. And some shopping malls, such as the Mall of America in Minneapolis and Sawgrass Mills Mall in Sunrise, Florida, are outstandingly large. But all contemporary malls share a similar look and feel.

A walk through a typical shopping mall provides a convenient window on the contemporary U.S. retail world. Along the way, we pass stores selling clothing, kitchen supplies, cosmetics, furniture, appliances, shoes, books, records, vitamins, greeting cards, and various other items commonly required for everyday living. The shopping mall is hardly the first place where one would look for sexual materials, and especially not erotica and pornography. A closer look, however, yields some surprising results.

One of the first display windows to catch the eye is Victoria's Secret, which has built its reputation by offering romantic and distinctly skimpy women's lingerie (although its current line also includes skirts, tops, dresses, pants, and other clothing). Victoria's Secret's merchandizing secret has been to sell "sexiness" along with its clothing—a type of sexiness that has come to be comfortable for most American consumers.[3] In her insightful book *At Home with Pornography* (1998), Jane Juffer cites Victoria's Secret as a primary example of the "domestication of pornography," in which pornography and erotica have been integrated into the everyday lives of women (and men as well). According to Juffer, sexually explicit products and materials have been socially legitimized in contemporary society, and not just by Victoria's Secret.[4]

Victoria's Secret has essentially "domesticated" the selling of sexy underwear, but in an earlier time, the sexy lingerie market was dominated by a more-daring, less-domesticated marketer: Frederick's of Hollywood (more on this later). By adding just a touch of subtlety and sophistication to their apparel and presentation, Victoria's Secret has created a shopping environment in which most American women can feel comfortable browsing (as well as being seen). Men, who are typically shopping for gifts for their wives or girlfriends, are also able to shop there, usually with only moderate levels of discomfort.

Today, the Victoria's Secret catalog has become a cultural icon, appearing in American mailboxes with some regularity. The shapely models in the catalog are sexually interesting to both the men and women of a household, as well as to teenagers. As a point of historical comparison, today's Victoria's Secret catalog typically features more sexually provocative photographs than those that appeared in the "girlie magazines" of mid-twentieth century America. In a sardonic observation about the catalog's sexual content, William Safire, a conservative political columnist and language/grammar maven, once wrote, "I spend an inordinate amount of time reading Victoria's Secret catalogues, looking for errors. To avoid disapproving stares from colleagues, I slip the catalogue inside my copy of *Hustler*" (Safire 2001, 28).

Some shopping malls feature specialty stores that go a step beyond Victoria's Secret, offering more explicit versions of sexy lingerie, along with a variety of other sex-related products. As we noted earlier, in the pre–Victoria's Secret era it was Frederick's of Hollywood that dominated the market of sexy lingerie, but with a distinctly raunchy style—picture a bra with the images of two hands coming from behind, each hand covering a breast. Frederick's stores were sometimes found in shopping malls and still are occasionally, but it has always been primarily a mail-order business.

In today's consumer world, imitators of Frederick's can be readily found, sometimes in shopping malls, but more often in out-of-the-way shopping areas. To locate them one can check the yellow pages under "lingerie-retail," or search the Web where one will find sites such as www.nightdreams.com and www.lockeddoor.com. The retail outlets usually have similarly suggestive names: "Forbidden Fruit," "Luv'N Time," "Taste of Indulgence." The merchandise includes such provocative items as women's panties with open crotches and bras with holes for the nipples, along with vibrators, dildos, ben wa balls, leather and latex apparel, and "exotic shoes."[5]

Another clothing merchandiser that flirts with sexuality is Abercrombie & Fitch. This upscale clothing store is aimed primarily at youthful customers and often features handsome young men, usually with bare chests revealed, waiting at the door of the store welcoming customers, especially young women. The sexual invitation is obvious.

Abercrombie & Fitch has sold various clothing items that have carried suggestive words and slogans. At one time, the store tried to market a line of thong underwear for preteen girls, with the words "Eye Candy" and "Wink, Wink" printed on the front. When enough parents objected to this item, it was withdrawn. Much more obvious was a T-shirt for young women with the words, "Who Needs Brains when You Have These?" written across the chest (http://en.wikipedia.org/wuju/Abercrombie_&_Fitch).

Abercrombie & Fitch's most blatant venture into sexuality came in 2003 when its quarterly catalog presented photographs of topless and bare-bottomed young women, often in group settings. The cover teaser promised "group sex and more." An article in the catalog, written by a sex educator, encouraged sexual experimentation, including sexual three-somes and group masturbation (Parvaz 2003).

Going back to other types of stores typically found in shopping malls, we may come across a bookstore with its wide array of books and maga-zines including many with sexual, erotic, and pornographic content. *Playboy*, *Penthouse*, and *Hustler*[6] have been standard fare in many book-stores for decades. But also on the racks may be an innocuously named magazine called *2: The Magazine for Couples*. This magazine provides another example of "the domestication of pornography." A recent article, for example, instructs couples on how to make their own pornographic video at home (or some other private setting). Readers are encouraged to bring a third party to do the filming and to operate the camcorder. The article also offers advice on potential logistical problems the couple may encounter along the way. For example: Is the camcorder to be handheld or placed on some stationary place, such as a tripod or on the night table? Each has its advantages and drawbacks for making a good pornographic video at home (Carlson 2004).

In addition to the large bookstores, there are a number of other retail stores that stock a wide variety of sexual and pornographic magazines. These are displayed along with hundreds of other special-interest maga-zines (e.g., *Barron's*, *Golf for Women*, and *Wired*). As one example, a Hallmark gift store in suburban Maryland offers the usual array of greet-ing cards, wrapping paper, and tchotchkes, but it also features at least a hundred sex and nudity magazines. While these particular magazines are partially covered and are often plastic wrapped, they are nonetheless clearly visible to all the customary Hallmark shoppers. The women behind the checkout counter, who usually appear to be middle class and oriented to selling greeting cards, seem to handle the sale of sexual and pornographic magazines with admirable aplomb.

Going back to bookstores, almost all will have a "classics" section that will be selling books that were once illegal in the United States. Titles that were once considered obscene but are now the standard fare of any well-stocked bookstore include James Joyce's *Ulysses*, D. H. Lawrence's *Lady Chatterley's Lover*, John Cleland's *Fanny Hill*, and Henry Miller's daring duo *Tropic of Cancer* and *Tropic of Capricorn*, and many others (see Chapter 4).

Among the best sellers in well-stocked bookstores one will find many books with sexually explicit material—some by major authors, others by unknowns. As an example, the prominent American novelist John Updike published *Villages* (2004), a book that has been described by one reviewer as "a wondrous sexual and social retrospective of small-town living over the last half-century" (Weldon 2004, 3). Among Updike's many published novels, quite a number describe in vivid detail the sexual practices of the residents of suburban and small-town America.

Other sexually explicit, but nonfiction titles available in a mall bookstore might include *A Mind of Its Own: A Cultural History of the Penis* (Friedman 2001) or, for gender balance, *Nymphomania: A History* by Carol Groneman (2000). Catherine Millet's (2002) sexual autobiography, *The Sexual Life of Catherine M.*, may also be on the shelves of the nonfiction section (Millet 2002). (This astonishingly explicit account of Millet's sexual life will be described in greater detail in Chapter 4.)

Browsing along a typical bookstore table for new novels, there are usually many other sexually explicit books. Some of the titles in this category might include *The Bride Stripped Bare* (Anonymous 2003),[7] *Candy Licker: An Urban Erotic Tale* by Noire (2005), and *Kiss and Tango: Looking for Love in Buenos Aires* (Palmer 2005). These along with dozens of other sexually provocative books can easily be found on the up-front displays of any major bookstore. The reader who is looking for sexual material in contemporary novels will have no difficulty finding it.

Today's bookstores also often devote an entire section to what is euphemistically called "erotica." Here one may find Marcy Sheiner's anthology *Best Women's Erotica* (Sheiner 2004), along with related Sheiner titles, *Ripe Fruit: Erotica for Well Seasoned Lovers* (Sheiner 2002) and *Best of the Best: Women's Erotica* (Sheiner 2005). Also in the erotica section, one might find *Rescue Me: An Erotic Novel* (Clark 2005), *Never Enough* (Lloyd 2003), *The Almond: The Sexual Awakening of a Muslim Woman* (Nedjma 2004), and *Secrets of a Gay Marine Porn Star* (Marritt 2005). The punningly titled *Love in Vein, II* (Brite 2004) is intended for readers with a special taste for vampire sex.

The young-adult sections of mall bookstores also feature some highly sexual materials, with many volumes providing realistic depictions of the sexual activities of contemporary young people (see Chapter 4).

The calendar and sports sections of mall bookstores may provide glimpses of the long-popular *Sports Illustrated* "swimsuit issue"; the title is, of course, a euphemism for the magazine's array of photographs of scantily attired, well-tanned female bodies. Judging from the yearly sales of this issue, sexy young women may have surpassed baseball and football as "America's national sport" (more on the swimsuit issue in Chapter 4).

Moving along through the shopping mall, we might come across a music emporium, offering CDs and tapes that also contain sexually explicit material. Contemporary recording artists like Lil' Kim, Concetta

Kirschner, Princess Superstar, and Janet Jackson often compete for having the most sexually daring lyrics.

As an example, Princess Superstar's "Bad Babysitter" is typical of the recordings on sale. (A video is also available.) The song has some detailed sexual language. It describes a babysitter who tells the young boy she is watching that at 6:00 P.M. it's time to go to to bed because her boyfriend has arrived and wants her to "give him head." She goes on to warn the boy that where he sits to watch TV may be sticky "cause I sucked his dicky" (Princess Superstar Is, Rapster Records, Berlin, 2001).

A typical shopping mall will also have a multiplex theater showing everything from action/violence and drama to romantic comedy, teenage adventure, and family films. With the exception of the latter, the rest generally offer some combination of nudity, sexual talk, or sexual activity (probably simulated but made to look real). Profanity is standard fare in many films, including the increasingly common "fuck" in all its possible forms (see Achenbach 2006).

For those who want even more sex in their movies, there is always the video store. In the major franchises, such as Blockbuster, the sexual fare is usually limited to mass-distribution, R-rated movies. But local "Mom & Pop" stores often have a partitioned-off section that provides abundant varieties of sexually explicit material. The sex presented in these X-rated films is not simulated (as it is in Hollywood films); it is the real thing. For heterosexual, gay, and lesbian viewers, there are plenty of choices. For those who are interested in something stronger, there are also sadomasochistic titles. (Chapter 7 will provide a more extensive examination of the pornographic film industry.)

Moving along in the shopping mall, we may come across a comic book store. The comic book store is one venue that many Americans would not readily associate with sex. Generally, comic books bring to mind the super heroes of the past: Superman, Captain Marvel, Batman, and Spiderman (Wright 2001). Today's comic book store, however, will probably feature an adult section much like the X-rated section of a Mom & Pop video store. Usually, the adult section is located near the back of the store, and young customers are shooed away if they happen to drift into the forbidden area. For adults, however, the selection of sex comics is abundant and the material is extremely graphic (see Chapter 4).

If walking through the mall has left one hungry, why not stop for a bite to eat at Hooters, a popular food franchise built on the principle that young women's breasts will bring in customers?[8] Despite (or because of) the blatant sexism of the Hooters concept, it is a franchise that continues to thrive. Started in 1983, Hooters Inc. now has more than 250 franchise locations in 40 U.S. states, as well as Asia, Aruba, Canada, England, Mexico, Singapore, Taiwan, the Bahamas, and Puerto Rico (http://www .hootersofamerica.com). The corporation's most recent commercial venture is a Las Vegas hotel/casino. Not among the glitzy mega-hotels of the Vegas Strip, but it does offer the possibility of "hanging out" with the "world-famous Hooters Girls."

Hooters' Web site describes its restaurants as having a casual beach theme featuring '50s and '60s jukebox music, sports on television, and a casual American menu. Hooters' public relations office is candid about the importance of the young women in short shorts who serve the food: "The element of female sex appeal is prevalent in the restaurants, and the company believes the Hooters Girl is as socially acceptable as a Dallas Cowboy cheerleader, *Sports Illustrated* swimsuit model, or Radio City Rockette" (http://www.hootersofamerica.com). The Web site further declares, "Sex appeal is legal and it sells."

## SHOPPING BEYOND THE MALL

Not all American retail stores are found in malls. Supermarkets, for example, are more likely to be found outside of malls, as are many other all-purpose stores (such as Wal-Mart, Target, K-Mart, and Costco). The latter group, along with the electronics, technology, and computer stores (Best Buy, Circuit City, Comp USA, and others), are commonly known as the "big-box" stores. These stores also offer American consumers a variety sexual materials and pornography. We will begin by examining the most conventional of American retail stores: the supermarket.

## THE SUPERMARKET

For most Americans, grocery shopping usually involves a trip to the supermarket, where the basic products are foods and drinks. The most "sinful" merchandise that one would expect to find are the cheesecakes in the bakery department and the Dove bars or the latest Ben and Jerry's concoction in the ice cream freezers. Plastic-encased copies of *Playboy*, *Hustler*, and *Penthouse* are often found in convenience stores, but one doesn't usually expect to find sexual materials among the bagels and the broccoli of an average supermarket.

But a closer look will turn up some sexual materials even in this innocent setting. We can begin at the checkout counter. As we wait, we scan the various tabloids (*National Enquirer*, *Star*, *Globe*, *Vibe*, *In Touch*), their front covers featuring photos of scandal-plagued celebrities, accompanied by lurid headlines. The troubles of celebrities include marriage breakups, adulterous affairs, sexual perversions, and various other types of sexual scandals. Inside the magazines are photos of female celebrities in their latest Versace, Armani, or Givenchy gowns, revealing more breasts, thighs, and belly buttons than might be seen on an average day at the beach.

The checkout-aisle display also includes *Cosmopolitan*, its cover featuring airbrushed photos that almost, but never quite, reveal the models' nipples. The magazine cover's teasing headlines are now such a familiar part of our culture that they have almost become self-parodies. Anyone can easily create fictitious versions of the *Cosmo* teaser, such as "Turn On Your Man by Using Duct Tape," or "Three Ways to Achieve an Orgasm While Driving (Safely)."

Other magazines found in most major supermarkets provide a smorgasbord of sex. Consider the venerable "men's magazine" *Esquire* and the contemporary mass-market men's magazine *Maxim*. Neither of these magazines is especially daring in today's sex-and-pornography world, but each has enough high-quality photographs of sexy, semi-clothed women to attract the interest (and dollars) of large numbers of male consumers. In July 2005, *Maxim* reported the results of its contest to find the "10 sexiest women in America," complete with photographs. *Esquire* in 2006 was searching for "The Sexiest Woman Alive," and in 2008 it was searching once again.

*Vanity Fair* is another mass distribution magazine with an abundance of sexual material. The March 2006 issue featured on its cover nude photographs of two popular young actresses, Scarlett Johansson and Keira Knightly. Their photos are part of "Tom Ford's Hollywood," which offers "47 steamy pages" of photographs of the hottest stars (*Vanity Fair* 2006, 34). Among the dozens of full-page photographs in the issue, one finds the ubiquitous Jennifer Anniston, who manages to pose decorously wearing only a pair of knee-high boots; Sienna Miller, who starred in the movie *Casanova*, is lying in repose, naked from the waist; young actor Jason Schwartzman, photographed with an unidentified naked female gazing at him; Pamela Anderson and Mamie Van Doren (the latter a sexual icon of an earlier era), both with their breasts falling from their costumes; George Clooney, as a director on a movie set, with a baker's dozen of female assistants, all in their panties and bras.

For years, magazine advertising has used sexual images of women as a way of attracting the attention of men. Today's magazine advertising is more blatantly sexual, whether it is directed at men or at women. Whether touting jeans, perfumes/colognes, or alcohol, sexual images are found in nearly every mass-circulation magazine on the market today.

This quick look at the supermarket has considered only a few of the many examples of sexual materials and products that pervade the everyday consumer marketplace. We haven't even mentioned the prominent condom displays that promise consumers the ultimate in sexual pleasures. Only a few decades ago, condoms could only be found under the counters of drugstores, with no visible advertising.

## ELECTRONICS, TECHNOLOGY, AND COMPUTER STORES

When looking for electronic and technological equipment (computers, big-screen televisions, CD, DVD, and VCR players, etc.), many Americans today shop in big-box stores. It would be natural to assume that such high-tech environments would be nearly pristine, until we examine the software section more closely to find video games that have moved far beyond the Pac Man and the Mario Brothers games of yesteryear. Recent news reports have revealed that the popular "Grand Theft Auto," already suspect among many media watchdogs and parents, can now be augmented with software that introduces sexual/pornographic images into the scenario.

A number of video games today are designed to provide access to sex and nudity. The video-game industry is now a 7 billion dollar business, and the game players are primarily teenagers. Many teenagers who started playing video games in the 1980s and 1990s are now young adults, who, according to the Entertainment Software Association, are now the marketing targets of the industry (Oldenburg 2004, C10). These adults can now purchase any video game they desire, including products with explicit sexual content.

The video-game industry has developed its own rating system with "E" for everyone, "T" for teenagers, "M" for mature, and "A" for adults. It is impossible to determine how diligent retailers are in following this rating system, but most interested teenagers or preteens can easily find someone eighteen or older to purchase an "M" or "A" rated game, or find access to such games in their own homes or the homes of friends.

One of the most popular "M"-rated video games to be found at the typical computer store is "The Guy Game," produced by TopHeavy Studios. The game features a quiz show in which an MC asks trivia questions of bikini-clad young women (real women, not computer generated images). The banter between the MC and the young women is suggestive and raunchy, but the real goal of the game is to answer the questions asked by the MC correctly and then to predict whether the young women will be able to answer the fairly simple questions as well. If a young woman fails to answer a question, she must take off her bikini top, but her breasts remain (at least temporarily) covered electronically by what male players call "knocker blockers" (Oldenburg 2004, C10). The pixels are gradually removed as the player answers more questions correctly, with the ultimate objective of removing all the pixels to reveal the woman's breasts. According to the game's developer, "The Guy Game" is "geared toward guys about things guys like–competing against your buddies and topless nudity" (Oldenburg 2004, C10).

"The Guy Game" is just one example of sex and nudity in the video game industry. The Playboy corporation is currently producing a game called "Playboy: The Mansion," in which the objective is to build up a financial empire like Hugh Hefner's. In the course of the game, Playboy bunnies are frequently on view. Another popular game, "Singles: Flirt Up Your Life," allows the player to develop sexual relationships. These relationships can be between men and women, women only, or men only, and the skill of the player determines how far the relationship will go sexually.

The primary merchandise of a computer store is, of course, the computer itself, which provides users access to the Internet and, therefore, unlimited sexual materials. We will discuss the enormous volume of sexual material and pornography on the Internet in Chapter 9. The Internet is easily the world's largest repository of sexual materials and pornography. The "secret museums" of Europe and the celebrated pornography collections of major museums (such as the French *Bibliotheque Nationale* in Paris or the British Museum in London) are paltry compared with the amount of pornography on the Internet today.

### SEXUAL EMPORIA

For those with more adventurous sexual tastes, there are the sexual emporia, large stores oriented completely to sexual materials. While not quite "big-box" stores on the order of Best Buy or Sam's Club, these stores are springing up today in various places around the country.

Just outside of Milford, Connecticut, for example, a large new store called "Penthouse Boutique" offers all manner of sexual materials (National Public Radio 2004), including adult videos, sex-related clothing and paraphernalia (whips, chains, leather suits, etc.), and a wide variety of additional sexual products.

Not everyone in Milford, Connecticut, is happy about this new business in the community. In a radio interview about the issue, one city official openly expressed his dismay about the new store, but also admitted that there was little he could do about it. "They are protected by the First Amendment of the Constitution," he acknowledged (National Public Radio 2004). In the same radio interview, a local minister in Milford said that he was less resigned to the existence of a large sex store in the community, suggesting that the existence of such stores could be limited or eliminated through restrictive zoning laws, a tactic that has been successfully used by many local communities to keep sex-related retail establishments away from schools, churches, and residential areas.[9]

Similar sex emporia have sprung up throughout the state of Ohio, including the "Erotic Empire" and "In the Mood," as well as a chain called "The Lion's Den." Some citizens regard the growth of such stores as an unstoppable trend in the commercial advance of sexual materials and pornography. One individual interviewed on NPR explained, "Sex stores are booming over the last decade. This is capitalism at its best."

This opening chapter has provided a brief look at the availability of sexual materials and pornography in the most immediate parts of the consumer world. Little has been said so far about commercial communications media, such as newspapers, radio, and television. Nor have we given attention to the academic community or the sex-therapy world, both of which contribute to the abundance of sexual material in America today. In the chapters that follow, we will explore all of these areas and their contribution our hypersexual society.

## A NOTE ON TERMS USED IN THE TITLE

The title of this book is *A Hypersexual Society: Sexual Discourse, Erotica, and Pornography in America Today*. The key terms in the title need to be defined and discussed before we can move on to the body of the book.

First and foremost is the term *hypersexual*. In the mass media and on the Internet the term hypersexual is now often found as an adjective to describe the level of sexual saturation in American society (key in "hypersexual society" on any Internet search engine). In the scholarly world, hypersexuality was introduced by the late French social theorist Jean Baudrillard as a prime example of his overarching theoretical concept "hyperreality." Hyperreality, according to Baudrillard, describes the simulated[10] images and representations of everyday reality (from magazine photographs to television programs to theme-based amusement parks) that have become increasingly pervasive in the United States and many other contemporary societies (Baudrillard 1986/1989). Because of our constant exposure to mediated simulations of reality (through the entertainment industry, corporate advertising, etc.), "reality" (the realm of unmediated, everyday activities and experiences) has been overwhelmed and displaced by "hyperreality." According to Baudrillard, society has become so inundated with the often-spectacular simulations and images of the hyperreal that it is now nearly impossible to distinguish what is real or to separate reality from the simulations. Simply put, we have become so consumed and captivated by the nonstop flow of simulated words and images around us that we can no longer tell the difference between our "real" lives and our lives as readers, viewers, and consumers. Or even if we can tell the difference, we may prefer the beauty, energy, and excitement of the representation over that which it represents. In the words of George Ritzer, Baudrillard's hyperreality is "a simulation that is more real than real, more beautiful than beautiful, truer than true" (Ritzer 1997, 96).[11] Not surprisingly, Baudrillard's favorite example of hyperreality is Disneyland, a fantasy world that far exceeds the real world as it exists around us (Baudrillard 1983).

For Baudrillard, the *hypersexual* is an extension of hyperreality into the realm of human intimacy. Just as the hyperreal has displaced the real world, so has the hypersexual (mediated simulations of sexual experience) overwhelmed and displaced the actual coupling of human bodies. "Sexuality," he explains, "does not fade into sublimation, repression and morality, but fades much more surely into the more sexual than sex: porn[ography] the hypersexuality contemporaneous with the hyperreal" (Baudrillard 1983/1990, 11).

Pornography and obscenity are therefore simulations (photographs, films, narratives, virtual experiences, etc.) that take the place of real sex. Baudrillard writes, "what is obscene is not the copulation of bodies, but rather the mental redundancy of sex, the escalation of truth which leads to the cold vertigo of the pornographic" (Baudrillard 1983/1990, 54). Hypersexuality for Baudrillard has two essential characteristics: (1) the overwhelming abundance of simulated sexual images, narratives, and representations at all levels of society; and (2) the tendency of these mediated simulations to undermine and take the place of unmediated sexual experience.

While we have gained some insights into hypersexuality from Baudrillard, this book will concentrate almost exclusively on the first of these characteristics (the increasing abundance of sexual materials, erotica, and pornography throughout society). We will not attempt to evaluate the impact of our hypersexual society on traditional, unmediated sexual experience, though we will give some attention to those critics of pornography who believe that pornography addicts have forsaken real sex for pornographic sex. Instead, our primary interest in this book will be to document the pervasiveness of sexual discourse, erotica, and pornography in American society today. From this perspective *a hypersexual society is a society in which sexual discourse, erotica, and pornography are persistently present in almost all aspects of the society.* The subsequent chapters of this book will provide ample evidence for labeling American society as a hypersexual society.

Two other prominent terms are used in the title: *erotica* and *pornography*. In the past, countless jurists, legislators, and theorists (as well as opponents and supporters of sexual materials) have tried to distinguish between the two terms. Many who have devoted their attention to this matter have tried their best to argue that erotica is one thing and pornography is something else. Their attempts to establish clear-cut and objective distinctions have not been successful.

Both erotica and pornography deal with explicit presentations of sexual activity, either through words or visual images, and attempts to distinguish between the two inevitably require discerning the motivations of the creator (which can often only be inferred) and the reader or viewer (which rely heavily on the subjective expectations and intentions of the individual). In short, to make a distinction between pornography and erotica, it is necessary to make inferences about the producer and the person who reads or views sexual materials.

As a brief example of how difficult it is to distinguish between erotica and pornography, we can employ a distinction made by many contemporary feminists. This distinction, which probably emanates from Gloria Steinem's 1970s, groundbreaking essay (see Chapter 3), is that erotica is sexual material that does not degrade women, while pornography does. As soon as one gets beyond the extreme examples, however, Steinem's distinction becomes hopelessly unclear. Most would agree that magazines such as *Hustler*, as well as similarly explicit Internet Web sites (e.g., www.bangbus.com, www.gangbangsquad.com) intentionally emphasize the degradation of women. For each of these examples, however, there are literally hundreds of other examples of books, magazines, and Internet Web sites that present explicit sexual material in which it is nearly impossible to discern whether women are being exploited or not. Consider, for example, romantic novels, which are almost exclusively purchased by women but often include sex scenes that some readers might interpret as degrading to women. As we will see in Chapter 4, romance novels are sometimes divided into five different categories: "sweet, spicy, steamy, sizzling, and savage." The "savage" category includes books that depict violence against women, including rape, kidnap, seduction, or prostitution (Bartlett 2001). Are "savage" romantic novels, then, to be considered pornography, while all other romantic novels are erotica? Some would say yes, but many devotees of romance novels might disagree.

As another example, consider the genre of lesbian literature that features sadomasochism between women. According to Califida (1994), sadomasochism is one dimension of lesbian sex, and thus lesbian erotic literature routinely includes sadomasochistic texts. Are such works to be considered pornography, or erotica?

As another example, heterosexual writer Daphne Merkin created a literary and cultural sensation when she wrote a 1996 article for *The New Yorker* magazine in which she described how being spanked by men sexually arouses her (more in Chapter 4). Is Merkin therefore being degraded as a woman when she acknowledges that it is sexually exciting for her to be spanked?

The pornography-versus-erotica question is even further confounded by the conflicting and haphazard ways in which the term pornography is used by different individuals and groups. Among culturally conservative people, especially religious conservatives, almost any reference to sex (including sex education and references to contraception) or any display of the nude body (even in celebrated works of art) is often labeled pornographic. When the word pornography is so loosely thrown around, it is impossible to settle on a workable definition.

For all of these reasons it has not been possible for us to escape the conclusion that both pornography and erotica are—like beauty—in the eye of the beholder. This leads to the conclusion that whenever sexual materials are viewed positively (for whatever reason) they are labeled as erotica, whereas sexual materials that are viewed negatively (again, for whatever reason) are labeled as pornography. In this book we will therefore make no hard and fast distinctions between the two terms. When we use either term it will be appropriate to the context of the discussion.[12]

A final term used in the title is *sexual discourse*. As we will explain more fully in Chapter 2, sexual discourse is a critically important concept in the work of Michel Foucault, the French philosopher/historian who contributed to the development of postmodern social theory and the historical study of sex (Foucault 1978, 1984/1985; Ritzer 1997). The word *discourse* in everyday usage simply means verbal statements or verbal exchanges, either in written or spoken form. Thus, sexual discourse is any written or spoken statement that involves sex, sexual behavior, and sexuality. Chapter 3 will elaborate on Foucault's crucially important idea that attempts to repress and censor sexual discourse invariably have the paradoxical effect of *increasing* the amount of sexual discourse. Sexual discourse, as we will see throughout this book, has many sources and speaks from many different perspectives. The sources of sexual discourse range from academic scholarship and research, to sex therapy, to legislation and judicial rulings, to the entertainment world, and increasingly to the cyber world. The perspectives of sexual discourse range from those that openly and enthusiastically support all forms of sexual material to those that oppose almost every form of sexual material. All of these sources of, and perspectives on, sexual materials contribute to the hypersexuality of American society.

CHAPTER 2

# THEORETICAL FOUNDATION AND CONCEPTUAL TOOLS

Political pundits, as well as many average Americans, today often divide the United States into two categories: the "Red" states and the "Blue" states. This distinction grew out of the 2004 presidential election in which the Red states were those that voted Republican (the entire South and much of the Midwest) and the Blue states, were those that voted Democratic (the population centers of California and New York, along with New England and the Mid-Atlantic states). In general, the Red states represent a conservative/traditional point of view, while the Blue states reflect a more liberal/progressive outlook. The Red state–Blue state divide is only a broad-brush characterization, but it does draw attention to the deep divisions among Americans about what has come to be called the "social values" debate.

For the conservatives/traditionalists social values tend to revolve around a commitment to traditional family life and religion (almost exclusively a belief in Christianity), while the liberals/progressives are more likely to be committed to social issues such as racial justice, economic equality, and personal freedom. Both sides have strong feelings about sexual matters, in particular issues associated with abortion, gay and lesbian lifestyles, sexual abstinence for the unmarried (especially teenagers), and the prevalence and availability of sexual material, erotica, and pornography.

While the conservatives/traditionalists and the liberals/progressives have very different views about these social issues, there is one point about which they agree: American society is saturated with sexual materials. In this sense, almost everyone agrees that American society is a hypersexual society, a society in which sexual discourse, erotica, and pornography are pervasive. Many writers, theorists, and social commentators have addressed the question of why sexual materials are so pervasive in today's society. Some of these analysts come at the question from an "anti-sex" perspective, while others take a "pro-sex" position.

Two twentieth-century intellectuals epitomize these opposing points of view: E. Michael Jones, a conservative Catholic scholar; and the French philosopher/historian Michel Foucault. The positions of these two scholars illustrate the two sides of the debate about sexual materials in contemporary society. Each offers an explanation for why sexual behavior and sexuality are so open and unrestrained in contemporary society

## E. MICHAEL JONES—AN ATTACK ON SEXUAL LIBERATION

E. Michael Jones is a leading representative of a relatively small set of intellectuals who deplore the sexual excesses of contemporary society (Jones 2000). His book, *Libido Dominandi: Sexual Liberation and Political Control*, is a scathing, six hundred–page attack on the sexual liberation in Western European countries, and especially in the United States. For Jones, the term sexual liberation is a pejorative that covers a variety of destructive social trends and activities, including birth control, abortion, acceptance of gay and lesbian sexual activities, unconventional sex (such as sadomasochism), and, most importantly, pornography.

For Jones, sexual liberation is historically rooted in the radical notions that anticipated and followed the French Revolution. It should be noted that Jones is not alone in viewing the French Revolution as a seminal event in European history that led to increases in sexual freedom and pornography in Western societies, though his assessment is more consistently negative than the positions of other social historians (see Hunt 1993c; Verstraete 1999).

Jones argues that before the French Revolution the Catholic Church maintained moral order and kept sexual behavior in check in continental Europe. The breakdown of religious authority opened the way for libertines, freethinkers, and all manner of immoral people who then flooded Western societies with "filthy" pornographic materials and "lewd" descriptions of sexual deviance.

Jones identifies a variety of other social theorists and activists who have contributed to the societal breakdown of moral authority. A special place is given to eighteenth-century English utopian William Godwin and his wife, the early feminist Mary Wollstonecraft (Gordon 2005). Jones also faults the writings of the early nineteenth-century social philosopher Auguste Comte, the founder of sociology. Even though most contemporary sociologists view Comte as politically conservative, Jones regards his creation of a "science of society . . . an ersatz religion" as an attempt to replace the Catholic Church (Jones 2000, 15–16, 92–93).

Not surprisingly, Jones charges the infamous Marquis de Sade, the eighteenth-century French aristocrat who wrote explicit sadomasochistic novels, with brutalizing sex and lowering moral values of French society. Jones credits Sade with "firing the first shot of the sexual revolution" (Jones 2000, 20).

Jones also selects three other individuals for special opprobrium: Sigmund Freud, the early twentieth-century Viennese physician who founded psychoanalysis; Wilhelm Reich, a German follower of Freud and author of *The Sexual Revolution*, which played a key role in the sexual revolution of the 1960s; and Alfred Kinsey, a biology professor at the University of Indiana in the 1930s and 1940s who revolutionized the scientific study of sexual behavior. All three, according to Jones, provided illegitimate scholarly arguments for sexual liberation. (We too will point out the important roles played by Freud and Kinsey in Chapters 6 and 5, respectively.)

Jones reserves a special rebuke for John D. Rockefeller III, who headed the Rockefeller Foundation, which gave financial support to Kinsey's research and subsidized the family planning (birth control) movement.

Jones also condemns several other twentieth-century notables, some famous, some now nearly forgotten. Among this list of culprits are: John B. Watson, the founder of psychological behaviorism; Edward Bernays, a pioneer of modern advertising; Betty Friedan, a leading advocate of mid-twentieth-century feminism; Hugh Hefner and Larry Flynt, prominent American publishers of sex magazines; Sallie Tisdale, a pro-pornography feminist and author of *Talk Dirty to Me*; and Annie Sprinkle, a pornography film star who has lately attained some success as a sexual performance artist. Jones fires his final flaming attack at former-president William Jefferson Clinton for his sexual transgressions while in the White House. All, according to Jones, have contributed to the unhealthy growth of sexual liberation.

## MICHEL FOUCAULT—THE EXPANSION OF SEXUAL DISCOURSE

In contrast to Jones, Michel Foucault represents a much more positive view of sexual liberation. Foucault devoted much of the last part of his life to exploring sexuality in societies around the world. In his writing he has given special attention to the amount and importance of sexual discourse and also to the increasing openness regarding sexual diversity. Foucault's work is crucial for understanding the hypersexuality of contemporary American society.

Foucault's last major scholarly project was the three volume *The History of Sexuality* (1978, 1984/85), a historical description and analysis of sexual discourse and sexual behavior in the world's societies. This work has had enormous influence on a wide range of scholars in the years since its publication.

As one major point of *The History of Sexuality*, Foucault rebuts the prevailing belief that sexual repression has been widespread in Western societies, particularly the nineteenth-century Victorian period. The Victorian era has been widely described as being averse to any discourse about sexual behavior and sexuality. Foucault claimed the opposite was true. Those who were committed to concealing, obscuring, and censoring all discussion of sexual matters during the Victorian period were in fact "inciting" sexual discourse, both by the public statements of their own positions and the opposing views they inspired. The later chapters of this book will provide numerous illustrations of Foucault's idea that almost every attempt to repress and censor sexual materials inevitably will have the effect of increasing discourse about sexual topics.

Foucault claimed that it was not his intention to make judgments about sexuality and sexual expression. He was not concerned with saying "yes or no to sex," formulating "prohibitions or permissions" about sex, "denying its importance and its effects, or quibbling about the words used to describe sex" (Foucault 1978, 11). His primary interest was in analyzing the factors contributing to the frequency with which sex has been, and still is, the subject of discourse. Foucault says his interest was in "who does the speaking, the positions and viewpoints from which they speak, the institutions which prompt people to speak about it and which store and distribute the things that are said. What is at issue . . . is the way in which sex is 'put into discourse'" (Foucault 1978, 11). Foucault identified three factors that he believed to be preeminent in stimulating sexual discourse: power, knowledge, and pleasure (Foucault 1978). The objective of *The History of Sexuality*, he declared, was to "define the regime of power-knowledge-pleasure that sustains the discourse on human sexuality" (Foucault 1978, 11). While each of these factors is equally important, Foucault's attention was clearly focused on power throughout *The History of Sexuality*, with particular attention to the continuing struggle for power among competing sexual discourses. For Foucault, power represents the capacity to name, define standards for, and regulate acceptable beliefs and behavior, along with the ability to critique, restrict, and repress opposing viewpoints and behaviors (Foucault, *History of Sexuality*, 82–85). In striving for power, all discourses inevitably provoke the resistance—and consequently the competing struggles for power—of those with different positions and interests (Foucault 1978, 95).

Our major interest here is on the three modes of sexual discourse and their ongoing struggle for power in our society. Our labels will be the *political-legal*, with its formal emphasis on power, the *rational-intellectual* (knowledge), and the *pleasure-hedonistic* (pleasure).

Although all forms of sexual discourse are concerned with power, *political-legal* sexual discourse is the form of discourse most openly and deliberately associated with power. Throughout our history, the political-legal system of American society, and the organizations and individuals working within it, have consistently tried to control, limit, and even censor sexual writing, speech, display, and behavior.

Political-legal actions and actors are vividly illustrated by the late-nineteenth–early-twentieth-century anti-sex zealot Anthony Comstock, who single-handedly tried to root out any reference to or display of sexual activity in American society. Chapter 3 will take a closer look at Comstock's anti-sex crusade.

Political-legal attempts to repress and censor sexual material have certainly not disappeared completely, even in our current hypersexual society. Chapters 3 and 8 will demonstrate how various organizations, some Congressional leaders, and the Federal Communications Commission have maintained a continuing vigilance over radio and television broadcasts that use the public airwaves.

While political-legal sexual discourse typically aims to control and restrict sexual discourse and sexual behavior, Foucault insightfully recognized that the opposite could also be true: the would-be sexual repressors frequently increase the overall volume of sexual discourse in a society, both by calling attention to the very materials that they find objectionable and through their own writings and public pronouncements about the issue.

A prominent recent example of Foucault's observation was the report issued by Special Investigator Ken Starr before the impeachment proceedings against President Clinton. President Clinton had allegedly engaged in sexual transgressions with White House intern Monica Lewinsky. Starr, in a multi-year investigation, assembled extensive testimony about Clinton's alleged sexual activities and then sent the complete record of his investigations to the Congress, which subsequently released all the material to the public. Major newspapers around the country published either the complete report or summaries of it. *The Washington Post*, a paper that generally avoids printing any words that readers might consider offensive, published every word of the Starr report, uncensored, where it could be read by anyone who bought a paper. After the Starr report was released to the public, many Americans labeled it "pornography" because of its detailed descriptions of various sexual acts in which President Clinton allegedly engaged. While Starr's report was ostensibly an attack on sexual misbehavior, it is difficult to avoid the conclusion that the report actually increased public discourse about sexual behavior at the time. Among the topics that engaged many Americans was whether or not oral sex and telephone sex were *really* sex.

*Rational-intellectual* sexual discourse (roughly corresponding to Foucault's "knowledge" category) insists that sex can be best understood through objective study and analysis. Our examination of rational-intellectual will focus on two overlapping intellectual worlds: academe and sex therapy.

In the academic world today, a wide variety of scholarly disciplines have adopted sex as an important part of their subject matter (see Chapter 5). In the humanities, for example, literary and artistic criticism frequently includes the analysis and evaluation of sexual materials in books, films (including pornographic films), and other forms of art and sculpture (both ancient and contemporary). Historical analyses of sexual materials range from studies of the classical periods of Greece and Rome, through the major civilizations of Asia, to the Renaissance of Western Europe, and on to the development of American society.

Rational-intellectual sexual discourse is firmly entrenched in the social sciences. Studies of sex include: cross-cultural ethnographies; sociological studies of sexual attitudes, values, and behavior; and psychological research on sexual responses to pornographic stimuli, and many other examples. Chapter 5 will provide a more detailed account of social scientific research on sexual behavior.

Sex therapy (see Chapter 6) covers a wide range of activities. Professional sex therapists typically earn advanced degrees from reputable academic institutions and establish practices in which they counsel and advise patients. Other sex therapists, however, often have less-impressive academic credentials, but still use their specialized "knowledge" about sex to influence people (and advance their personal careers). Many of these pseudo-sexual therapists are little more than hucksters. Many can be found today on the Internet where they offer advice about sex or promise to solve sexual problems.

The rational-intellectual perspective provides the underpinning for academic and therapeutic sexual discourse. From a Foucauldian perspective, the rational-intellectual perspective is as much about power (aiming to define and legitimize sexual attitudes, values, and behavior) as it is about objective analysis.

*Pleasure-hedonistic* sexual discourse emphasizes the naturalness and the pleasure of sex, even the types of sex that differ from the predominant cultural standards (homosexuality, sadomasochism, fetishes, and so on). The pleasure-hedonistic view has become increasingly prominent in the United States since the middle of the twentieth century, but it should be noted that many cultures have emphasized how pleasurable and interesting sex is. Archeological scholars and historians have repeatedly revealed how important sexuality has been for humans in all cultures. Wherever written records have been preserved, especially in the centuries after the invention of printing, documents of all types provide ample evidence that sexuality has always been of interest to people.

Modern writings extolling sexual pleasure can be found in printed materials of all kinds, including *haute* literature and poetry, romance novels, popular magazines, and various types of erotic-pornographic publications. Modern visual arts have also depicted the pleasures of sex through paintings, photographs, films, videotapes, and Internet Web sites.

## THE ONGOING INTERPLAY AMONG THE THREE TYPES OF SEXUAL DISCOURSE

In every society, there is an ongoing interplay and competitive tension among these three forms of sexual discourse, with all three striving for power. "Where there is power," wrote Foucault, "there is resistance" (Foucault 1978, 95). The classic power relationship, explained Foucault, "depends on a multiplicity of points of resistance: these play the role of adversary, target, support, or handle in power relations" (Foucault 1978, 95). This means that each mode of sexual discourse regularly competes with the others for the right to define what is and is not acceptable in the sexual realm. These contests for power take various forms, from reasoned arguments, to legal challenges, to hostile, even violent, exchanges between individuals and groups.

Again according to Foucault, "[T]here is a plurality of resistances, each of them a special case: resistances that are possible, necessary, improbable; others that are spontaneous, savage, solitary, concerted, rampant, or violent; still others that are quick to compromise, interested, or sacrificial; by definition, they can only exist in the strategic field of power relations" (Foucault 1978, 95–96). At any given historical-societal moment, one or the other of these forms of discourse is likely to have hegemony. Today's sexually saturated society, for example, is increasingly dominated by the pleasure-hedonistic and the rational-intellectual modes. Following Foucault's observation, however, all public discussions of sexuality, including those specifically designed to repress and censor sexuality and sexual behavior, do in fact contribute to the total amount of sexual discourse in society.

This competing quest for power can be further illustrated by using a metaphor from the world of the theater. Among the three modes of sexual discourse, those who speak from the pleasure-hedonistic perspective command the stage today, they are the stars (literally in the mass-media world and the entertainment industry). Those who speak for the rational-intellectual point of view, which are found primarily in the worlds of academe and sex therapy, are the supporting actors, though they may occasionally enjoy their moments of semi-stardom through the mass media and in the entertainment industry (e.g., Dr. Phil). Those who represent the political/legal perspective act primarily as bit players today, though, for brief periods, even they are able to command the national limelight. During the 1980s, for example, feminist scholars Catherine MacKinnon and Andrea Dworkin made a vigorous legal and political effort to halt the production and distribution of pornography in the United States. While they ultimately failed in their campaign against pornography, they did command the national spotlight for nearly a decade. (Chapter 3 will provide a fuller description of the MacKinnon/Dworkin campaign.)

## FOUCAULT AND POLYMORPHOUS SEX

Near the end of his life, Michel Foucault gave increasing attention to sexual behavior, as contrasted with his earlier focus on sexual discourse. In his own life experiences, he uncovered "a world saturated with sex" (Miller 1993, 292) and was surprised and pleased to find an increasing social acceptance of diverse forms of sexual behavior in many contemporary societies, particularly the United States. During the 1970s, he participated in the gay-male sexual scene in San Francisco, California, where he explored the world of anonymous sex, including sadomasochism (Miller 1993). The emergence of AIDS in the 1980s subsequently led to the closing of the San Francisco bathhouses and perhaps had some dampening effect, at least for a while, on the more extreme and promiscuous versions of gay sexual behavior.

Today, however, the practice of polymorphous sexuality has become increasingly common, the urban bathhouses having been replaced in New York, San Francisco, and other cities by sex clubs, party circuits, and Internet hookups (Specter 2005). The mass media have exhibited a remarkable degree of sexual openness, especially in the range of discourse about sex in today's society. Foucault would probably have been astounded by the television fare of recent years, such as *Queer as Folk*, *The*

*L Word*, *Queer Eye for the Straight Guy*, or even the relatively mild sitcom *Will and Grace*.

Not only have gay and lesbian sex become commonplace, but also a variety of other sexual identities and activities (sadomasochism and bondage, cross-dressing, transvestism, and fetishes of all kinds) are now a common part of sexual discourse in today's world. Each of these will receive our attention in later chapters.

## SOCIETAL TRENDS AND HYPERSEXUALITY

An historical view of hypersexuality must take a long-range perspective as it identifies the societal trends that have made it possible for modern society to become saturated with sexual discourse, sexual materials, and sexual activity. Postmodern social theorists have pejoratively labeled this type of broad historical approach as the "grand narrative." Grand narratives, in simple terms, are ideas that identify particular historical events and trends that produce or contribute to subsequent societal developments. The grand narrative we will employ here will give special importance to three historical developments that have significantly contributed to the hypersexuality of contemporary society:

1. Economic development and personal affluence,
2. Political democratization and personal liberty,
3. Technological advances and personal accessibility.

## ECONOMIC GROWTH AND PERSONAL AFFLUENCE

Nations throughout the Western world, especially in North America and Europe, have made dramatic economic advances over the last century and a half. These nations have had either predominantly capitalistic economies or some combination of free enterprise and state economic planning, but regardless of the particular economic systems, almost all have enjoyed significant economic advances. One major result is the personal affluence of a great many people in their populations.

For the most thoroughly capitalistic countries, market forces govern the goods offered for sale to consumers. Entrepreneurs in these societies use capital to make products for the public to purchase, and these products include sexual materials.

Jeffrey Weeks argues in his book *Sexuality and Its Discontents* (1985) that capitalism has three central imperatives: "expansion, realization of surplus value, and profit" (Weeks 1985, 21). He continues, "[I]f we take a central strand of capitalist expansionism—its tendency to penetrate and colonize ever-increasing areas through its commodification and commercialisation of social life—then we can discern certain key points of articulation between changes in the structure of capitalism and changes in sexual life—the unintended consequences of capitalist growth" (Weeks 1985, 22). For Weeks, capitalism leads to what he called "pornocracy," by which he means that sexual and pornographic materials in a capitalistic society become available upon demand. In less theoretical terms, this thesis may be expressed with the slogan *sex sells*.[1] In nearly every economy in which merchants have produced written or visual sexual materials, their products have sold for a profit.

Profits are generated because producing sexual or pornographic materials can be done at a relatively low cost compared with many other products in the marketplace. Though not every sex merchant or pornographer in history has become rich, many have. Throughout this book we will see example after example of how lucrative it can be to sell sexual materials, including erotica and pornography.

Some capitalist societies, especially in the nineteenth and early twentieth centuries, used the legal system to restrict the sale of sexual materials and pornography. Governments in the United States, England, Ireland, and other European countries placed rigid restrictions on the production and distribution of sexual materials. Under such restrictive conditions, trafficking in pornography was limited to those few people who were willing to challenge the existing laws and risk punishment. Such risk-taking often resulted in substantial profits.

Even today, tensions remain between those who produce sexual and pornographic products and those wishing to censor or restrict such materials. But generally, those who produce sexual materials continue to be successful—both legally and financially. In contemporary capitalistic societies around the world, sexual materials and pornography are now found in abundance, often yielding enormous profits for those who produce them.

A revealing contemporary example is the increase of sexual and pornographic materials in the former Soviet Union (now, specifically, Russia). Throughout much of the twentieth century, the communist government of the Soviet Union vigorously prohibited the production, sale, or possession of sexual materials and pornography. After the fall of communism, however, entrepreneurs in Russia began to produce and sell sexual materials and pornography in abundance (Goldschmidt 1999). Today, on the Internet, Russian pornography reaches all parts of the world.[2]

## PERSONAL AFFLUENCE

At the individual level, increased personal affluence has dramatically increased the availability of sexual materials and pornography in contemporary society. Whenever individuals have wealth, personal property, and material goods, they generally have greater-than-average access to sexual materials. Historians have shown that sexual materials in Western societies have been largely limited to wealthy and high-status individuals (Hunt 1993a; Kendrick 1987). In *The Secret Museum* (1987), Walter Kendrick illustrates this phenomenon in nineteenth century European society, where wealthy males were the only citizens allowed to view sexual and pornographic materials held by the major museums and libraries of Europe.

Kendrick recounts the eighteenth-century unearthing of objects from the city of Pompeii, the Italian town that was covered by ash and debris from the eruption of Mount Vesuvius in 79 A.D. The work of digging out Pompeii did not begin until nearly seventeen hundred years after it was buried. The early hunters of antiquities chose Pompeii because of the comparative ease of the excavation; the entire city had been covered by stone and ash, but not by the mud that had covered two other cities—the mud later hardened to stone (Clarke 2003, 148).

As early as 1758, rumors circulated about "lascivious" frescoes (wall paintings) that had been uncovered in the Pompeiian excavations (Kendrick 1987, 6). As the digging at Pompeii continued, it soon became clear that sexual representations, in mosaics and sculptures as well as wall paintings, were much more than rumors. Early excavators typically removed the frescoes and mosaics from the walls and sent them to their wealthy patrons. In some cases, the excavators deemed the material too obscene or offensive, and destroyed them (Clarke 2003, 148).

The Pompeii wall paintings and frescoes depict male-female couples in foreplay and engaged in various positions of sexual intercourse. Others show males and females engaged in cunnilingus and fellatio. Some wall paintings show threesomes (two men and one woman) and foursomes (two men and two women) engaged in various sexual acts. Even in contemporary society, many people would still consider the Pompeiian art objects to be pornographic.

Many of these paintings were found on the walls of public baths (places of leisure and pleasure), and some in what were probably houses of prostitution. But also, some of these erotic objects were found in the homes of private citizens, often in bedrooms or other rooms where the inhabitants might have been expected to engage in intimate activities. Yet

others have been found in entryways or rooms where they would easily
have been seen by any and all visitors to the home (Clarke 2003).

Sexual representations were also part of the everyday lives of the people of Pompeii in other ways. Common and useful objects such as lamps,
vases, and other household utensils were frequently decorated with copu-
lating couples and other sexually explicit scenes (Clarke 2003).

In the eighteenth century, royal families and other society elites were
the people who were most likely to come into possession of the sexually
explicit paintings, frescoes, sculptures, and other artifacts from the historical past. Often these privileged members of society were faced with the
question of who should see or even know about these sexual materials.
The problem became especially acute when explicitly sexual objects were
given to public museums and libraries because of their obvious historical
value. Museum curators often decided that these objects, while they
might be safely viewed by men of education and sophistication, were
inappropriate for the lower classes and women (Kendrick 1987). English
curators and cataloguers in the nineteenth century tended to omit the
sexual materials entirely from their catalogs, or referred to them with
oblique labels. In the British Museum, for example, such materials were
part of the "Private Case" (Kendrick 1987, 70).

Other curators, especially on the European continent, often listed the
sexual objects in separate publications, exclusively devoted to the special
collections sections of the library. Even today, certain sexual materials are
not available for general circulation in some American university libraries.

The secret museums and libraries of the eighteenth and nineteenth
centuries highlight two important issues related to sexual materials and
pornography. For one, access to sexual and pornographic materials of
antiquity was typically restricted to the elite members of the society:
members of the royalty, the educated, and the economically powerful.
Secondly, these elites, who were almost invariably males, generally saw it
as their social responsibility to keep such materials out of the hands (and
away from the eyes) of the lower social classes, women, and youth.
Explains Kendrick: "[A] gentleman with appropriate demeanor (and
ready cash for the custodian) would be admitted to the locked chamber
where controversial items lurked; women, children, and the poor of both
sexes and all ages were excluded" (Kendrick 1987, 7).

Even before the eighteenth and nineteenth centuries, the privileged
people of society already enjoyed exclusive access to sexual and pornographic materials. As early as the seventeenth century, books, lithographs
and paintings with sexual content were becoming increasingly available in
European societies. Such materials were not inexpensive, however. Sexual

and pornographic materials typically had to be purchased from artists, printers, or dealers who specialized in such items. Only the few with sufficient discretionary funds could afford them.

Samuel Pepys, the well-to-do London diarist of the seventeenth century, is an example of a man who had sufficient means to obtain pornography. In his celebrated diaries, Pepys scrupulously described everything he did: the good, the noble, the scandalous, and the dishonest, even recording a number of his adulterous seductions, liaisons, and love affairs.

In one of his diary entries, Pepys describes purchasing a copy of *L'Ecole des filles* in 1668 from his regular book dealer. This volume is usually credited with being the first work in the French-language pornographic tradition (DeJean 1993). Pepys received the book in a "plain binding" and he resolved at the time of purchase to burn it after reading it. Pepys describes the book as "the most bawdy, lewd book I ever saw," further reporting that he had an erection through most of his reading of it. "[A] mighty lewd book," he says in his own defense, "but yet not amiss for a sober man once to read over to inform himself in the villainy of the world." After all, he was saying, a man of his stature in the community had a civic responsibility to inform himself about the wicked ways of the world of pornography.

After sufficiently informing himself (and masturbating to ejaculation), Pepys fulfilled his initial resolve and burned the book in his fireplace (Coote 2001). Not only would a man of lesser means probably not have been able to afford such a book, but once having obtained it, he would not likely have burned it on the evening of the day of purchase. Also, since the book was written in French, only an educated Englishman would have been able to read it.

An example from the art world offers another illustration of how sexual representations and pornography have historically been the province of the wealthy. The Spanish artist Lucientes de Goya produced some beautiful paintings of women, including a number that are openly erotic. A recent American exhibit of Goya's work, which features some of his most sensual paintings, was titled, "Goya: Images of Women" (Roberts 2002). The exhibition centerpiece, "The Naked Maja," is arguably Goya's most famous painting and possibly also his most erotic. The painting depicts a full-frontal view of a naked young woman reclining on a lounge.[3] It is one of Goya's "gentleman paintings," which were painted for wealthy patrons who would then have shown them to their gentleman friends in what was then called a "secret cabinet."

Goya also painted "The Clothed Maja," appropriate for showing to larger audiences, including women. The curator of the contemporary

Goya exhibit called the Maja painting "pornographic," and a newspaper columnist described the entire exhibition as "definitely R-rated." She assisted newspaper readers by suggesting in her headline that they: "Think Playboy centerfold, circa 1800" (Roberts 2002).

Whether it was access to the antiquities excavated from Pompeii and stored in the "secret museums" of Europe, books published by French pornographers, or the paintings of Goya, the pattern has historically been the same. Elite males have always been the ones with the greatest access to sexually explicit materials.[4]

### AFFLUENCE AND PORNOGRAPHY IN THE TWENTIETH CENTURY

In the United States, as late as the first half of the twentieth century, people with the most money and education still enjoyed the greatest access to sexual materials and pornography. In the early decades of the twentieth century, the burgeoning immigrant populations of America's cities lived in ghetto-like conditions and struggled to make an adequate living for themselves and their families. In the rural areas of the country, most of the millions of people eked out livings on small homesteads or made meager profits as small-town merchants. Such individuals simply did not have enough disposable income to indulge in the purchase of the few sexually explicit materials then available.

In 1920s America, an exception occurred when a small, sexually explicit comic book became available even to low-income men (Adelman 1997). These crudely produced, raw-sex comics, which came to be called "Tijuana Bibles," could be purchased for a few dollars and were thus available for men with low incomes. (The Tijuana Bible will be described more fully in Chapter 4.)

Today, however, sexual materials of all types are not limited to the wealthy. Almost all Americans can afford magazines and books that have both sexually explicit materials and pornography. Even many public libraries provide access to books, magazines, and videotapes with sexual content, at no cost to library patrons. Cable and satellite television and personal computers, all of which are within the economic means of most Americans, also provide an abundance of sexual material. As American society has become progressively wealthier, and a higher percentage of the population has attained some level of affluence, sexual materials and pornography have become economically accessible to virtually anyone who is interested.

## POLITICAL DEMOCRATIZATION AND PERSONAL LIBERTY

The growth of political democracy in modern times has given many people, both in the United States and in countries around the world, greater influence in the selection of their political leaders. Along with increased democratization, citizens have also achieved greater personal liberty, including greater access to sexual materials. This personal liberty has also extended to greater freedom in individual sexual behavior (but this freedom is not unlimited).

In the United States, the Declaration of Independence and the Constitution both provide strong verbal support for individual freedom and liberty. However, the ringing words of the Declaration of Independence (extolling "life, liberty, and the pursuit of happiness") and the First Amendment's guarantee that "Congress shall make no law . . . abridging the freedom of speech, or of the press" have not always applied to speech about sex or to sexual behavior. Only since the 1970s have these freedoms become gradually more assured. Even today, some forms of sexual speech and behavior continue to be challenged.[5]

In the past few decades, the U.S. Supreme Court has generally ruled that Americans have personal freedom when it comes to having access to sexual materials (Moretti 1984; Roysner, Morales, and Barrett 1999). The only major exception is sexual materials relating to minors (Jenkins 2001). Most personal freedoms regarding sexual materials in the United States have been established by the courts, and thus a brief review of twentieth-century court decisions will help to explain how this has happened.

### AMERICAN COURTS AND SEXUAL MATERIALS/PORNOGRAPHY

Throughout the last half of the nineteenth century, U.S. courts were greatly influenced by an 1868 British legal ruling, *Regina v. Hicklin*, which made obscenity illegal but said little about pornography. As U.S. courts followed the *Hicklin* decision, obscenity continued to be a crime while other sexual materials, such as pornography and erotica, were protected (Berger, Searles and Cottle 1991; Hyde 1965; Moretti 1984).

The major problem has been that it has been virtually impossible for judges, legislators, or any other citizens to distinguish between obscenity and pornography (and also between pornography and erotica). Most importantly, distinguishing between obscenity and pornography has proven to be a persistent and nettlesome problem for the courts. As legal scholar Daniel Moretti has observed, "defining obscenity has been, and continues to be, a most difficult task . . . the judicial effort to find an acceptable definition of obscenity constitutes one of the longest and most arduous struggles in the history of American jurisprudence" (Moretti 1984, xi).

The *Hicklin* case's original test for obscenity involved judging whether or not the material "tended to deprave and corrupt those whose minds are open to immoral influences" (Moretti 1984, 1). This definition includes several ambiguous terms (deprave, corrupt, immoral), but it also has a hint of nineteenth-century elitism. In expressing concern about those "whose minds are open to immoral influences," the courts may have been referring to children and adolescents, but they may also have been reflecting the then-prevailing view that obscene material and pornography should only be viewed by the educated upper classes—especially educated, upper-class males.

Through the early years of the twentieth century, the "*Regina/Hicklin*" test continued to prevail in American courts, but as early as 1913, Judge Learned Hand had already identified crucial flaws in the logic of this obscenity definition. As he observed, if the reference to "minds . . . open to immoral influences" referred to children, then adults would be legally limited to reading only the contents of a child's library. Judge Hand also noted that a work of science or literature could be banned under the ruling for a containing a single instance of obscenity.

The first real challenge to the *Hicklin* test occurred in 1933, when a case involving James Joyce's *Ulysses* came before the Supreme Court. This groundbreaking case, *United States v. One Book Entitled Ulysses*, established a new standard for obscenity (Moretti 1984, 3); it ruled that a work should be judged as a whole, "not on the alleged obscene nature of isolated passages" (Moretti 1984, 3). The *Ulysses* case was not the end of the Hicklin obscenity standard, however, since the Court also ruled that a work was obscene if it was *intended* to "stir . . . lustful thoughts." "Intention" turned out to be an equally ambiguous standard for determining obscenity because it has been nearly impossible to determine with certainty what the intent of an author might be. Unless an author explicitly states his or her intention it may be impossible to determine what it is. Most authors, especially those who write (or otherwise produce) pornography, do not voluntarily provide this information.

Through the middle years of the twentieth century, American courts at the state and federal levels ruled on a variety of cases in which defendants had been charged with obscenity. The outcomes of these cases were inconclusive because the rulings varied from case to case. For example, the courts in one state might rule that a book or magazine was obscene, while another court in another state might rule that it was not obscene.

An important watershed in this sometimes-yes–sometimes-no legal process was reached in the late 1950s, when the case of a New York mail-order book and magazine merchant named Samuel Roth reached the Supreme Court. Roth and his court case hold a significant place among those American authors, publishers, and distributors who fought to achieve freedom of the press in the United States. Roth's personal story will be told in greater detail in Chapter 3. Here we need only note the importance of Roth's Supreme Court appeal of a lower court ruling in which he had been found guilty of mailing obscene pictures, photographs, magazines, and books (Hyde 1965, 185). In *Roth v. United States*, the nation's highest court ruled against the controversial book and magazine merchant, upholding his earlier conviction by a six to three vote. The court ruling was a victory for the prosecutors but also, ironically, a victory for those who would follow in Roth's footsteps.

Justice William Brennan wrote the decision in the *Roth* case, reaffirming that obscenity was *not* protected by the First Amendment. In his ruling, however, Brennan also tried to do what many other jurists had avoided—to define obscenity. Brennan's test for obscenity involved asking whether an average person, applying contemporary local standards, would find that the dominant theme of the material, taken as a whole, appealed to prurient interests (Moretti 1984, 8). Most importantly, Brennan declared that, in order to be ruled obscene, a product or work of art must be "utterly without redeeming social importance" (Moretti 1984, 8).

Thanks to Brennan's ruling, lawyers who were defending other producers and distributors of sexual and pornographic materials could now defend their clients by arguing that the works of their clients were not "utterly without redeeming social importance." As a prominent example, D. H. Lawrence's *Lady Chatterley's Lover* had been banned in the United States because it contained many explicitly sexual scenes and vulgar language. Yet Lawrence's book also contained copious amounts of political, social, and philosophical material. Following the *Roth* decision, *Lady Chatterley* became one of the first of a series of long-suppressed books that could be legally published and distributed in the United States.

In 1967, the Supreme Court augmented the *Roth* decision in the case of *Redrup v. New York*. A New York newsstand operator named Robert Redrup had been arrested for selling two suggestively titled and sexually laden books: *Lust Pool* and *Shame Agent*. Redrup had been convicted of selling obscene books, but the Supreme Court heard the case and reversed the conviction without any additional comment. Therefore, the court was tacitly agreeing that the books in question were not obscene.

The *Redrup* ruling was a critically important case because, thereafter, literary censorship was virtually dead in the United States (Slade 2005). Within a short time, thirty other obscenity convictions were overturned by American courts. Publishers of sexually oriented materials quickly recognized the new opportunities emanating from the *Redrup* ruling. Magazine publishers were especially quick to take advantage of the increasingly permissive legal climate. This was contemporaneous with major social changes occurring in American society; in particular, the "sexual revolution" of the late 1960s was already well underway.

In 1973, however, the case of *Miller v. California* imposed partial limitations on the publication and distribution of sexual material and pornography. In its ruling on this case, the Supreme Court, then under Chief Justice Warren Burger (a conservative Nixon appointee), attempted to reinstate restrictions on the distribution of sexual materials and pornography.

The details of the *Miller* case are not exceptional. Marvin Miller, a Los Angeles publisher of pornographic materials, sent a mass mailing of brochures depicting men and women engaging in a variety of sexual acts (Moretti 1984, 30). Miller was brought to trial and convicted under a California law that prohibited the distribution of obscene material. He then appealed all the way to the U.S. Supreme Court (Lane 2000).

In its ruling, the Burger court provided the following criteria for judging whether or not a work was obscene:

1. If the average person, applying contemporary community standards, would find that the work, taken as a whole, appeals to prurient interests;
2. If the work depicts or describes, in a patently offensive way, sexual conduct specifically defined by the applicable state law;
3. If the work, when taken as a whole, lacks serious literary, artistic, political, or scientific value.

Despite the obvious similarities to Justice Brennan's decision in the *Roth* case, the Burger court made a few important changes. In the first place, the *Miller* test did not require that the material be "utterly without redeeming social value," as *Roth* had specified. Instead, the *Miller* test simply required that the material must lack "serious value" in order to be judged obscene (Moretti 1984, 31). The *Miller* decision also spelled out specific details of what would be "patently offensive," all of which were more restrictive than the *Roth* decision. Finally, and most importantly, the *Miller* ruling made it clear that obscenity was to be judged on the basis of individual "community" standards, not a national standard (Moretti 1984). Following this last point, any community in the United States, however conservative, could essentially demand that any given book, magazine, or film be ruled obscene—a community-based standard that could potentially apply to the entire country. In short, the most conservative community in the country could possibly set the limits for the entire society.

The *Miller* decision substantially reduced the distribution of sexual materials in the United States in the 1970s. Publications such as *Playboy* and *Penthouse*, for example, reacted by modifying their covers or having them displayed half hidden.

Despite the *Miller* decision, the legal gates for the production and distribution of sexual materials and pornography had long since been opened in the United States. Even though, in specific communities where the population was especially conservative, prosecutors were able to close pornographic bookstores and adult theaters, in most places, sexual materials and pornography remained legally available. Americans who had an interest in such materials now had the freedom to read and see almost any form of sexual material they wanted, including pornography.

## TECHNOLOGICAL ADVANCES AND PERSONAL ACCESSIBILITY

Professor Joseph Slade, a respected scholar of sexual materials and pornography, has advanced (perhaps with some irony) Slade's Law: "whenever one person invents a technology, another person will invent a sexual use for it" (Slade 2000b, 9). Slade's numerous illustrations include the vulcanization of rubber, which quickly led to the latex condom, a contraceptive (and disease-control device) that was much cheaper and probably more reliable than sheaths made of sheep intestines. But it is in the realm of communication technologies that the greatest sexual applications have occurred.

In 1455, Johann Gutenberg invented what would become the most influential device in advancing communication: the printing press. Gutenberg's printing press, which was actually a hand-set metal type, allowed its users to print multiple copies of printed material. Books and pamphlets could thereafter be produced in abundance.

Before the fifteenth century, the Christian Church effectively controlled the written word in Europe; only writings approved by the church could be printed and published. As Lane has written, "[T]he only books produced during [the Middle Ages] were made by monks hunched over in a monastery scriptorium" (Lane 2000, 7).

Gutenberg's invention allowed words, and eventually pictures, to be produced beyond the controlling hand of the Catholic Church in Europe,[6] depicting anything a writer or artist chose to create, including sexual materials. Pornography now became at least potentially available to large numbers of people. "It was only when print culture opened the possibility of the masses gaining access to writing and pictures," writes historian Lynn Hunt, "that pornography began to emerge as a separate genre of representation" (Hunt 1993b, 13).

Printing was only the first of many technological advances contributing to the greater availability of sexual and pornographic materials. In the last 150 years, photography, motion pictures, recordings, radio, television, and the Internet have all increased and expanded accessibility to sexual and pornographic materials. Not every new technological advance has led to immediate increases in sexual materials, however. The telegraph, for example, was a very influential advance in communication in the nineteenth century, but it had almost no uses that advanced sexual discourse. Similarly, the telephone, sound recording, and radio, in their early years, provided little sexual content. Nor did television in the 1950s, constrained as it was by the restrictive codes of the movie industry. With the exception of the telegraph, however, all of these technological innovations eventually helped to increase the sexual and pornographic content of American society.

The telephone, for example, which was virtually sex free in its early days, has now generated a booming "phone-sex" industry. Lane has described the phone-sex industry as a remarkably simple and profitable business. Its infrastructure consists of "a few large national companies" that can afford highly complex telephone systems and huge advertising budgets, as well as a number of small independent operators who can make a good living. Lane provides the example of a small operator named "Heather" who intentionally keeps her business small. She employs a few women part-time to answer the calls, but takes most of them herself. By her own account, she "now grosses around $4,300 per week" (Lane 2000, 161).

As early as 1997, phone sex yearly revenues were estimated to be one billion dollars a year (Lane 2000, 163). Even the auxiliary profits (revenues generated by the calls made on 800 and 900 numbers, phone charges added to home telephone bills, and fees added to hotel and motel bills) contribute to the total. And there are also the profits earned by the companies and individuals who provide the sex talk for callers.

Telephone technology has now moved far beyond the simple fixed-in-place receiver. Today's cell phones have small screens and allow Internet access. These technological developments provide hand-held devices with immediate access to all the pornography now available on the Internet (Musgrove 2005a).

Movies and television have completely broken away from their earlier years of self-censorship and now provide sexual material and pornography in limitless variety. Radio, which was also heavily restricted in its early years, now routinely features shock jocks and raunchy music lyrics, though not without occasional interventions by federal communications agencies (see Chapter 8).

The newest communication technology, the Internet, provides a cornucopia of sexual material (see Chapter 9). Its impact has been summarized by *Time* magazine:

> [T]he modern concept of pornography was invented in the 19th century by European gentlemen whose main concern was to keep obscene material away from women and the lower classes. Things got out of hand with the spread of literacy and education, which made pornography available to anybody who could read. Now, on the computer networks, anybody with a computer and a modem can not only consume pornography but distribute it as well. (Elmer-Dewitt 1995, 45)

The accessibility of pornography on the Internet has essentially negated the potentially limiting effects of many of the Supreme Court decisions discussed earlier. Since the Internet generally provides sexual and pornographic materials to users who *choose to view it* the question of community standards becomes moot.

Lane has explained how the Internet avoids judicial restrictions on the distribution and viewing of sexual materials:

> The Internet . . . poses in fairly stark terms the extent of a local government's obligation or duty to protect its citizens from themselves. While it can be argued that a local government can and even should protect its citizens from the unwanted risk of seeing explicit sexual materials in a storefront or bookstore window on Main Street, it is less clear that the same obligation exists to protect citizens from what they might see on their personal computer screens in the privacy of their homes. In addition, the purchase and consumption of pornography from the Internet dramatically reduces the visible effects of pornography on a community. When someone uses a computer to access pornography on the Internet, it does not increase the risk that a criminal element will be attracted to the community, nor does it decrease the property values of surrounding homes. (Lane 2000, 288)

Lane's argument clarifies how technological innovations have actually changed the way that pornography affects communities. This new technological impact started with the VCR, which became available in the 1980s. Soon thereafter, most American households were able to rent and play movies in their homes, including easily accessible pornography videos (and, more recently, DVDs). Today, X-rated videos and DVDs can be found in video stores, purchased on cable or satellite television, or purchased on the Internet and delivered directly to one's mailbox

Technological advances, from the printing press to the Internet, have given ever-larger numbers of people access to written and visual sexual/pornographic materials. Access to such materials is no longer limited to the elites of the society.

Economic development, political democratization, and technological advances have been the driving societal forces in producing our hypersexual society. Societal forces do not operate in the same way as natural forces, however. In the physical world, the actions of individuals are not required to keep the planets of the solar system rotating around the sun. In societies it requires individuals to act in order for change to occur. Human actors, in the context of societal trends, are essential elements of that process.

The Gutenberg printing press, by itself, changed nothing. Individual decisions still had to be made about what to print and for what purpose. This point is clearly illustrated by historian Lynn Hunt in her book *The Invention of Pornography*. Pornography, Hunt explains, was invented in the sixteenth century when various writers and revolutionaries were already searching for ways to challenge the authority of the Catholic Church (Hunt 1993a). The printing press gave them the technological means to do so.

Similarly, the formal guarantees of freedom of speech and freedom of the press in the American Constitution did not automatically translate into the free distribution of sexual materials and pornography. Only when individual twentieth-century actors demanded these freedoms (by defying existing laws and raising legal challenges to censorship) did sexual materials and pornography finally become broadly available in the society. The part played by individuals in this process will be given special attention in this book

Some individuals have played minor roles in increasing the freedom of sexual expression in contemporary society; others have been trailblazers or pioneers; and some have changed our entire way of looking at sexual materials and pornography. In the chapters that follow, we will give special attention to these key players, sex pioneers, and paradigm breakers.

## KEY PLAYERS, SEX PIONEERS, AND PARADIGM BREAKERS

Sexual discourse in every historical period is shaped and changed by a relatively small number of individuals. Some of these people may fight for the status quo, or even for regression to previous times. Others will break existing rules and norms (or sometimes establish new rules and norms) and challenge authority. Some will introduce fashions and trends. A few will create new paradigms. The terms key players, sex pioneers, and paradigm breakers will be used to describe the various actors who have played a significant role in creating today's hypersexual society.

Anthony Comstock (mentioned briefly earlier in this chapter and described in greater detail in the following chapter) played a crucial role in creating America's version of Victorian sexual repression and prudishness. Through the last part of the nineteenth and early part of the twentieth century, he campaigned relentlessly—and often successfully—to suppress all forms of sexual discourse in the United States.

In contrast, Helen Gurley Brown is an example of a key player in promoting sexual discourse in mid-twentieth-century America by convincing single girls that they too could enjoy sex. Her earliest contribution was the best-selling book *Sex and the Single* Girl (Brown 1962). Brown later reinforced her theme of sexual freedom for women through her many successful years as editor of *Cosmopolitan* (Streitmatter 2004). (Brown's story will be told more fully in Chapter 4).

More than just key players, some individuals can be best described as *sex pioneers*. Sigmund Freud, for example, is described as a sex pioneer because of his introduction of the themes of sexual behavior and sexuality into the worlds of psychology and mental health. His influence on sex and therapy will be described further in Chapter 6. Another sexual pioneer is Alfred Kinsey, who brought sex into academe by firmly establishing sexual behavior as a legitimate field for scientific and scholarly research (Chapter 5).

A few rare individuals are influential as "paradigm breakers." For example, Michel Foucault's revolutionary and influential work on the history of sexuality changed the views and approaches of intellectuals and scholars about sexuality and sexual discourse.

Throughout the rest of the book, the concepts and ideas introduced in this chapter will be used as a general guide for examining the various realms in which sexual material and pornography are commonplace today: print publications, academe, therapy, the entertainment world, and the Internet. Chapter 3 will begin, however, with an overview of the historical and continuing opposition to sexual discourse in the United States. Attempts to repress and censor sexual material and pornography have always been present in American culture, and these attempts continue in various ways in the twenty-first century. Repression and censorship may not have succeeded, but they have continued as an important part of American culture. In so doing, they have inevitably contributed, as Foucault observed, to the continuing discourse about sex.

## CHAPTER 3

# REPRESSION AND CENSORSHIP

## EARLY AND CONTINUING ATTEMPTS TO SUPPRESS SEXUAL MATERIALS AND PORNOGRAPHY

John Ashcroft served as U.S. Attorney General from 2001 until 2005. As the nation's chief law enforcement officer, Ashcroft had primary responsibility for fighting crime, cracking down on corporate wrongdoing, and guarding the nation against potential terrorists. The last of these was a particularly important responsibility after September 11, 2001. With all of these awesome duties, Ashcroft still found time during his tenure to take care of one more important task: ordering that two larger-than-life-size bronze statues in the Department of Justice building be hidden behind draperies. Why? The official press release stated that the statues created a distraction when Ashcroft stood in front of them while holding news conferences. And why were the statues so distracting? News reporters and political columnists suspected that the distraction was that one of the statues was of a bare-breasted woman, which Ashcroft, a self-proclaimed Christian fundamentalist, might have found offensive. Nudity, especially female nudity, is often objectionable to fundamentalist Christians.

Two insights can be drawn from this relatively trivial Justice Department episode. First, people in power often try to repress or censor sexual materials to protect or justify their personal values and beliefs. Second, attempts by those in power to conceal, obscure, and censor sexual displays or materials usually incite greater amounts of discourse about sex—the very topic they wish to suppress.

When the Justice Department statues were covered during Ashcroft's tenure as Attorney General, the event received widespread attention throughout the mass media. Even months later, when Ashcroft appeared on the David Letterman show to promote a compact disk of his singing, Letterman pressed him about the issue. Ashcroft claimed to know little about the placing of the drapes, but said they might have been hung in the hall to hide construction.[1] Skepticism about the truthfulness of Ashcroft's response produced even more sexual discourse in the American media (in the form of jokes, cartoons, commentaries, and editorials about the infamous nude statues).

Ashcroft's decision to censor the nude statues represents a contemporary example of an attempt by a political authority to gain power over sexual discourse (in this case, sexual representation) in our society. Power, for Foucault, is that which rejects, rules, prohibits censors, or normalizes behavior at all levels of social life (Foucault, *History of Sexuality, Vol. 1*, 83–85). This chapter will focus primarily on power as exercised by those in positions of authority (i.e., political-legal actions that attempt to control, limit, or censor sexual materials and sexual discourse).

If a government, for example, acts on the conviction that pornography contradicts prevailing religious beliefs, then religious doctrine can be used to control the population's access to sexual material. Such was the case when the Taliban, around the year 2000, controlled Afghanistan and imposed its rigid Islamic beliefs on the population. The Taliban's strict beliefs prohibited all forms of sexual display (women were made to wear burkas, photographic images of women in any mode of dress or undress were strictly forbidden). This gave the fundamentalist Islamic party power over what the Afghan people could see or do. After the NATO forces, led by the U.S. military, invaded Afghanistan and ousted the Taliban from power, these restrictions were lifted and sexual materials quickly became available and, in the process, eliminated the Taliban's control over sexual access in Afghan society.

As the case of Ashcroft illustrates, however, U.S. political, legislative, and judicial authorities have also frequently tried to limit the sexual materials that citizens can or cannot see. What follows is a brief look at some historical attempts to suppress sexual materials in American society.

## HISTORICAL ATTEMPTS TO REPRESS SEXUAL MATERIAL IN THE UNITED STATES

Through much of American history, political-legal discourse about sexuality and sexual behavior has very often been directed toward repression and censorship. This reached a peak in the last years of the nineteenth and first half of the twentieth century. The major forms of repression have consisted of laws passed by different levels of government, arrests and prosecutions by law enforcement agents, presidential commissions established to investigate and castigate pornography, court decisions aimed at restricting sexual materials and pornography, and public opinion campaigns waged against sexual materials, especially pornography.

Before moving on to the story of sexual repression and censorship in the United States, we should point out again how attempts to limit sexual discourse contribute to the hypersexuality of the society. First, when governments have tried to prosecute individuals for producing and distributing sexual materials, especially erotica and pornography, the court rulings have often gone against the government. This was especially true during the last half of the twentieth century. Second, whenever attempts have been made to suppress sexual materials, it almost always provokes other individuals and groups, who then take a stand in opposition to censorship and repression. As Foucault observed, opposition to sexual discourse inevitably contributes to the overall amount of sexual discourse about sex.

This chapter will focus on the leading individuals and groups who have tried to suppress and censor sexual materials and sexual activities—and the forces that fought against them. The quest for power over sexual discourse, according to Foucault, always produces resistances.

Historian Jay Gertzman's book *Bookleggers and Smuthounds* (Gertzman 1999) nicely illustrates Foucault's point. Gertzman studied the publishers and sellers of erotic and pornographic materials during the first half of the twentieth century. He concluded that a "symbiotic relationship" existed between the purveyors of sexual material and the moralists who tried to suppress them. "I have become convinced," he explained, "that the publishers of erotica and the moralists who attacked them during the early twentieth century had (as they continue to have) a subtle symbiotic relationship" (Gertzman 1999, 1).

Gertzman's argument can be expressed even more simply: each camp in the antipornography versus pro-pornography struggle reaped benefits from the other's position. To increase the appeal of their products, sellers of erotica and pornography promoted the merchandise as fascinating, off-limits, and obscene. Moralists who tried to suppress sexual and pornographic materials loudly denounced the vileness and obscenity of such products, which made the books and magazines all the more attractive for many buyers of pornographic products. And the viler the products distributed by the "smut peddlers," the easier it was for moralists to justify their antipornography crusades.

The symbiosis argument is clearly illustrated by the now antiquated phrase, "banned in Boston," which was used for decades by twentieth-century book publishers to entice readers to purchase their "banned" books. In a more contemporary example, rap singers such as Eminem, Lil' Kim, and many others include sexual material in their lyrics that many adults find offensive. The more adult moralists rail against the lyrics, the more attractive they become for adolescents and young adults who enjoy challenging the limits of the forbidden. Similarly, Internet pornographers routinely use descriptions such as "barely eighteen" or "barely legal" to suggest that their models are just old enough to avoid prosecution under child pornography laws.

## ANTHONY COMSTOCK: THE EXTREME
## ANTI-SEX CRUSADER

The history of censorship in the United States can best begin with Anthony J. Comstock (1844–1915), whose name has become synonymous with censorship. Comstock was so relentless in his fight against sexual material and pornography that his name finally became a part of the English language. The word *Comstockery* is defined in modern dictionaries as "a strict censorship of materials (as books and plays) considered to be obscene" (*Merriam-Webster's New Collegiate Dictionary*). The definition hardly does justice, however, to the vehemence of Comstock's crusade against sexual material.

George Bernard Shaw, the early twentieth-century English playwright, first coined the word Comstockery in 1905, after the written versions of some of his plays were not allowed to be circulated freely by the New York City Public Library. Incensed, Shaw wrote a letter to the *New York Times* in which he described Comstock's crusade as "the world's standing joke at the expense of the United States," which he condescendingly referred to as "a provincial place, a second-rate country-town civilization" (Kendrick 1987, 148). Ironically, Comstock had nothing to do with the restrictions placed on Shaw's works by the New York Public Library. Yet Comstock fully deserved the eponymous label, since he devoted his adult life to fighting what he called "smut," "obscenity," "lewdness," and "filth." Between the early 1870s and 1913, Comstock waged a one-man crusade against the sale and distribution of anything that had the slightest connection with sex. He supported the passage of numerous state and federal laws to suppress what he described as "the scourges of society."

Scholars and historians differ on whether Comstock was a lone activist or speaking for a broad spectrum of the American people. Kendrick (1987) argues that Comstock did not have wide public support for his anti-sex activities and that most Americans around the turn of the twentieth century were largely indifferent to his fight against obscenity (Kendrick 1987, 143). Historians John D'Emilio and Estelle Freedman reached a different conclusion. "Comstock could not have managed his campaign," they argue, "without broader public support" (D'Emilio and Freedman 1988, 160). For instance, several nineteenth-century organizations, such as the Women's Christian Temperance Union, the suffrage movement, and the "social purity" movement, were already on record as opposing "vicious literature" (D'Emilio and Freedman 1988, 160). Some of these organizations, for example, the suffrage movement, were among the progressive forces of their time, and historians generally agree that Comstock was supported by progressives as well as conservatives during the early years of his crusade against sexual materials. Ultimately, Comstock did not win the battle against sex and pornography, but he did have a repressive impact on sexual expression in the early decades of the twentieth century.

## THE COMSTOCK STORY

Anthony Comstock was born before the Civil War in New Canaan, Connecticut, to parents of Puritan heritage. As a young man, he was devoutly religious and utterly convinced of the rightness of his faith. At age nineteen he wrote in his diary that he was not afraid of death because he was confident that after death he would be near to Jesus. He did, however, express the fear that he might not be joined in heaven by his relatives and friends, because their faith might not be as strong as his. This illustrates Comstock's lifelong conviction that his views were correct, along with his doubt that others could live up to his standards.

When he was only eighteen, Comstock carried out an act of civil disobedience in his home community. One night he broke into the store of a local merchant who had been accused of selling whiskey to women and children. He emptied the owner's liquor supply onto the floor and left a note warning the merchant that if he didn't stop selling liquor, "he might expect the entire building to come down" (Broun and Leech 1927, 41).

In the early 1870s, Comstock had a modest epiphany when he first learned about the existence of "obscene literature, pictures, etc." (Kendrick 1987, 131). He immediately concluded that these materials would have an adverse effect on young men and perhaps on other people as well. For the rest of his life, Comstock tried to eradicate every bit of sexual material from American society. He made no distinctions about what was being said or shown about sex, or the context in which sex materials appeared. If sexual references were found in a publication—whether pornographic, literary, scientific, or artistic—Comstock tried to destroy it, along with the individuals who produced or distributed it.

Comstock was surprisingly successful in getting organizational support for his crusade against sexual materials, including the active support of Congress. In 1873, he received financial support from the Young Men's Christian Association (YMCA) of New York. His plan was simple: use the money to purchase the publications he considered obscene and then physically destroy them.

Comstock's greatest successes came with the passage of laws governing the U.S. Postal Service. In 1873, Congress passed and President Ulysses S. Grant signed "An Act for the Suppression of Trade in, and Circulation of, Obscene Literature and Articles for Immoral Use." Comstock had labored for a year to get Congress to pass the act, which became popularly known as the "Comstock Law" (Kendrick 1987, 134). According to Kendrick, the law ensured "That no obscene, lewd, or lascivious book, pamphlet, picture, paper, print or other publication of an indecent character, or any article or thing designed or intended for the prevention of conception or procuring an abortion . . . shall be carried in the mail" (Kendrick 1987, 134). This provision, which prohibited the U.S. Postal Service from transporting "indecent" material, gave Comstock his greatest strength as he carried out his campaign against sexual material in the United States. The bill also empowered the Postmaster General to appoint Comstock as a "special agent" to enforce the new law. Comstock held this position until his death in 1915.

Comstock never received a salary for his work as a federal agent, apart from the governmental funds necessary to "defray his expenses." His expenses must have been considerable, however, since he seized and destroyed, by his own estimate, at least 160 tons of material that he found objectionable. He claimed to have convicted "persons enough to fill a passenger train of sixty-one coaches" with sixty persons in each coach (Kendrick 1987, 136), and also boasted that he had hounded quite a number of peddlers of "smut and filth" until they committed suicide. In his zeal to obliterate anything having to do with sex, Comstock often violated the civil rights of those he opposed. For example, he frequently used what is today called entrapment in order to arrest people he believed were trafficking in obscene materials.

Comstock was especially concerned about the damaging effects of obscene literature on young people, and in particular young men who might be tempted into masturbation. In his 1887 annual report to the New York Society for the Suppression of Vice, Comstock listed the materials that had to be eradicated for the protection of children: "books, pamphlets, leaflets, songs, pictures, and . . . articles in rubber, wax, and other materials—all designed and cunningly calculated to excite the imagination and inflame the passions of youth into whose hands they may come" (quoted in Beisel 1997, 53). Comstock had great success in controlling and limiting the distribution of sexual literature and materials in the United States (including birth control information being distributed by the early feminist crusader Margaret Sanger). But his influence waned after his death. By the 1920s, many Americans were starting to react negatively to Comstock's extremism. The word Comstockery soon became a kind of joke, at least among the more sophisticated and intellectual parts of the American population (Broun and Leech 1927).[2]

This negative reaction against censorship has been repeated frequently in the decades that followed. Critics of sexual materials and pornography have often overplayed their hands, exaggerating the negative impact of such materials. As a result, many Americans have rejected and ridiculed their overheated claims.

## REPRESSION IN THE POST-COMSTOCK YEARS

After Comstock left the national stage, the battles against obscenity and pornography were fought mostly in the legal system. During the 1920s, a small number of literary entrepreneurs started challenging the prohibitions against publishing and selling sexual material. Samuel Roth was among the most influential of these early sex pioneers. Roth has been variously described as a defender of freedom of the press, a shrewd businessman, a criminal, a smut peddler and a pornographer, and in some respects, all of these labels are applicable. Labels aside, Roth was undeniably a man who challenged the sexual standards of publishing and selling sexual materials in American society and in his efforts he made a significant contribution to the hypersexuality of American society.

## SAMUEL ROTH: THE ENTREPRENEUR WHO FOUGHT FOR SEXUAL FREEDOM

Samuel Roth was born in Poland in 1895 and came to the United States as a small boy when his parents emigrated. Reaching adulthood in the 1920s, he fancied himself a "man of letters" (Gertzman 1999, 225). In this capacity, he founded the Poetry Bookshop in Manhattan, which he used as a base for publishing the literary magazine, *Lyric*. In *Lyric* he published his own poetry and essays, as well as the work of his literary friends. He also wrote and published articles and poems in other publications, including the *Nation*, *Harper's Weekly*, *Poetry*, and the *Menorah Journal* (Gertzman 1999, 225).

Through his bookstore and publishing business, Roth met some of the most important literary figures of his time, including the aging Frank Harris, who had published a notorious erotic autobiography *My Life and Loves* (Harris 1963/1922); the American poet Edna St. Vincent Millay; and the acclaimed Yiddish writer Solomon Asch. Roth also met the poet Ezra Pound, through whom he made contact with the Irish writer James Joyce (Gertzman 1999).

In the late 1920s, Roth published some pirated excerpts from Joyce's *Ulysses*, which is now considered one of the twentieth-century's literary classics. In the 1920s, Joyce's novel was thought to be pornographic because it contained some unforgettable sexual episodes.[3] For publishing excerpts from Joyce's book, Roth was arrested and subsequently sentenced to jail for sixty days.

After this conviction, Roth aggressively shifted his bookselling business toward works that were unabashedly pornographic (Hyde 1965, 185). It was a financially successful move for Roth, but also a personally costly one. Over the next three decades, he was vilified in the press as a "peddler of smut" and relentlessly hounded by police and prosecutors.

In 1932, *Vanity Fair* featured Roth as a public enemy in its series: "We Nominate for Oblivion." Roth was charged with being a book pirate, a publisher of a book that attacked President Herbert Hoover, and as a distributor of pornography. Among some other highly vilified nominees "for oblivion" in *Vanity* Fair was Adolf Hitler (Gertzman 1999, 222–23).

Roth's biggest problems were not with bad publicity, but with the law, however. In the years following his initial jail term he served three other prison sentences for selling obscene materials. He attempted, with only partial success, to elude the law by frequently changing his name and the names of his business. From the 1920s to the 1950s, Roth used sixty-two different names in an effort to evade law-enforcement authorities (Hyde 1965). Roth's frequent name changes once led *New Yorker* writer and humorist Dorothy Parker to author an article describing "an imaginary conversation between Roth and his many pseudonyms" (Gertzman 1999, 361; quote from Hamalian 1974). Roth was arrested again in 1954, when he was nearly sixty years old. He was indicted on twenty-six counts of mailing obscene pictures, photographs, magazines and books (Hyde 1965, 185). He was convicted, fined five thousand dollars, and sentenced to five years in prison. Roth's appeal of this conviction eventually made its way to the Supreme Court in the *Roth v. United States* described in the last chapter. Though the Supreme Court upheld Roth's conviction,

Justice Brennan's 1957 restatement about what constitutes obscenity contributed to the breakdown of pornography restrictions in the United States (Lane 2000, 25).

As a result, the 1960s witnessed a new era of sexual openness in magazines (*Playboy* and *Penthouse*), books (*Lady Chatterley's Lover* and *Fanny Hill*), movies (Russ Meyer's *The Immoral Mr. Teas* and the Swedish film *I Am Curious Yellow*), and the theatre (*Oh Calcutta* and *Hair*). These magazines, books, movies and plays were followed by a predictable outcry from political conservatives, religious leaders, and other concerned individuals and groups. American presidents Johnson, Nixon, and Reagan responded to the increase in pornographic materials by creating commissions to study "the problem."

## GOVERNMENTAL COMMISSIONS AND PORNOGRAPHY

In 1967, President Lyndon Johnson concluded that the increase in "pornography" had become "a matter of national concern" and therefore established a "Commission on Obscenity and Pornography" (Berger, Searles, and Cottle 1991, 22). The final report, *The 1970 Commission on Obscenity and Pornography*, was released three years later, but by that time Richard Nixon was the president.

Commission members included legal professionals, social scientists, religious leaders, and mass media specialists.

The commission was divided into four groups, each of which investigated a specific aspect of the pornography issue: the effects of pornography, the traffic and distribution of pornography, legal issues relating to pornography, and actions that might be taken with respect to pornography (Berger, Searles, and Cottle 1991).

For many commission supporters the major objective was to demonstrate that pornography led to sex crimes and sexual violence.[4] These expectations were disappointed, however, as the commission reported that no research could be found supporting the hypothesis that pornography increases sexual violence or sex crimes. According to some scholars, the report essentially, "gave pornography a clean bill of health" (Donnerstein, Linz, and Penrod 1987, 23). While that conclusion may have been overstated, the report did provide producers of pornography, erotica, and other sexual materials with a defense that had something of an official imprimatur. During most of the 1970s, producers of sexual materials, including pornographers, were shielded by the commission's conclusions (Berger, Searles, and Cottle 1991).

President Nixon received the commission's report unenthusiastically, and the U.S. Senate passed a resolution condemning the conclusions.

Nixon called the report "morally bankrupt," and further proclaimed, "So long as I am in the White House there will be no relaxation of the national effort to control and eliminate smut from our national life" (Kendrick 1987, 219).

Nixon went even further in his condemnation of pornography, saying, "pornography is to freedom of expression what anarchy is to liberty; as free men willingly restrain a measure of their freedom to prevent anarchy, so must we draw the line against pornography to protect freedom of expression" (Kendrick 1987, 219). Despite Nixon's disapproval, the flow of pornography in the United States continued unabated. One important response came in 1985 when a new Republican president, Ronald Reagan, created another commission to study pornography and its effects. Chaired by Edwin Meese, President Reagan's Attorney General, this commission and its report is generally called the "Meese Commission."

## THE MEESE COMMISSION ON PORNOGRAPHY

President Reagan established the Meese Commission "to officially' over-turn the earlier [1970 Commission] report and spearhead a national effort to increase enforcement of antipornography laws" (Berger, Searles, and Cottle 1991, 25). The Commission's membership was even more broad-based than the 1970 commission, including: "persons with back-grounds in law, behavioral medicine and psychiatry, broadcasting and publishing, and market research" (Berger, Searles, and Cottle 1991, 25). Reagan's appointments to the commission were not completely impar-tial, however. Among the commission's members were "a legal counsel for Citizens for Decency through Law, a leader of the fundamentalist organization Focus on the Family, and a Franciscan priest" (Berger, Searles, and Cottle 1991, 25), all well-known opponents of pornography. Reagan also knew very well that Meese, the man he had appointed to chair the commission, was vehemently opposed to pornography. Meese had been a California prosecutor when Reagan was governor of that state and had been praised by Reagan for "closing down every adult bookstore in his district" (Berger, Searles, and Cottle 1991, 25).

The Meese Commission primarily used public hearings, held in vari-ous cities across the country, to collect data on pornography and its effects. The witnesses who appeared at these hearings were overwhelm-ingly opposed to pornography. Law enforcement officers and religious opponents of pornography were prominently represented, along with Linda Lovelace, the former porn star movie actress, who testified about how she had been abused, victimized, and coerced into appearing in the movie Deep Throat and other pornographic films. (A fuller Linda Lovelace story will be told in Chapter 7.)

The Meese Commission members were especially sympathetic to the witnesses who spoke out against pornography, while those who were less critical were treated more abruptly and dismissively. Even the antipornography feminists Andrea Dworkin and Catherine MacKinnon, whose efforts to outlaw pornography will be described later in this chapter, were treated in a somewhat hostile manner (Berger, Searles, and Cottle 1991).

It was no surprise when the report of the Meese Commission on Pornography was released in 1986 and offered a much more negative assessment of the effects of pornography than had the 1970 commission. The report concluded that violent and degrading pornography (defined as oral, anal, group, masturbatory, and homosexual sex) was definitely harmful (Berger, Searles, and Cottle 1991). Some of the more conservative members of the commission argued that *any* sexually explicit material (even if not violent or degrading) was harmful; they argued that even simple nudity might provoke people to engage in illicit sex (Berger, Searles, and Cottle 1991).

Meese, for whatever reasons, soon distanced himself from the more extreme views of the ultra-conservative members of the commission, proclaiming publicly that as a young man he had read *Playboy* and that it had apparently had no serious impact on his morality. On a more legalistic note, Meese stated publicly that, to his knowledge, "there has not been any court that has held *Playboy* or *Penthouse* to be within the Supreme Court definition of obscenity" (Jones 2000, 583).

In spite of Meese's personal observations, the report did negatively impact the sale of popular magazines like *Playboy* and *Penthouse*, as well as successful books such as *The Joy of Sex* by Dr. Alex Comfort (Strossen 1995). In April 1986, the Southland Corporation, then the owner of forty-five hundred 7-Eleven stores, announced that it would no longer sell *Playboy*, *Penthouse*, or *Forum* magazines (Jones 2000, 578). The president of Southland reported that his decision was based on testimony given before the Meese Commission.[5]

These negative impacts on the distribution of sexual materials were relatively short term, however. Earlier court rulings had cleared the way, and as the country moved into the 1990s, the deluge of sexual and pornographic materials moved relentlessly forward (Weinstein 1999).

During the same time that the Meese Commission was attempting to stop pornography, a vigorous feminist fight to redefine pornography as a violation of women's civil rights was also taking place under the leadership of two key players: Catharine MacKinnon and Andrea Dworkin.

## Feminism and Pornography

During the 1960s and early 1970s, feminists generally supported the idea of greater sexual freedom for women and for men. Many feminists accepted, and some actively supported, the distribution of erotic and even pornographic materials. Tolerance for pornography began to fade among some feminists, however, as they increasingly defined pornography as exploitive of women; other feminists made a direct connection between pornography and violence against women. Feminist Robin Morgan memorably proclaimed: "Pornography is the theory, rape is the practice" (Morgan 1978).

Gloria Steinem, the preeminent journalistic feminist of the era, made a similar argument against pornography in a boldly titled article, "Erotica and Pornography: A Clear and Present Difference" (Steinem 1980). Steinem, who was attuned both to feminism and the sexual revolution, supported sexual freedom for women. This led her to favor erotica, but disapprove of pornography, which she condemned as one more example of the domination of women by men.

Steinem asserted that it was possible to discern whether an image is erotica or pornography simply by looking at any photograph or film of two people "really making love." Real lovemaking (and hence erotica), she believed, includes scenes of "sensuality and touch and warmth, an acceptance of bodies and nerve endings."

In addition to these vague criteria for identifying erotica, Steinem also added the criterion of motivation, defining the erotically engaged couple as "people who are there because they want to be, out of shared pleasure." In contrast to the positive image of the erotic couple, she condemned the physical, emotional, and economic exploitation involved in the making of pornography: "Now look at any depiction of sex in which there is clear force, or an unequal power that spells coercion. It may be very blatant, with weapons of torture or bondage, wounds or bruises, some clear humiliation, or an adult's sexual power being used over a child" (Steinem 1980, 37). Morgan's and Steinem's early feminist critiques of pornography laid the groundwork for an all-out legal attack on pornography by MacKinnon and Dworkin.

## Pornography as a Violation of Women's Civil Rights

Catherine Mackinnon and Andrea Dworkin made an imposing team in their legalistic fight against pornography. The two had very different family backgrounds and career patterns, both before and after their antiporn crusade. MacKinnon came from an upper-middle-class Minnesota family (see Finan 2004). Her father was an influential Republican Congressional representative from Minnesota who ran unsuccessfully for Governor of Minnesota and was later appointed as a federal judge. MacKinnon attended Smith College, from which she graduated magna cum laude with distinction in 1969. She later earned both a law degree (1977), and a PhD in political science (1987) from Yale.

"Dworkin was born in Camden, New Jersey" Andrea Dworkin had her primary success in life as a writer, authoring fourteen books (two coauthored with MacKinnon). By her own description, she did not have an easy life, but one filled with hardships, controversy, and sometimes violence. Dworkin's most recent autobiographical book is revealingly titled *Heartbreak: The Political Memoir of a Feminist Militant*. She concluded her brief preface with these poignant words: "I am ambitious— God knows, not for the money; in most respects, but not all, I am honorable; and I wear overalls: kill the bitch. But the bitch is not yet ready to die, she says, alone in a small room" (Dworkin 2002, xvi). Dworkin was born in Camden, New Jersey, where her father was a schoolteacher who held a second job unloading mail trucks for the post office (Dworkin 1995). After a somewhat rebellious high school career, she was admitted to the expensive—and very liberal—Bennington College on a scholarship. "I stayed there one year, left, returned for two years, left, mailed in my thesis from Amsterdam" (http://www.nostatusquo.com/ACLU/dworkin/AutobiographyII).

At Bennington, Dworkin frequently challenged the rules of the school's administration. She also joined protests against the Vietnam War in New York City, which landed her in jail. It was in jail that she first talked with women who had been jailed for prostitution and where she also learned about the other wretched experiences in the lives of women (http://www.nosatusquo.com/ACLU/dworkin/AutobiographyII).[6]

From the time she was a young child, Dworkin wrote constantly, but it was not until 1974 that she published her first book: *Woman Hating: A Radical Look at Sexuality* (1974). This book was followed two years later by *Our Blood: Prophecies and Discourses on Sexual Politics* (1976). In 1981, she published *Pornography: Men Possessing Women*, a book in which she first connected pornography and the degradation of women. In 1983, she moved to the University of Minnesota, where she co-taught a course on pornography with Catherine MacKinnon.

## CREATING AN ANTIPORNOGRAPHY ORDINANCE

MacKinnon was on a one-year appointment at the University of Minnesota Law School when she and Dworkin teamed up to teach the course on pornography. The two were invited by the Minneapolis Zoning Commission to testify on a proposed ordinance that would restrict the location of businesses selling sexually explicit materials. When MacKinnon and Dworkin met with the Zoning Commission, they offered a much more radical proposal about pornography. In addition to recommending the relocation of businesses selling pornography, they also urged Minneapolis officials to pass an ordinance that would ban the sale of pornography completely. They based their argument on the claim that pornography is a form of sex discrimination that violates the civil rights of women. In drafting an antipornography ordinance for the city, they defined pornography as "the sexually explicit subordination of women, graphically depicted, whether in pictures or words." This included:

> women . . . presented dehumanized as sexual objects, things or commodities; . . . presented as sexual objects who enjoy pain or humiliation; . . . presented as sexual objects who experience pleasure in being raped; . . . presented as sexual objects tied up or cut up or mutilated or bruised or physically hurt; women's body parts are exhibited . . . such that women are reduced to these parts; women . . . presented as whores by nature: . . . presented being penetrated by objects or animals . . . presented in scenarios of degradation, injury, abasement, torture, shown as filthy or inferior, bleeding, bruised or hurt in a context that makes these conditions sexual. (Finan 2004)

In December 1983, the Minneapolis City Council passed an ordinance that authorized any woman to sue the producer or distributor of pornographic materials, as defined by MacKinnon and Dworkin. On December 30, despite tremendous pressure from feminists and other antipornography forces, Donald Fraser the mayor of Minneapolis vetoed the ordinance, arguing that its descriptions of pornography were so inclusive and ill-defined that the ordinance would probably be declared unconstitutional. "The definition of pornography in the ordinance," he explained, "is so broad and so vague as to make it impossible for a bookseller, movie theater operator, or museum director to adjust his or her conduct in order to keep from running afoul of the law" (Finan 2004, 9).

When Minneapolis failed to pass the proposed ordinance, even after a second try, MacKinnon and Dworkin turned their attention to another city, Indianapolis, Indiana. Indianapolis city officials were generally much more politically conservative than those in Minneapolis and they quickly passed the antipornography legislation. The new Indianapolis law imposed civil sanctions for the distribution of sexually explicit material demeaning to women and prohibited the distribution of pornography, which was defined as "the graphic sexually explicit subordination of women, whether in pictures or words" (Weinstein 1999).

Immediately after its passage, the bill was challenged in court by "booksellers, publishers, librarians, magazine wholesalers and distributors" and other advocates of civil rights (Finan 2004, 10). In 1985, the case was heard in the U.S. District Court by Judge Sarah Evans Barker, who declared it invalid because it violated the First Amendment of the Constitution. The City of Indianapolis appealed the decision, and the U.S. Court of Appeals affirmed the district court ruling, with Judge Frank Easterbrook writing the opinion.

Judge Easterbrook's ruling hinged on his observation that the Indianapolis ordinance unlawfully discriminated against a particular "point of view" in how women are treated in the depiction of a sexual encounter. According to the ordinance, when a sexual encounter is described or shown in an "approved" way (i.e., equality between the sexes), then it is lawful. When a sexual encounter shows a women being treated in a disapproved way—(domination, humiliation, etc.) then it is not lawful. "The Constitution," ruled Easterbrook, "forbids the state to declare one perspective right and silence opponents." In enforcing the law, the state would be prohibiting one viewpoint about sexual encounters, while accepting another.

Judge Easterbrook further ruled that the state cannot lawfully suppress words and images that present women in submissive and humiliating conditions, even if such words and images might lead to negative consequences (subordination of women in the workplace, lower pay, insult and injury in the home, battery and rape on the streets), unless the danger produced by such material is clearly established as "not only grave, but imminent." Easterbrook's ruling reflects Justice Howard Taft's oft-quoted judicial judgment that free speech does not allow a person indiscriminately to shout "fire" in a crowded theater, since such an action would present "a grave and imminent danger" to other people. All other speech, whatever its potential negative effects on particular individuals, is constitutionally protected.

After the Court of Appeals ruled the Indianapolis ordinance unconstitutional, the city appealed the decision to the U.S. Supreme Court. In 1986, the Supreme Court affirmed the Appeals Court decision without hearing oral arguments or issuing an opinion (Weinstein 1999).

## OTHER FEMINIST VIEWS ABOUT THE
## MACKINNON AND DWORKIN ARGUMENT

Feminist writers during the 1980s and into the 1990s generally supported MacKinnon and Dworkin's position that pornography is harmful to women. Catherine Itzin, for example, edited the anthology, *Pornography: Women, Violence, and Civil Liberties*, which assembled more than two dozen articles supporting MacKinnon's and Dworkin's view (Itzin 1992a). Itzin's personal experiences, both in her own country, the United Kingdom, and in the United States, led her to accuse pornography of exploiting women and children both economically and sexually. Poor women, she claimed, are especially likely to be exploited because they have fewer opportunities for earning a living and are sometimes coerced into pornography where they may be hurt physically or psychologically (Itzin 1992b).

More recently, Dines, Jensen, and Russo (1998), have vigorously and effectively defended the feminist case against pornography, dedicating their book to Andrea Dworkin, "whose writing and commitment to fighting the pornography industry have made this work possible" (Dines, Jensen, and Russo 1998, v). Despite their ongoing support for MacKinnon and Dworkin's position, the authors seem to despair about the lack of success in the fight against pornography. More than a decade after the MacKinnon/Dworkin legal challenge had been struck down by the American courts, the tide of pornography had not been turned back. The United States is described in Robert Jensen's introductory chapter as a "hypersexualized pornographic culture" and "a culture saturated with pornography" (*Jensen* 1998, 6–7).

Feminists fighting to eliminate pornography from society have reason to despair. Not only was the battle lost in the courts, but many feminist writers have also spoken out against those who would censor pornography. The following is just a sampling of these books: Alison Assiter and Carol Avedon (1993) *Bad Girls and Dirty Pictures: The Challenge to Reclaim Feminism*, Carol Avedon (1994) *Nudes, Prudes and Attitudes: Pornography and Censorship*, Wendy McElroy (1995) *XXX: A Woman's Right to Pornography*, Pamela Church Gibson and Roma Gibson (1993) *Dirty Looks: Women, Pornography and Power*, Nadine Strossen (1995) *Defending Pornography: Free Speech, Sex, and the Fight for Women's Rights*, and Lisa Palac (1998) *The Edge of the Bed* (informed by her own experiences as a pornography participant and producer).

## A CANADIAN FOOTNOTE ON MACKINNON/DWORKIN

While the Mackinnon/Dworkin legislation failed in U.S. courts, the opposite occurred in Canada. In 1992, the Canadian Supreme Court concluded, in *Butler v. the Queen*, that pornography degrades and dehumanizes women. MacKinnon provided a brief for this case, which apparently influenced the decision of the Canadian court (Strossen 1995, 19). The Canadian interpretation of obscenity laws does contain the provision, however, that "no material will be deemed obscene if it has an artistic purpose or is a part of the serious treatment of a sexual theme," which parallels the position of U.S ruling that "excludes serious literary, artistic, political, or scientific value" (Strossen 1995, 231). Also following U.S. law, Canadian law states that obscenity laws only apply to works as a whole—not to individual parts that include sexually explicit materials (Strossen 1995).

Even though the Canadian legal interpretation was based on the Mackinnon/Dworkin formulation, its execution has had some notably antifeminist results. According to a 1993 issue of the Canadian *Feminist Bookstore News*, "Within the first two and a half years after the *Butler* decision, well over half of all Canadian *feminist* [emphasis added] bookstores had materials confiscated or detained by customs" (Strossen 1995, 231). During the same period, mainstream and franchise bookstores that carried sexually explicit materials were rarely bothered. Madonna's book, *Sex*, which contained many erotic scenes, was openly sold in many bookstores with no interference by the Canadian authorities (Strossen 1995).

In one application of the Canadian antipornography law, two books written by Andrea Dworkin (*Pornography: Men Possessing Women* and *Women Hating*) were confiscated by customs agents at the Canadian-U.S. border (Strossen 1995; Weinstein 1999). The confiscated books were written in opposition to pornography, as their titles clearly reveal, but Canadian authorities, following the letter of the law, would not let them pass into Canada (Strossen 1995).

According to most observers, the feminist legal challenge to pornography has failed (Dines, Jensen, and Russo 1998; Itzin 1992a; Lederer 1980; Russell 1993). The failures of past efforts do not mean, however, that attempts to repress sexual materials and pornography have ceased. Today, politicians, special interest groups, and individuals are using various means (community meetings, newspaper ads, direct mailings, and the Internet) to fight against pornography and other sexual materials.

## CONTINUING EFFORTS TO SUPPRESS
## SEXUAL MATERIALS AND PORNOGRAPHY

The U.S. Congress and the legislatures of individual states continue trying to censor or repress sexual/pornographic materials. These actions are most often in response to high-profile news events involving controversial sexual displays, such as the Janet Jackson Superbowl halftime incident, *Desperate Housewives'* Nicollette Sheridan's infamous dropped towel on a Monday Night football broadcast commercial, or any number of Howard Stern's on-air comments. Public outcry following such events has prompted politicians in Washington to demand ever-larger monetary fines when television and radio broadcasts on public airwaves exceed their standards of decency (Ahrens 2005a). These will be discussed more fully in Chapter 8.

Politicians also respond to complaints from special interest groups and organizations created to fight pornography and various forms of sexual licentiousness. The following are brief descriptions of some of the most prominent organizations and individuals dedicated to repressing sexual material and pornography today.

### THE AMERICAN FAMILY ASSOCIATION

The Rev. Donald E. Wildmon leads one of the largest, strongest, and most wide-ranging antipornography organizations in the United States. An ordained United Methodist minister, Wildmon holds a Master of Divinity degree from Emory University (1965). During the 1970s, Wildmon served as the pastor of First Methodist Church in Tupelo, Mississippi, from which he retired in 1977 to found the National Federation of Decency. In 1988, this organization was transformed into the American Family Association.

On the current Web site for the American Family Association (http://www.afa.net), Wildmon provides a personal account of the epiphany that led him to his current antipornography crusade: "One evening in 1977 I sat down with my family to watch TV. On one channel was adultery, on another cursing, on another a man beating another over the head with a hammer. I asked the children to turn off the TV. I sat there, got angry, and said, 'They're going to bring this into my home, and I'm going to do all I can to change it'" (http://www.afa.net/about.asp). Today Wildmon's organization, after being in existence for more than 30 years, claims more than 2.5 million members. To spread his message, Wildmon has appeared on Good Morning America, The Today Show, The MacNeill Lehrer Report, Nightline, The 700 Club,

Meet the Press, Crossfire, and Focus on the Family (http://www.afa .net/about.asp).

The major targets of Wildmon's American Family Association are sexual displays and pornography, especially on television and radio. AFA claims, for example, to have led the fight to clean up the Howard Stern Radio Show (though the impact on Stern's career has hardly been noticeable—see Chapter 8). Other AFA efforts have included: helping to remove pornography magazines from forty-three federal prisons, getting thirty thousand convenience stores to pull sexually oriented magazines from their shelves, and convincing Burger King, Clorox, and S. C. Johnson to pull their advertising from television programs that contain sexual material.

AFA also sponsors programs that support people fighting "sexual addiction" to pornography. A complementary program is designed to help the "victims of pornography," including family members of "pornography addicts," as well as women who have engaged in the production of pornography (http://www.afa.net/pornography).

## FOCUS ON THE FAMILY

The Focus on the Family Web site begins by asserting that up until recently, "Americans have intuitively understood the danger to family and community posed by pornographic and obscene material" (http://www.family.org/cforumn/fosi/pornography). According to the Web site, this situation has changed, and today, sexual materials and pornography appear unabated throughout our society. Pornography is characterized as treating human beings not as "unique creations with inherent dignity," but "more as objects to be manipulated to further personal aims" (http://www.family.org/cforumn/fosi/pornography). This perspective reflects the intellectually sophisticated perspective of David L. Weiss, the organization's major spokesperson.

Weiss's publications focus primarily on pornography on the Internet and the presumed deleterious effects of Internet porn on married couples. Along with the American Family Association, Weiss believes that pornography is addictive, especially for males. He also recommends counseling for married couples whose lives have been negatively affected by pornography.

## MORALITY IN MEDIA

In 1962, Father Morton A. Hill established Morality in Media to "combat obscenity and uphold decency standards in the media" (http:// www.moralityinmedia.org).[7] Though Father Hill died in 1985, the organization he created continues to be active. MIM's primary focus is television programming that it considers "indecent," even if it is not considered obscene (and thus illegal) by constitutional criteria. MIM actively encourages supporters to send their objections about indecent television programming both to the Federal Communications Commission and directly to companies that sponsor indecent television programming through on-air advertising. Other recommendations include contacting national media executives, as well as local television affiliates and cable operators, directly (http://www.moralityinmedia.org/fighttv.htm).

<h2 style="text-align:center">PARENTS TELEVISION COUNCIL</h2>

L. Brent Bozell III started Parents Television Council in 1995 with a focus on television programming. The PTC Web site states as its objective: "reducing graphic and gratuitous sex, violence and profanity in the media" (http://www.parentsstv.org). According to its Web site, PTC currently claims to have twenty-eight chapters across the country.

Judging from the media coverage of Bozell and his organization, Parents Television Council is among the most successful of the antipornography organizations. A recent Time magazine cover story, "The Decency Police" (Poniewozik 2005; see also, Thompson 2004), prominently featured Bozell and PTC. In just ten years from its inception, PTC grew to a million-member organization, with sophisticated methods of monitoring the media and mobilizing its members. The organization boasts a mailing list of 125,000 "online members," and its Web site offers complaint form letters and "streaming video clips" of TV episodes that visitors can watch. If they find them offensive, they have only to click to zap off a letter (Poniewozik 2005, 27).

Bozell continues to issue position statements on news events and television programming. In response to recent legislation by Senator Ted Stevens of Alaska to bring cable and satellite television under the control of the Federal Communications Commission, Bozell has stated that "he would support legislation that would subject cable to the same decency regulations as broadcast television" (http://www.parentsstv.org). Recently, he wrote a scathing attack on MTV, describing the popular music network as "a 24-hour hangout selling easy sex, swagger and swearing—all aimed, directly and deliberately, at children (http://www.parents stv.org/PTC/publications/1bbcolumns/2005/0204.asp). PTC also provides statistical analyses of television programming. On MTV, for example, PTC analysts identified "3,056 depictions of sexual dancing, gesturing, or various forms of nudity, and another 2,881 verbal sexual references" during a recent 171-hour period (http://www.parentsstv.org/PTC/publications/1bbcolumns/2005/0204.asp).

## CITIZENS FOR COMMUNITY VALUES

This Cincinnati-based organization was started by Dr. Jerry Kirk in 1983 as a challenge to "the pandering of pornography—and the harmful toll it was taking on the lives of men, women, and children" (http:// www.ccv.org/About CCV.htm). The organization's major objective is to monitor and take "action against pornography outlets" (http://www .ccv.org/About CCV.htm).

While strongly opposed to pornography, CCV also supports the First Amendment right of free speech. "In all our efforts, we resolve to abide by existing Supreme Court decisions, oppose unauthorized censorship, and defend the rights of free speech and community involvement" (http:// www.ccv.org/About CCV.htm). The critical term in this statement is "community involvement."

Working within the Supreme Court Miller decision, which ruled that obscenity should be judged on the basis of individual community standards, Citizens for Community Values has mobilized community opinion to eliminate the sale or rental of many sexual materials in the greater Cincinnati community. Today, the organization's Web site claims that 95 percent of the twenty-eight hundred stores that sell magazines in the greater Cincinnati area do not sell *Playboy*-type magazines and that 95 percent of stores that sell or rent videos do not handle X-rated videos. Topless bars and strip clubs have also been nearly eliminated in the Cincinnati area. In the seventeen counties in the Greater Cincinnati area, only five such businesses are still in operation, the smallest number for any major metropolitan area in the country (http://www.ccv.org/About CCV.htm).

The Citizens for Community Values is also actively involved in campaigns against same-sex marriage. The group's first organized effort was the National Campaign to Protect Marriage that mobilized national and local pro-family leaders in all fifty states to work together to defend traditional "'one-man—one-woman" marriage (http://www.ccv.org/About CCV.htm). The organization's support for this cause has extended to various "defense-of-marriage" laws in thirty-six states.

Other groups that have been created to reduce or censor sexual materials and pornography in the United States include: Authentic Relationships International, Concerned Women for America, Exodus International, Family Research Council, Enough is Enough (see Donna Rice Hughes in the next section), American Decency Association, Center for Reclaiming America, National Coalition for the Protection of Children and Families, and Faith to Action.

While organizations are the principal sources of opposition to sexual material and pornography in the United States, individuals around the country are also waging their own personal battles against pornography: writing letters or e-mails to the editors of their local newspapers, organizing picket lines in front of adult book stores, creating Web sites, and even writing books (often self-published) to state their positions. One such individual is Donna Rice Hughes.

## DONNA RICE HUGHES

In 1988, Senator Gary Hart, a Democrat from Colorado, was seeking the nomination for the presidency of the United States. In the course of the campaign, rumors abounded that the married Senator Hart was having an extra-marital affair. Senator Hart vigorously denied the reports and foolishly challenged the press to show proof that the rumors had validity. Newspapers were soon reporting Hart's comings and goings, including his visits to the Washington, DC, townhouse of a young woman named Donna Rice. A short time later, a photograph appeared on the front page of *The National Inquirer*, showing Rice seated on the lap of Senator Hart as they were about to set sail on the appropriately named pleasure boat, *Monkey Business*.

All of this adverse publicity forced Senator Hart to withdraw from the presidential race; Donna Rice, who had now had her fifteen minutes of fame, faded from public view. But Rice has re-emerged, with her new name Donna Rice Hughes, and now she is an antipornography crusader, working to protect children from sexual material and pornography on the Internet. In the late 1990s, she established a Web site and coauthored the book *Kids Online: Protecting Your Children in Cyberspace* (Hughes 1998), coauthored with Pamela T. Campbell.

Hughes currently serves as the president of "Enough is Enough," described on its Internet Web site as "a national nonprofit educational organization whose mission is protecting children from the harms of predators and pornography and the links to sexual violence" (http://www.enough.org/who.htm). In her current public role as a guardian of children who are threatened by sexual material and pornography on the Internet, Hughes has appeared on *Dateline*, *The Today Show*, *Oprah*, and *20/20*, and stories about her have also appeared in many of the country's major newspapers (http://www.protectkids.com .donnaricehughes/bio.htm).[8]

Hughes is just one of many people in the United States fighting against the pervasiveness of sexual material and pornography in society. Some, like Hughes, work independently, while others lead or join organizations that are trying—usually with only limited success—to repress sexual material and pornography through the Internet, radio, television, or some form of print media. In the twenty-first century, sexual expression is restricted in only limited ways, with the resulting free flow of sexual material, erotica, and pornography contributing to the formation of our current hypersexual society.

# SEX ON THE PRINTED PAGE

## FROM LITERARY CLASSICS TO *PLAYBOY* AND X-RATED COMICS

In 2002, a book titled *The Sexual Life of Catherine M.* hit the American book scene (Millet 2002). The book, an autobiographical account of the extraordinary sex life of a French woman named Catherine Millet, was widely reviewed (generally positively) in major American publications, and achieved sales that put it on some of the most prestigious best seller lists. Millet, though highly esteemed in the art/literary world, did not make her reputation as an expert on sex, and certainly not as a writer of pornographic materials. For many years, she has been an eminent Parisian art critic and the editor of the highly respected magazine *Art Press*.

When Millet's book was published in the United States, some reviewers were shocked by the raw details of the author's sex life, but others found her story riveting. Many reviewers cited the redeeming literary or social value in Millet's introspective, analytical examination of her promiscuous sexual experiences. "An extraordinary story," wrote a reviewer for *Newsweek*, "An eloquent, graphic—and sometimes even poignant—account." A reviewer from *The Philadelphia Inquirer* enthused: "This exquisite, philosophical, imaginative, precisely reported memoir . . . offers a wholly unique voice. . . . The excellence of Millet's memoir rests not in numbers . . . but in Proustian memories and perceptions suffused with sex and insights" [1]

Millet's literary description of her sex life was certainly explicit and was probably shocking for many readers. She began her account with a very long chapter titled "Numbers," an innocuous word that she used to signal her many sexual experiences with multiple partners. "In the biggest orgies in which I participated" she recalled, "there could be up to 150 people . . . and I would take on the cocks of around a quarter or a fifth of them in all the available ways: in my hands, my mouth, my cunt and in my ass" (Millet 2002, 10). Many of her partners were at the time and still remain unknown to her. "I can only account for forty-nine men whose sexual organs have penetrated mine and to whom I can attribute a name or, at least, in a few cases, an identity" she confesses (Millet 2002, 10).

A surprising number of these multiple-partner sexual experiences were arranged, or at least condoned, by whoever might have been her primary lover at the time. She would often go to a back room of the Chez Aime' bar in Paris where she would lie on a rough-hewn table, the room illuminated only by overhead lights, to receive the men from the bar. "Always the same configuration: hands running over my body, me grabbing at cocks, turning my head from left to right to suck, while other cocks rammed into me, up toward my belly. Twenty could take turns in an evening." (Millet 2002, 19).

Only a half century ago Millet's book would have been labeled obscene and pornographic and would probably have led to arrests and prosecutions. To date, no such actions have been taken. This explicitly sexual book is now an acceptable, and even respectable, part of American book publishing.

## UNDERSTANDING THE ACCEPTANCE OF MILLET'S AUTOBIOGRAPHY

The three major societal trends we introduced in Chapter 2 have led to the general acceptance of Millet's book, as well as to the widespread availability of all forms of sexual material in American society. As described before, these include:

1. Economic development and personal affluence,
2. Political democratization and personal liberty,
3. Technological advances and personal accessibility.

Of these three societal trends, political democratization and personal liberty have played the most important role in changing the attitudes of producers and consumers of sexually explicit publications. During the past half century, the expansion of the idea of personal liberty has transformed the social, legal, and cultural context, so that today previously forbidden materials have become increasingly available to adult Americans.

The shift toward more personal freedom can be traced to a number of social/historical sources. First, the movement away from living in small communities to living in more urban places has given Americans more personal freedom. Small-town life may have a nostalgic appeal for many people, but, in fact, many more Americans than ever live in cities and even suburbs where they have relative anonymity—or, at the very least, greater personal privacy.

A second source of personal liberty has a more normative character. During the cultural upheaval of the 1970s, Americans increasingly accepted the view that each person has a right to do what he or she wants, as long as it doesn't harm anyone else. Individuals were urged by counter-cultural leaders to "do their own thing" and "march to their own drummer." "Whatever turns you on" became the rallying cry for what came to be known as the "sexual revolution."

This expanding notion of personal liberty was consistent with the traditional American cultural value of individualism, particularly the uniquely American version of individualism known as "expressive individualism" (Bellah et al. 1985). Expressive individualism is the recognition or discovery of "one's unique identity and the freedom of individual self expression" (Bulman 2005, 20). Expressive individualism has reinforced Americans' emerging freedom to purchase and read whatever sexual materials they wish.

Libertarian values have also played an important role in forming Americans' attitudes toward and use of sexually explicit materials. Libertarians are especially concerned about the ways in which governments infringe on the personal lives of individuals. They believe that individuals should be able to make personal decisions about their lives without interference from others. They are especially resistant to interference by the government. Libertarian beliefs, whether in pure or modified form, have contributed to an increased sense of freedom for individuals to read or view whatever they wish, as long as their behavior does not harm others.

Economic development and technological advances have also increased the availability and consumption of sexually explicit materials in American society. General economic prosperity has provided individuals with more disposable income to spend on the products delivered by traditional and emerging media technologies—from books and magazines to movies and CDs, and the explosion of materials on the Internet. As we shall see in the following discussion, technological advances have had the unanticipated effect of reducing the importance of the once-dominant forms of pornography (e.g., magazines). As video, digital, and interactive technologies have dramatically increased the accessibility and affordability of sexually explicit materials, they have made earlier forms of print pornography less significant. But for most of the middle part of the twentieth century magazines and books were the primary source of erotic and pornographic materials.

## PORNOGRAPHY AND EROTICA IN AMERICAN MAGAZINES

For many years, American magazine publishers provided much of the available pictorial erotica and pornography in the United States. The content of most of these magazines was generally limited to photographs of nude women in various poses, but some of the more hard-core magazines also featured photographs of men and women engaged in sexual intercourse and other sexual acts. A much smaller number of magazines presented photographs that were directed toward gay males, and a few depicted females engaging in sex. One of the key players in the distribution of pornographic magazines (as well as other pornographic materials as his enterprise expanded) was Reuben Sturman.

### REUBEN STURMAN: AN EARLY PURVEYOR OF PORNOGRAPHIC MAGAZINES

Sturman was a first-generation American, the son of Russian immigrants. After serving three years in the Air Force, he returned to civilian life in the early 1950s in Columbus, Ohio, where he was looking for opportunities to make his fortune (Schlosser 2003). He first took a job as a salesman for a candy and tobacco distributor, but soon went into business for himself when he acquired a large quantity of remaindered comic books. He successfully sold these to candy stores for a profit, which started him in the wholesale magazine business. He soon was selling automobile magazines, movie magazines, and crossword puzzle magazines, but eventually, he moved on to selling sex magazines and "sex-pulp" novels. These last two categories proved to be more profitable than the other printed products (Schlosser 2003).

As Sturman's distribution of sex publications increased in the early 1960s he had his first encounters with the law. In 1964, a Sturman-owned warehouse in Cleveland was raided by the FBI. Authorities confiscated 590 copies of Sex Life of a Cop, an explicit fictional account of the sexual escapades of two police officers. During the raid, the FBI also seized copies of Jack Kerouac's *The Subterraneans*, a classic of the Beat Generation that is still being sold and read today.

In the face of these early legal challenges, Sturman made what would remain a lifelong commitment. In the words of his biographer: "After thinking long and hard, Reuben Sturman came to a conclusion that he would defend at great cost for the next thirty years: Americans should have the freedom to read or to view whatever they wanted, in the privacy of their own homes—and he should have the freedom to sell it" (Schlosser 2003, 118). Sturman took his case all the way to the Supreme Court, which ruled in 1967 that *Sex Life of A Cop* met the legal standard of having "some social value."

During the next quarter of a century, Sturman established adult magazine stores throughout the country, which provided profitable innovations such as peep shows (coin-operated film projections displaying short loops of sexually explicit film, shown in small cubicles) and X-rated videotapes. As he expanded his pornography business throughout the 1970s and 1980s, Sturman became enormously wealthy. But the more his wealth increased, the more he became visible to authorities. Eventually, it was a tax evasion charge—and not a pornography charge—that led to Sturman's arrest and conviction. In 1992, he was sentenced to four years in prison and fined one million dollars (Schlosser 2003).

Sturman's career represents only a small part of the growth of pornographic publications during the last half of the twentieth century. By the 1970s, adult bookstores had opened throughout the country, usually in the gritty areas of large cities, but also in the fringe downtown areas of smaller cities, in some small towns, and along the streets and highways of the suburbs. Adult bookstores can still be found today, but many have gone out of business due to competition with sexual material that is now more easily available on VCRs, DVDs, and the Internet.

Mass-circulation sex and nudity magazines, as opposed to the strictly pornographic, are a different story. This is a story that begins with Hugh Hefner and *Playboy* magazine.

## Hugh Hefner, the Perennial and Aging Playboy

Hugh Hefner's story has been told so many times that it has become a part of American cultural and sexual folklore. He has now attained such celebrity status that America's media (newspapers, magazines, and television) routinely report on his lifestyle and his activities (Sales 2001; Waxman 1999).[2]

Hefner's rags-to-riches story began around 1946 when, only twenty years old, he was discharged from the Army. Enrolling at the University of Illinois, courtesy of the GI Bill, he earned a bachelor's degree. After college he moved from one job to another, before finally enrolling in the graduate program in sociology at Northwestern University, where he lasted only one semester. At this time in his personal life Hefner had only one serious girlfriend, and that was the woman he eventually married. By his own account, Hefner did not have sexual relations until he was twenty-two years old (Talese 1980).

Following his abortive foray into sociology, Hefner worked at an advertising agency and then for the Chicago-based magazine *Coronet*. After that job ended, he worked for another magazine publisher, who was just entering the "girlie" magazine field, which provided the young Hefner with his first exposure to a promising new field of publishing.

In 1953, Hefner ventured into the publishing world, putting up six hundred dollars, which he had borrowed against his apartment furniture, to publish the first issue of *Playboy*. The introductory issue featured a nude calendar photograph of Marilyn Monroe, at that time a nearly unknown actress. The Monroe photograph helped to catapult Hefner's magazine into the center of American popular culture. "Prior to *Playboy*," explains Gay Talese, "few American men [or women] had ever seen a color photograph of a nude woman" (Talese 1980, 27).

Hefner's career has now gone into the twenty-first century, and though there have been a few economic bumps along the way, his creation, now Playboy Enterprises International, Inc., still thrives. Hefner is billed as the editor-in-chief of the magazine, but his daughter Christine runs the Playboy Corporation and the magazine. Now in his eighties, Hefner has devoted himself to living a hedonistic sexual life in his Los Angeles Playboy mansion. Since ending his second marriage (to a previous *Playboy* Playmate), he has surrounded himself with a variety of beautiful blonde-haired young women (at one time numbering seven nineteen to thirty year olds). Hefner has said, "I'm leading the fantasy life of an adolescent boy" (Sales 2001, 245).

The *Playboy* philosophy, which Hefner embodies, encourages readers to maximize their sexual pleasures and adventures. Over a half century, the number of male readers who have absorbed some of *Playboy*'s self-indulgent, hedonistic philosophy is incalculable, but Hugh Hefner is arguably the most important single individual to have advanced and legitimized the pleasure-hedonistic mode of sexual discourse in American society.

## BEYOND *PLAYBOY*

After the success of *Playboy*, many lookalikes and wannabes made their appearance on the magazine racks of the nation. *Penthouse*, published by Bob Guccione, has been one of the most successful of these competitors.

*Penthouse* was first published in Great Britain but Guccione brought it to the United States in 1969, where it enjoyed substantial success during the 1970s and 1980s (Bosworth 2005). By 1979, *Penthouse* had gained a circulation of 4.7 million, providing Guccione with an estimated net worth of 200 million dollars

Like *Playboy*, *Penthouse* featured soft photographic images of naked young women (called "Pets" to parallel *Playboy*'s "Playmates"). *Penthouse* has the distinction of being the first large-circulation magazine to publish photographs of female pubic hair, spread vaginas and erect penises.

The popularity of *Penthouse* began to decline, however, after the publication of the Report of the Meese Commission on Pornography in 1986 (see Chapter 3). The Meese Report caused many retail outlets, especially convenience stores, Wal-Mart, and other large retail outlets, either to remove or partially hide sexually oriented magazines from their shelves. *Penthouse* experienced its greatest losses during the late 1980s and 1990s when the technological changes began to cut into the market. As soon as Americans were able to rent or purchase X-rated videos, which they could play on their home VCRs, the sales of *Penthouse* and similar magazines started to decline (Bosworth 2005). The advent of cable and satellite television, followed by the Internet, provided even more conveniently available sexual material, all of which negatively impacted the sex-magazine market.

## LARRY FLYNT AND *HUSTLER*

A more infamous follow-up to *Playboy* was provided by the introduction of Larry Flynt's *Hustler* magazine in 1973 (Flynt 2004). *Hustler*'s photographs had a much rawer edge than did those in *Playboy* or *Penthouse*. "At *Hustler*," Flynt recently recalled, "we were being outrageously vulgar by design" (Flynt 2004, 6). This policy, which featured everything from spread-legged models to the cartoon image of a nude woman being forced through a meat grinder, has proven successful for nearly four decades, and has made Flynt a multimillionaire.

Flynt's personal history is another rags-to-riches story, though certainly not one with the virtues of Horatio Alger books. After a teenage hitch in the Navy, Flynt returned to his home state of Ohio in the early 1960s. He worked double shifts in a factory and soon accumulated enough money to buy a bar that was owned by his mother. Within a few years, Flynt owned eight bars, which he named "Hustler Clubs." To advertise his clubs, he put out a newsletter featuring photographs of the go-go girls who worked there. The newsletter eventually morphed into *Hustler* magazine (Flynt 2004).

While Hefner and Guccione made their greatest contributions to the pleasure-hedonism form of sexual discourse, Flynt has become increasingly involved in the political-legal side of sexual discourse. In recent years, he has become something of a First Amendment celebrity, noted as much for his high-profile court battles as for his salacious and sexist publications.[3]

In the late 1980s, Flynt published a satirical fiction piece about the late Rev. Jerry Falwell, founder of the fundamentalist political organization Moral Majority. This piece, suggested that Falwell had had incestuous sexual relations with his mother. Falwell filed a 50 million dollar lawsuit against Flynt and his magazine. A lower court ruled that Flynt should pay Falwell two hundred thousand dollars, but Flynt refused to pay and appealed the decision to a higher court. Ultimately, the case reached the Supreme Court, where all nine justices ruled in favor of Flynt, establishing much more liberal legal standards regarding libel.

In 1978, Flynt was shot by an assailant, leaving him a paraplegic. Flynt's physical limitations have not prevented him from publishing *Hustler* and more than thirty other adult magazines. He has also become a champion for free speech and is a popular speaker on college and university campuses across the country (University of Southern California, Harvard, and others).

Larry Flynt is a self-described "pornographer" and "smut peddler," and though he is anathema to many people he has been a key player in the political-legal form of sexual discourse and, in his own way, an effective advocate for personal liberty. In the process, he has achieved what many Americans strive for: wealth and celebrity.

## OTHER SEXUALLY ORIENTED MAGAZINES TODAY

In 1974, Hefner introduced *Playgirl*, the supposed female answer to *Playboy*, which followed Guccione's 1973 *Viva*, another glossy magazine featuring naked male bodies. Even though these magazines were created for women, many in the publishing world suspected that the primary consumers were gay males. According to Patricia Bosworth, a former editor of *Viva*, "I heard rumors that much of the readership was made up of gay men who liked [the nude male] pictorials" (Bosworth 2005, 158).

While *Playgirl* and *Viva* may have a mixed and uncertain clientele, men are clearly the targeted audience for many of today's newsstand (and Internet-advertised) magazines featuring nude male models. The magazine *Men*, for instance, describes itself as "America's largest selling erotic magazine for men who love men," while *Freshman* bills itself as "the monthly erotic magazine all about young men . . . a mix of great nude photography and fiction . . . all with youth appeal." Another magazine, *Instinct*, proudly proclaims itself to be "America's #1 gay magazine," and sees itself as a "clever mix of *Cosmo* and *Maxim*."

SCREW, THE MAGAZINE

A discussion about American sex magazines would not be complete without a brief mention of *Screw* magazine and creator/editor Al Goldstein. From the late 1960s through the early years of the twenty-first century, Al Goldstein was the undisputed king of bad-taste pornography in print. Goldstein's major life accomplishment was the creation of a tabloid-like newsprint magazine that was universally acknowledged as the raunchiest, most in-your-face sex publication that could be found in the United States (Paumgarten 2005). The title, *Screw*, said it all—the magazine was about sex and screw anyone who didn't like it. Eventually, Goldstein took his pornography product to cable television in New York City, where for a few years he hosted a late-night show called *Midnight Blue*. One writer described Goldstein as "the foulmouthed host of the scruffy . . . pornography program." (Paumgarten 2005, 23), while another reporter simply described *Midnight Blue* as "an X-rated cult show" (Zawadzinski 2005, C9).

Goldstein enjoyed enormous financial success in the heyday of his publication. He amassed a fortune estimated at 11 million dollars and with his riches he hosted parties at some of New York's hottest clubs during the 1970s. But Goldstein eventually fell on hard times, bankruptcy and at one point homelessness (Paumgarten 2005; Zawadzinski 2005; Reinholz 2004). He sometimes slept in homeless shelters or in Central Park, but eventually got back on his feet, and now lives on Staten Island with his 28-year-old fifth wife (Zawadzinski 2005).[4]

Goldstein's economic downfall was at least partially the result of his abrasive and tendentious personality and his eagerness to file costly lawsuits. His most successful sexual publication, *Screw*, eventually became obsolete with the advent of new technologies that could provide pornography more effectively. People became less interested in Goldstein's old-fashioned newsprint publication once that they were able to rent or purchase X-rated videos or watch sexual scenes on cable/satellite television. And then along came the Internet with all of its pornography. Goldstein understood what had happened: "The Internet made pornography available for free, and I couldn't compete" (Zawadzinski 2005, C9).

SEX IN POPULAR MAINSTREAM AMERICAN MAGAZINES

Sex has also left its mark on America's popular, mass distribution magazines, many of which have increasingly made sexual content a mainstay of their monthly fare.

In the pre-World War II era of American culture, popular magazines, such as Saturday Evening Post and *Colliers*, were unrelentingly wholesome, with virtually no sexual content. Popular weekly magazines that featured photographs, such as *Life* and *Look*, occasionally offered mild sexual display in the form of starlets or debutantes gamboling around in one-piece bathing suits or low-cut gowns. In 1941, *Life* pushed the boundaries even further with a provocative full-page photograph of movie star Rita Hayworth, kneeling on a bed, dressed only in a lacy slip that outlined her ample breasts. The photograph became a popular pinup among American military men during World War II and remained unsurpassed until *Playboy's* nude calendar photograph of Marilyn Monroe appeared in the 1950s.

Perhaps the most sexually suggestive general-circulation magazine of the pre–World War II era was *Esquire*. Promoted as the "Magazine for Men," *Esquire* featured articles and stories by noted authors of the time, such as Ernest Hemingway, D. H. Lawrence, Theodore Dreiser, F. Scott Fitzgerald, and Langston Hughes. The sex came primarily in the full-page drawings of George Petty and Vargas, featuring ultra-shapely, seductively clad young women. Many of the *Esquire* cartoons also drew their humor from sexual suggestiveness and double entendres.[5]

### Cosmopolitan

*Cosmopolitan*, which started as a conventional women's magazine in the early twentieth century, made some big changes in the 1960s. With the magazine foundering, the magazine's publisher made a brilliant publishing move in 1965 by hiring a forty-three-year-old woman named Helen Gurley Brown as its editor-in-chief.

A creative thinker and talented writer with a background in business, Brown had published the popular advice book *Sex and the Single Girl* in 1962. According to her later autobiographical accounts, the book was based on her own personal experience (Brown 1982; Brown 2000). The book's concept was simple, but extremely farsighted for the early 1960s. Published four decades before "Sex and the City" hit television, Brown's book argued for a similar approach to life. A single woman, the book proclaimed, could and should have sexual relationships. And she should enjoy those relationships as completely as possible and not feel guilty about having done so.

When she took over as editor-in-chief of *Cosmopolitan* in 1965, Brown transferred the philosophy of her successful book to the magazine. Since that time, *Cosmopolitan* has stayed unwaveringly with the idea that young unmarried women should enjoy guilt-free, uninhibited sex. Over time, the magazine has included married and cohabiting women as part of its target audience, but always with the theme that sex should be enjoyable.

*Cosmopolitan*, under Brown's editorship, brought sex prominently to the front cover, and to the articles inside the magazine, and it became the most successful women's magazine in the last forty years of the twentieth century. In supermarket checkout lines, millions of Americans take a glance at the featured story headlines, even if they don't buy the magazine.

Brown stepped down from her position as editor-in-chief in 1996, but her imprint on *Cosmopolitan* endures. Some recent cover headlines include: "100 Sex Tips from Guys: Including the Best Ice-Cube Trick We've *Ever* Heard" (September 2004); "Our New Sex Position Named 77, It's as Mindblowing as That *Other* Naughty Number" (November 2005); and "40 Girlie Moves that Make Guys Melt" (March 2006).

### Tina Brown Brings Sex to The New Yorker

*The New Yorker* came into existence in 1925, the brainchild of Harold W. Ross, who personally controlled its style and content for a quarter century. Ross initially conceived of his publication as a humor magazine, and over the years the magazine has published some of the most amusing cartoons and cover art of any American magazine. But *The New Yorker* has been much more than a humor magazine. Its articles soon became noted for their authoritative reports on places, people, and events written by the best American writers and journalists. Many of the greatest writers of the twentieth century—including F. Scott Fitzgerald, Alexander Woollcott, James Thurber, Ernest Hemingway, John O'Hara, John Cheever, Vladimir Nabokov, J. D. Salinger, Rebecca West, and John Updike—have published in the magazine. *The New Yorker* also had the most renowned, and feared, critics writing about books, theater, film, dance, and architecture.

Within two decades of its beginning, *The New Yorker* had achieved tremendous prestige in the publishing industry and in American society generally. To have *The New Yorker* on one's coffee table became a sign of cultured sophistication, perhaps even intellectualism, even if one never bothered to read the magazine other than looking at the cartoons.

Regarding the place of sex in *The New Yorker*, the founding editor Ross insisted there should be nothing in his magazine that would "bring a blush to the cheek of a twelve-year-old girl" (Gill 1975, 32). "This is a family magazine, goddammit," he once famously said. Ross decreed that the magazine should publish no "offensive material," either in words or pictures. Under the rubric of "offensive material" Ross is said to have included promiscuity, homosexuality, and adultery (Kunkel 1995). Even after his death in 1951, Ross's strong influence continued to shape the magazine's pristine content, because the new editor, William Shawn had a similar aversion to "offensive material." *The New Yorker* continued its prohibition of sexual material through four more decades, including five additional years (1987–92) under Robert Gottlieb.

In 1992, the publishing world was shocked when Si Newhouse, the owner of the Condé Nast publishing empire, which now owned *The New Yorker*, abruptly hired Tina Brown as editor. Though still a relatively young woman, Brown had already made a name for herself in publishing, first in England where she edited a successful celebrity/gossip magazine and then in the United States as the editor of *Vanity Fair*.

When Brown was named editor of *The New Yorker*, "all hell broke loose" said one staffer (Seabrook 2000, 27). With Brown as editor sexual material was no longer forbidden in the magazine. To many observers, in fact, sex now seemed to be a major theme of the magazine (Seabrook 2000). One of the first articles that signaled a change in the magazine's style was "High-Heel Neil" (Berendt 1995). The article described a twice-married man of sixty-one years who was handsome, the father of three children, a businessman, a Republican, and a member of the social elite in Nashville, Tennessee. As normal as he seemed on the surface, Neil had one personal eccentricity: he liked to dress up in women's clothes, and not just any old clothes but chic, showy dresses, along with pantyhose and high heels. He often relied on his wife in making his clothing choices. The story of Neil, the cross-dresser, did not contain any sexually explicit material, but it definitely covered a topic that would not have been touched by previous editors.

Also in 1995, *The New Yorker* published Susan Faludi's article describing the pornographic film industry in the San Fernando Valley north of Los Angeles. Faludi wrote about the personal lives of the men and women who performed sexual acts for the camera. She provocatively titled her article, "The Money Shot," which in porno-film argot refers to the *de rigueur* climax of a sex scene when the male actor interrupts his climax and ejaculates onto the body or face of the female actor.

A more explicitly sexual article appeared in *The New Yorker* in 1996 when Daphne Merkin wrote a "personal history" revealing that she was sexually aroused when spanked by her male partners (Merkin 1996). For feminists, who had fought for many years against the myth that women liked to be abused by their male partners, Merkin's sexually explicit confession was anathema.

Perhaps the most explicitly sexual article appeared in 1998, the last year of Tina Brown's reign as the editor, when Paul Theroux (1998) described the work, life, and clients of "Nurse Wolf," a New York City dominatrix. Theroux, a noted travel writer, reported in great, sometimes painful, detail what Nurse Wolf did to (and for) her mostly male clientele. Theroux's descriptions of sadism and masochism sometimes rival the work of the Marquis de Sade.

The Nurse Wolf story was accompanied by a dazzling photograph by Helmut Newton, a fashion photographer whose fame was based on his many daringly sexual images. Nurse Wolf is pictured in a skimpy leather outfit and high spike heels, one of which is planted firmly on a bed, while Newton's camera, positioned at floor level, aims directly at her barely covered crotch. Adding to the dominatrix ambience, Nurse Wolf holds a black whip in her upraised right hand.[6]

Throughout Brown's tenure at *The New Yorker*, the undressed bodies of women (and, in some cases, men) were frequently shown in photographs and drawings. During this period the magazine's employees held a weekly betting pool, in which they tried to guess how many times a woman's nipple would appear in that week's issue (Seabrook 2000, 32).

Tina Brown's tenure as editor of *The New Yorker* ended in 1998 when she agreed to edit a new magazine (*Talk*, which failed). Since then the new editor, David Remnick, has toned down the sexual content of the magazine, but in stories, cartoons, and photographs sexual material is now routinely found in *The New Yorker*.[7]

*Sex Sells Magazines: From Sports Illustrated to National Geographic*
The *Sports Illustrated* "Swimsuit" edition was first published in February 1964 and it was an immediate success. It has appeared every year since and, according to *The Christian Science Monitor* Web site, an estimated 50 million copies of the swimsuit issue are sold each year (http://www. csmonitor.com). Since the first year's publication, the swimsuits have become skimpier and the pretense that this issue has anything to do with sports has nearly disappeared.

The magazine's Web site home page (http://www.sportsillustrated .cnn.com) links to a Web page devoted exclusively to the swimsuit issues and the models. The site offers a complete visual history of the covers from 1964 to the present and vignettes of the cover models, along with a videocam peek at a photo shoot with one of the recent models. DVDs and videos featuring the models are promoted, as are calendars, autographed photographs, posters, and even trading cards featuring the models.

In addition to the enthusiasm of the swimsuit issue's many fans, this publication has provoked considerable counter-sexual discourse. Critics and would-be censors abound and have led to a number of Web sites exclusively devoted to attacking the swimsuit issue and trying, with no apparent success, to suppress its publication. Linnea Smith, of Chapel Hill, North Carolina, maintains a one-woman crusade against *Sports Illustrated*. The logo of Smith's Web site has a logo that features a circle with the familiar slash through the silhouette of a bikini-clad woman and then a tagline that plays off *Sports Illustrated* initials S.I. (*S*ocially *I*rresponsible, *S*eriously *I*nequitable, and *S*exually *I*mmature). The site's home page proclaims: "Pornography-influenced media is [*sic*] a public a public health concern and a social justice issue," and also asks rhetorically: "How are sexual shenanigans portrayed by the swimsuit issue different from old school porn attitudes at their worst?"

The Web site of Americans for Fair Sports Journalism uses feminist and athletic arguments against *Sports Illustrated*: "The `swimsuit issue' is an insult to female athletes and an insult to all women. . . . Mimicking the photo layouts in magazines like *Playboy*, *Penthouse*, and *Hustler*, the *Sports Illustrated* 'swimsuit issue' presents women as ineffectual and submissive sex objects." This organization urges petitions and boycotts against *Sports Illustrated* and sixteen other Time Warner publications. Once again, we have an example of Foucault's observation that those who object to sexual materials have the unintended consequence of promoting more discourse about sex.

### Et Tu, National Geographic?

Throughout its century-old history, *National Geographic* has built its reputation on excellent photographs and informative stories about out-of-the-way geographic regions and exotic cultures. With its stellar, unblemished image, *National Geographic* shocked the publishing world when it published its own special swimsuit issue in February 2003, placing itself in direct competition with *Sports Illustrated*. The special issue was not mailed to regular subscribers and could only be purchased at newsstands or via the Internet. Ostensibly, the issue was devoted to the history and evolution of swimwear, and it did, in fact, cover swimming costumes from Victorian times to the present, as well as photographs of swimwear in other societies (e.g., the women of Kathmandu bathing in the Bagmati River and the nearly obligatory bare-breasted women of the Marquesas Islands in Polynesia). The issue's primary focus, however, was on modern and contemporary swimsuit styles in the developed world, especially the United States and Europe. Provocatively, the cover featured a young woman lying in shallow water wearing a bikini made of three small scallop shells strategically arranged and secured by thin cords. One reviewer dubbed the issue "babes in bikinis" (Kurtz 2003, C1).

The magazine's editors were forthright about their motivations when interviewed by journalists. "We wanted people to loosen up a little on the concept of what *National Geographic* is," observed editor Bill Allen. "A lot of young men of a certain age grew up with *National Geographic* and they were always waiting for the pictures of natives to come along" (Kurtz 2003, C1, C4). Allen's comment, of course, was a reference to the photographs of indigenous bare-breasted women depicted in stories about exotic cultures, which have been prominent in the magazine's history.

Although there was no organized objection to this issue of *National Geographic*, America's newspapers and magazines had plenty to say about the excursion of this venerable travel magazine into suggestive sexual content—further increasing sexual discourse in contemporary American culture.

## BOOKS AND NOVELS

In the 1950s, a relatively small number of American fiction writers were beginning to write more openly about the sexual lives of their characters. Writing about sex was one thing, but getting the material published was quite another. Major publishers in mid-twentieth century America were fearful of being charged with producing and distributing obscenity, which was illegal, and therefore rejected the manuscripts of the more adventurous writers. One major exception was Grove Press.

### GROVE PRESS

In the early 1950s, a new publishing company called Grove Press came into being. In 1951, Barnet Rosset, while still a 29-year-old college student, purchased a fledgling publishing company named Grove Press for three thousand dollars (http://www.groveatlantic.com).[8] Barney, as he was called by nearly everyone who knew him, ran Grove Press for more than three decades. Because he was independently wealthy, he could publish the books he believed in, even though they might not be profitable. His publications ranged from the work of obscure American poets to avant-garde European novelists.

But the books for which Grove Press became noted were novels that had explicit sexual content. These books were written by serious American and European fiction writers. Often, these were books that other American publishers were afraid to publish.

In 1959, Grove published an American edition of D. H. Lawrence's *Lady Chatterley's Lover*, a controversial novel that had been banned in the United States (even though it had been published privately in England since 1928). This book was a serious literary work by an established author, but the book broke new ground for earthy sexual language and vivid descriptions of sexual acts.[9]

In 1961, Grove followed with the publication of Henry Miller's *Tropic of Cancer*, a book that was almost completely devoted to semi-autobiographical accounts of Miller's sexual adventures in 1920s Paris (Ferguson 1991). Miller's book had been published in Paris by Obelisk Press nearly thirty years earlier (1934) but had been banned in the United States since the 1940s. The publication of *Tropic of Cancer* in the United States eventually led to an important 1964 court decision, *Grove Press v. Gerstein*, which vastly expanded the rights of Americans to read literature with sexually explicit content.

During this early period, Grove also published several other noted books containing vividly described sexual activity. These include the autobiographical *My Life and Loves* by Frank Harris; the sadomasochistic classic *The Story of O*; and *Fanny Hill*, which has been described as "The first masterpiece of English pornography" (Hyde 1965, 97).

In addition to classical pornographic fiction and long-suppressed novels, Grove published a new wave of daring American authors who, in spite of a growing following in Europe, had remained unpublished in their own country. Among Grove's most notable publications by young American authors were William Burrough's *Naked Lunch* (1959), Terry Southern and Mason Hoffenberg's *Candy* (1958), John Rechy's *City of Night* (1963), and Robert Gover's *One Hundred Dollar Misunderstanding* (1961). Although these books were not blatantly pornographic, they did describe fictional characters engaging in various sexual activities. The sex was generally heterosexual, but homosexuality played important parts in the books of Burroughs and Rechy.

HAROLD ROBBINS: KING OF THE TRASHY AIRPORT NOVEL

In 1948, Harold Robbins published his first book, *Never Love a Stranger* (Robbins 1948) and his publisher was the highly reputable Alfred A. Knopf.[10] Nearly everyone agreed, especially the critics, that the book was not a work of great literary merit. In fact, most of the extraordinarily successful Robbins' novels were usually panned by the literary critics. But Robbins's books did sell (an estimated 750 million copies) because the stories were engaging and they were filled with raw sex (Wilson 2007). *The Carpetbaggers* was his most noted book, in part because it was later made into a movie. Robbins's biographer has written, "In today's sex-saturated society it's difficult to imagine the effect that Robbins's books had on the popular consciousness" but he has been called "a pioneer in the field" (Wilson 2007, 5).

## PEYTON PLACE

While Grove Press was leading the way in the publication of sex novels, another American publisher, Julian Messner, Inc., took a gamble and published a novel by an unknown writer named Grace Metalious. Metalious was the wife of a high school English teacher in a small New England town. She had no formal training as a writer and no previous publishing experience. Her book, *Peyton Place*, was released in 1956 and became a national bestseller. For a time, the author became almost as notorious as the book she had written (Toth 1981).

*Peyton Place* was a story about the people in a New England small town, but the story focussed primarily on the sex and violence that existed beneath the surface of a seemingly placid American community. The violence was nothing that could not have been found in other novels of that era, but the sex and the dialogue associated with sex (nipples described as "hard as diamonds," references to a man's erect penis), were shocking to many Americans.

Though literary critics found little merit in *Peyton Place*, the American public bought enough copies to put it on the best seller list, where it remained for twenty-six weeks, selling one hundred and four thousand copies within a month of its publication (Toth 1981, 131).

In 1957, Peyton Place was made into a movie, which starred some major Hollywood stars of the era (Lana Turner, Hope Lange, Lloyd Nolan). In 1964, the name was used again for a television series featuring the young actors Mia Farrow and Ryan O'Neal. Both the film and the television program were highly sanitized versions of the novel, but the name has continued to have a sexual connotation. The mere mention of Peyton Place evokes images of latent sexuality just beneath the surface of American society.

## LOLITA

Also in the 1950s, another controversial novelist created an uproar in the American publishing world. The author was Vladimir Nabokov and his book was *Lolita* (1955). *Lolita* told the story of the sexual obsession of a middle-aged man for a twelve- year-old girl. Unlike Metalious, Nabokov, a Russian emigre, had already gained considerable literary fame in Europe and the United States by the time he published *Lolita* (Nabokov 1955). Like *Peyton Place*, the novel's name quickly became part of the sexual lexicon of American society. Today, the name Lolita designates a sexual nymphet, or a prepubescent girl who is sexually precocious. In the Internet pornography world, a Lolita is a young, "barely legal," girl, and in child pornography chat rooms on the Internet, a "Loli-lover" is a pedophile who prefers preteen girls (Jenkins 2001, 118).

After Nabokov completed writing *Lolita*, it took him two years to find a publisher. During that time, the manuscript was offered to Viking Press, Simon and Schuster, New Directions, Doubleday, and Farrar, Straus, all of which rejected it. While a number of editors recognized the brilliance of the writing, they were fearful about the subject matter (Boyd 1991).

Eventually, Nabokov's agent submitted his manuscript to the editor of Olympia Press in Paris. Olympia Press had earlier published the works of Samuel Beckett, Lawrence Durrell and Jean Genet, along with both of Henry Miller's sexually explicit novels *Tropic of Cancer* and *Tropic of Capricorn*. In 1955, Olympia Press, because of financial problems, was publishing nearly anything that came along, including some admittedly pornographic books. After it became an international best seller, *Lolita* was finally published by the American publisher Putnam (Quennell 1980).

## PORTNOY'S COMPLAINT

By the 1960s, a large part of the general reading public in the United States expected and probably wanted a certain amount of sex in the novels they were reading. One of America's most famous twentieth-century authors, Philip Roth, was among the first to meet that demand. In 1959, Roth published *Goodbye, Columbus and Five Short Stories* (Roth 1959), but his most successful early novel was *Portnoy's Complaint* (Roth 1970).[11] The novel's protagonist, Alex Portnoy, provides his psychiatrist with a detailed first-person account of his sexual experiences, beginning with his unrelenting youthful masturbation and continuing through numerous sexual encounters with a variety of women. One of the more memorable episodes involves a woman he calls "The Monkey," about whom he tells his psychiatrist, "just saying her name, just bringing her to mind, gives me a hard-on on the spot!" (Roth 1970, 172).

### SEXUAL MATERIAL AND PORNOGRAPHY IN
### OTHER PARTS OF THE PRINT WORLD

The list of contemporary sex-laden American novels numbers in the thousands. Most of these books will never be described as literary classics; many, in fact, would probably be regarded as trash by most readers. These books are read by millions of Americans, however, with both males and females openly expressing interest in reading books with explicit sexual content. This is true even for publications in which sex has not previously played an important role. A brief discussion of three types of print publications will illustrate the pervasiveness of sex in the print medium: romance novels, young-adult fiction, and comic books.

## ROMANCE NOVELS

Romance novels are the mainstay of the American publishing industry, regularly making up more than half of all book sales. In 1999, 55.9 percent of mass market and trade books sold in North America were romance novels (Regis 2003, xi). In 1996, romance novels produced approximately 1 billion dollars in sales from 182 million books sold. The novels of Janet Daily alone, one of the most prolific and successful of the romance novelists, boast total sales of more than 300 million (Regis 2003, 159).[12]

The romance novel goes back to the eighteenth century, when in 1740 Samuel Richardson's *Pamela* was published. But the more familiar romance titles came in the nineteenth century with the publication of Jane Austen's *Pride and Prejudice* in 1813, Charlotte Bronte's *Jane Eyre* in 1847, and Anthony Trollope's *Framley Parsonage* in 1861 (Regis 2003). These early romance novels were about courtship and romance, not about sex. Until recently, the romance novel did not feature any explicit sexual content (Regis 2003, 55).

In the classic romance novel, a heroine tells the story from her own perspective. According to the tried-and-true formula, she meets a male hero, with whom there is a mutual attraction, but a barrier of some kind keeps them apart. Eventually, the two surmount whatever obstacles they have encountered. It is at this point that the either marry or commit to marriage (Regis 2004; Reiss and Reiss 1990).

The sexual dimension of most twentieth-century romance novels has customarily been left to the reader's imagination. The most vivid sex occurred when the hero would impulsively tear some clothing off the heroine (inspiring the term "bodice rippers") and carry her off to bed. At this point in the narrative, the story usually ended leaving the rest to the reader's imagination.

But romance novels have changed considerably in the last couple of decades. Today, some of the most famous authors of romantic novels are writing steamy sex scenes that leave little or nothing to the imagination. In a recent romance novel by best-selling author Beatrice Small, the first sexual intercourse of a new bride is described in the following manner:

> He plundered her sweetness, reveling in her tight, hot sheath. . . . Her silken thighs gripped him firmly. . . . Now he began to piston her with a careful measured cadence. . . . He plunged and withdrew over and over again until he felt the storm rising within her. When he thought he could bear the tension no longer she cried out, and he released his love juices, flooding her body. (Small 2001a, 209).

The heroine of Small's book, a historical romance novel set in seventeenth-century France and England, retains a modicum of virtue throughout, although she is often boldly and appealingly randy. In the space of four hundred pages, the heroine's love life is described in a baker's dozen sex scenes. Her lovers include two kings—one English, one French—who are sandwiched in time between two husbands. The first, a much beloved husband, is tragically killed, opening the way for encounters with the two royal lovers. On the last page of the book, the heroine ends up happily married, now to her second husband, since a happy-marriage ending is nearly obligatory in the romance novel.

People who pay attention to this form of romance novel writing categorize the authors on a five-step alliterative scale: sweet, spicy, steamy, sizzling, and savage. Going from sweet to sizzling the sex scenes become ever more explicit. The savage category is still steamy and sizzling, but also involves some level of violence, such as rape, kidnapping, seduction, or prostitution (Bartlett 2001).

## YOUNG-ADULT FICTION

Fiction for "young adults" is a nebulous category, created by publishers and booksellers to suggest books appropriate for an age group somewhere between childhood and adulthood. The fact that booksellers are not using the term "teenage books" suggests that the book industry is striving to appeal to adolescents eager to read more adult material. On the bookshelves of major American retailers (Barnes and Noble, Borders, and others), as well as on the Internet (www.amazon.com), it is easy to find young-adult books with explicit sexual content (Weeks 2001a).

The young-adult novel, Plunking Reggie Jackson, published as part of Simon & Schuster's "Young Reader" series for "ages 12 and up," includes the following passage:

> They made love on his bed, after practice, when the house was empty. Bree's lean body might have suggested adolescence, but there was nothing juvenile about her manner of participation in the sex act. She was as focused and fearless in the pursuit of her passion as any grown woman.

Since she was only fifteen, Coley wanted to believe in her innocence, but it wouldn't be easy. In the heat of the moment he didn't even remember to use a condom. (Weeks 2001a, A16)

It is not surprising that today's teenagers, who enjoy easy access to equally vivid sexual material on cable television, and in video games, magazines and DVDs, would be eager to read books with explicit sexual content. Publishers are quite willing to provide this type of sexual material to teenagers—in some cases, even younger children—since there are no legal restrictions on who can buy books classified under the innocuous heading of "young-adult" fiction.

## SEX IN THE COMICS

Comic books are not usually associated with sex and pornography. In the relatively short history of comic books, the heroes (and the few heroines) have generally been wholesome and asexual.[13] Despite these innocent images, however, comic imagery has always demonstrated the potential for pornographic content. Some of the earliest examples of pornography in Western societies took the form of sketches and drawings (Hunt 1993a). More recently, the "Tijuana Bibles" or "Blusies" of the 1920s and 1930s (tiny sexual comic books about the size of an elongated credit card) were a notorious forerunner of today's adult comic books. Despite the Tijuana label of these underground publications most were issued by marginal publishers in the United States, though some were printed in Cuba (Horn 1985). They were generally sold "under the counter," at places where men congregated (taverns, barbershops, garages, gas stations). The prices ranged from a quarter to as much as five dollars (Adelman 1997).

The standard format of the eight-page story featured a curvaceous, beautiful female. In the first panel, she was usually wearing clothing, but whatever she was wearing would soon be removed. Pubic hair was always shown, underarm hair, usually. The comic sometimes featured the cartoon image of a celebrity of the era (e.g., Mae West, Claudette Colbert, Rita Hayworth), or simply a pretty and shapely young woman. Often the characters were knock-offs of well-known comic strip characters, such as Dick Tracy and his girlfriend Tess, Popeye and Olive Oyl, Superman and Lois Lane, or even, in one Tijuana Bible, Mickey Mouse and Minnie Mouse. Drawings of sexual organs were explicit. Men usually had large erect penises, unless the artist was making fun of the man or showing him after having sex, in which case the female would usually be pleading for more sex. Sexual intercourse and fellatio were the most common forms of sex depicted in the comic strips, and the two often appeared in the same eight-page strip. Cunnilingus and anal intercourse appeared less frequently. Sex between two women was occasionally shown, while gay-male sex was extremely rare.

The artwork in Tijuana Bibles was crude and unaccomplished, even by comic strip standards, and the print quality was poor. Dialogue between characters was often ungrammatical, and misprints were numerous. Racial and ethnic stereotypes were common, as well as every conceivable type of sexism and gender stereotyping (Adelman 1997). While these little comic books were distributed illegally in the heyday of their popularity, today they are readily available in glossy-paper anthologies at any major bookstore or on amazon.com (Adelman 1997).

*Pornographic Comics Today*

Most of today's comic books still feature action heroes, though in more exotic forms than the Superman, Captain Marvel, and Batman heroes of the past. But along with the action heroes, any well-stocked comic-book store today is likely to have comic-book pornography, depicting males and females engaged in every imaginable sex act, with the sex organs vividly explicit and often exaggerated.

The artistic work in these contemporary pornographic comic books is not crudely done, but is the work of skilled artists. Unlike the conventional comic book, which has soft covers and pulp paper pages, the pornographic comics of today often have covers much like high-quality paperback trade books. Most pornographic comics today are in color. The price of these sexually explicit comics ranges between ten and fifteen dollars, while conventional comic books still cost between two and three dollars.

Pornographic comic books are not just offered in "brick and mortar" stores but are also advertised on the Internet. The "Last Gasp Online Catalog," for example, offers 608 titles in the adult comics category. This San Francisco—based publisher produces a wide range of exotic materials, and bills itself as providing "Mind Candy for the Masses" (http://www.lastgasp.com). Although the site's checkout point clearly states, "You must be over the age of eighteen to purchase this adult item," it is unlikely that many underage youngsters are intimidated by the admonition.

The sexual images in comic books cannot be rivaled by any other medium for explicitness and exaggeration. The comic book, Pinocchia, for example, features a bawdy takeoff on the classic Pinocchio story. In this version, Giuseppe creates a beautifully proportioned female out of wood. After she comes to life, Giuseppe enters her while she is on her hands and knees. Her face, reflected in a mirror urges Giuseppe, "Deeper,

Harder." Next frame, the now wide-eyed Pinocchia, murmurs, "MMM-MMM!" The story goes on from there (http://www.nbmpub.com).

Although comic books only interest a small percentage of the American population, it is significant that conventional comics today are often found side by side with pornographic comics, since they provide young kids (mostly males), who inevitably drift into the "X-rated" section of comic book stores, with early exposure to explicit sexual material.

## PRINTED SEXUAL MATERIALS IN AMERICA TODAY

In the United States today, nearly anything sexual or pornographic can be published and sold (child pornography is the only major exception). Changes in the political-legal realm account for most of the increased availability of printed words and pictures with sexual content. Several societal and cultural trends have paralleled the court cases that opened the way for the publication of sexual materials. Americans were increasingly living in urban and suburban places where they had increased individual freedom, self expression, and a libertarian political philosophy that emphasized the right of people to live their lives as they chose without interference, especially by the government. All these trends have added to the increases in sexual materials, thus adding to the hypersexuality of American society.

CHAPTER 5

# SEX IN ACADEME
## FROM KINSEY'S RESEARCH TO PORN STUDIES

In the autumn of 2004, the movie *Kinsey* was released in theaters across the country. The film provided millions of Americans with their first look at the research and personal life of the bow-tie wearing professor at Indiana University who devoted the last half of his life to the scientific study of sexual behavior. With Liam Neeson playing Alfred Kinsey and Laura Linney playing his wife, the movie told the story of how Kinsey, an entomologist, gave up his early professional obsession with studying the gall wasp and plunged into a new fascination: the study of human sexual behavior.

The movie provided a glimpse at Kinsey's research on sexual behavior but it also hinted at a darker side of his personality. Roger Ebert, the noted film critic, praised the portrayal of Kinsey's sexual research, but also recognized some of Kinsey's shortcomings. Ebert saw that Kinsey "had tunnel vision, and it led him heedlessly toward his research goals without prudent regard for his image, his family and associates" (http://www.rogerebert.com). David Denby concluded a rave review of the movie in the *New Yorker* with the observation: "Kinsey is definitely a hero, but he's also a neurotically driven man with a messianic streak, a sacrificial figure: wearing himself out in the pursuit of knowledge and experience, *he died for our pleasure*" (Denby 2004b, 173; emphasis added). Kinsey was certainly among one of the most influential and fascinating characters of twentieth century America: a true pioneer in the field of sex.

Kinsey was also a preeminent American spokesperson for Foucault's rational-intellectual form of sexual discourse, the objective analysis and scientific study of sexual matters. Kinsey devoted the last part of his life to introducing a rational-intellectual view of sex to American society, mostly through his work in academe.

## How Kinsey Brought Sex
### to American Universities and Colleges

In 1938, Kinsey, then a professor of biology at the University of Indiana, made the first steps toward his pioneering work on sexual behavior. The University of Indiana was then, and still is, a well-respected state university, but it was an unlikely place for innovations in teaching and research about sexuality and sexual behavior. Indiana was, after all, a Midwestern state, a state that was relatively rural and had agriculture as its primary economic enterprise. The values of the people of Indiana were then, as now, generally traditional and conservative.

In the spring of 1938, the leaders of the Association of Women Students at Indiana University met with Professor Kinsey to discuss their interest in a course on sex education. At Kinsey's urging, the organization submitted a petition to the university administration asking for a course on marriage and the family, a course that would include a unit on sex. Kinsey readily volunteered to organize and coordinate such a course (Jones 1997a, 1997b; Pomeroy 1972).

University administrators approved the marriage course, which soon became one of the most popular courses on campus, with hundreds of students enrolling each semester. Kinsey taught the unit on sex and also provided individual counseling to students on their personal questions about sex and marital relations. During a single semester, he conducted as many as 280 such counseling sessions with students.

Kinsey soon realized that many of the students' questions about sexuality and sexual behavior were unanswerable on the basis of sound scientific data. Prompted by this lack of scientific information on sex and also his own personal curiosity, Kinsey began to collect sexual histories from his students.[1] He reported in a letter to a friend that during the two years he was teaching the marriage course he accumulated more than 350 sexual histories. From this time on the collection of personal sexual histories became an insatiable quest for Kinsey; he took advantage of any and every opportunity to interview people (not just students) about their sexual lives. By the time Kinsey and his research associates published their two most famous books on sexual behavior, *Sexual Behavior of the Human Male* (Kinsey et al. 1948) and *Sexual Behavior of the Human Female* (Kinsey et al. 1953), they had collected over eleven thousand sexual histories.

Although Kinsey was forced to withdraw from teaching the marriage course at Indiana because of negative reactions from other faculty members

and critics in the community, he pushed ahead with his newfound interest and soon established the Institute for Sex Research. It was through this
Institute that Kinsey continued his studies of sexual behavior until the time
of his death in 1956. While the Institute has sometimes had difficulty
obtaining research funding, it has remained in existence to the present day.
Now called the Kinsey Institute, it continues to be devoted to scholarship on
"sexuality, gender, and reproduction" and is one of the world's greatest
repositories of sexual materials (http://www.indiana.edu/~kinsey).

Kinsey's research findings about sex have not always withstood the
criticisms of other scholars, including social scientists. And criticisms
have also come from another direction. A recent biography of Kinsey,
published more than forty years after his death, has somewhat tarnished
his reputation and even called into question his motives for relentlessly
pursuing research on sexual behavior (Jones 1997a). While Kinsey always
claimed that his motives for conducting sexual research were strictly
objective and scientific, the facts of his personal life suggest that he also
had a personal stake in breaking down the sexual limitations imposed by
conventional society (Jones 1997a).

In his personal life, Kinsey was both bisexual and masochistic. In his
early career as an entomologist, he often took his male graduate students
on extended field trips where it was not uncommon for him to walk
naked in the evening hours and to raise topics of sexuality with his students. A number of his friends have reported that Kinsey was inclined to
expose his sexual organs at the slightest provocation.

At his home, he and his wife often had private sex sessions with his colleagues, their wives, and other trusted friends. On these occasions everyone was encouraged to engage in different forms of sexual activity. Kinsey
was fascinated with sadomasochism and subjected himself to various
forms of pain when he masturbated, often tying a rope around his scro-
tum or placing objects (a toothbrush handle, for example) in the urethra
of his penis when he masturbated.

Over the years, Kinsey voiced ever-more-liberal views about all varieties of sexual behavior. According to one biographer, "Kinsey came to
believe that many sexual perversions, however repugnant to the public,
were basically harmless in the sense that they did not pose a threat to public safety. He even questioned "society's condemnation of pedophilia"
(Jones 1997a, 512). Kinsey also concluded from his case histories that no
serious long-term harm occurred from incest. But the unconventional
sexual category toward which Kinsey had the greatest sympathy was
homosexuality. In his published writings, his private counseling, and in

letters, he gave encouragement and support to those who were sexually attracted to members of their own sex.

Consistent with Foucault's observation that knowledge equals power, Kinsey clearly tried to use his scientifically acquired knowledge about sexual behavior to gain influence over sexual standards and behavior in American society. Beyond his long-term, mostly indirect influence on society at large, his impact on the study of sexual matters and sexual behavior in the scholarly world is immense. Because of his pioneering efforts, scholarly research about sexual matters, along with the teaching of courses about sex and pornography, is now an accepted part of the curricula of most American colleges and universities. For this reason alone Kinsey was truly a sex pioneer. But also, throughout all levels of society, the knowledge that Kinsey provided about sex contributed to a new form of sexual discourse. This increase in sexual discourse has included, just as Foucault postulated, the criticisms of Kinsey's research when he first published it and the words of a number of contemporary critics (we have already seen the criticism of Jones in Chapter 2).

The remainder of this chapter will demonstrate how sex and pornography have become accepted subject matter in the academic world—both in the classroom and in scholarly research. Many individual scholars have contributed to the current interest in sexual material and pornography, but Kinsey deserves special recognition as the sex pioneer who brought sex to American academe.

## THE SOCIETAL CONTEXT OF THE STUDY OF SEX AND PORNOGRAPHY IN ACADEME

While Kinsey championed the rational-intellectual approach to the study of sexual matters, a major societal trend during the last half of the twentieth century also made it possible for scholars and teachers to specialize in sexual research and scholarship. The political democratization and increased personal liberty described in Chapter 2 were occurring in the United States in the decades following Kinsey's work.

Supreme Court decisions relating to published materials gradually opened the way for the publication of all manner of sexual topics. The importance of these rulings cannot be overemphasized. From James Joyce's *Ulysses* to Larry Flynt's *Hustler*, the publication of sexual texts became available to the reading public, including books and articles written by scholars. It is no exaggeration to say that hundreds of publications being read by college and university students today, including some of the material in this book, could never have been published in the first half of the twentieth century in America.

## UNIVERSITY SEX RESEARCH AND COLLEGE COURSES ON SEX

After Kinsey opened the doors, a limited number of professors at colleges and universities around the nation turned their attention to sexual matters and the number has continued to grow over the years. Today, many professors have been able to carve out respectable, and in some cases highly successful, academic careers in areas related to sex.

Academicians specializing in sex—including in some cases pornography—now routinely teach courses, conduct research, publish articles in academic journals, write scholarly books, and present papers at professional conferences (Atlas 1999). The scholarly disciplines in which studies of sex and pornography find a home most easily are in the humanities, the social sciences, and the arts.

## SEX AND PORNOGRAPHY IN THE ARTS AND HUMANITIES

In the arts and humanities (in particular classical studies, history, literature, drama, and the fine arts), sex and pornography have become legitimate areas of study. Many professors in these fields consider sex and pornography their primary scholarly specialties; they teach undergraduate courses in these subjects, conduct graduate seminars, carry out research, and publish papers and books.

Consider, for example, the classics, a scholarly field that is often thought to be at the apex of scholarship because of its focus on the cultures of ancient Greece and Rome. In recent decades, classical scholars have discovered sex and pornography in the surviving written and visual materials of these wellsprings of Western civilization. Greek and Roman cultures provide ample amounts of sexual and pornographic material for scholarly analysis (Clarke 2003; Hallett and Skinner 1997; Richlin 1992a, 1992b; Skinner 1997; Toepfer 1991).

Marilyn B. Skinner, in her introduction to the edited volume *Roman Sexualities* (Hallett and Skinner 1997), describes the study of sexuality in the field of classics as a "subject that has only lately been sanctioned as appropriate for academic discussion" (Skinner 1997, 6). Skinner joins other scholars in crediting Foucault for the recent emphasis on sex in classical studies. "Current excitement over ancient erotics," she explains, "dates primarily from the appearance of the English translation of the second and third parts of Foucault's *Histoire de la sexualite*" (Skinner 1997, 6).

Amy Richlin's book, *Pornography and Representation in Greece and Rome* (Richlin 1992a), is another example of scholarly work on sexuality that is indebted to Foucault. Richlin, a classics professor at the University

94     A HYPERSEXUAL SOCIETY

of Southern California, acknowledges the seminal importance of Foucault's work in opening classical studies to sex, but at the same time she deprecates the quality of his scholarship. Classicists, Richlin argues, need to give more attention to erotica and sexuality precisely because these areas have been usurped by nonclassicists such as Foucault. Contemporary classicists, according to Richlin, should employ their superior knowledge of Greek and Roman texts to clarify how Foucault's selections of material are limited and his interpretations are questionable (Richlin 1992b, xvii). Similar critiques of the inadequacy of Foucault's work can be found in essays by Holt N. Parker (1992) and Madeleine M. Henry (1992), which also appear in Richlin's book.

Karl Toepfer's (1991) *Theater, Aristocracy, and Pornocracy* is devoted to descriptions and analyses of sexual orgies that have been presented in theatrical and artistic works dating back to the earliest times of Western history. In his summary of sexual orgies from the time of the Greeks to present-day movies, Toepfer concludes, as have other historians of pornography, that theatrical orgies have almost always been produced for aristocratic audiences and not for the masses.

In the academic field of history, Lynn Hunt's *The Invention of Pornography: Obscenity and the Origins of Modernity, 1500–1800* (1993a) has contributed the plausible thesis that pornography in European societies emerged after the development of the printing press, at which time pornographic works were a political protest against the elite authorities of the society (Hunt 1993b). Other influential historical studies of pornography include H. Montgomery Hyde's *A History of Pornography* (Hyde 1965), Walter Kendrick's previously discussed *The Secret Museum: Pornography in Modern Culture* (Kendrick 1987), Patrick J. Kearney's *A History of Erotic Literature (Kearney 1982)*, and Helen Lefkowitz Horowitz's *Rereading Sex: Battles Over Sexual Knowledge and Suppression in Nineteenth-Century America*. A twentieth-century historical study of American pornography also previously discussed is Jay Gertzman's: *Bookleggers and Smuthounds: The Trade in Erotica, 1920–1940* (Gertzman 1999).

While only a few historians have focused on pornography, many have studied sexual behavior and sexual attitudes. The potential for historians to study sex was recognized more than four decades ago in a scholarly journal article titled "American Historians and the Subject of Sex" (Burnham 1972). One of the most ambitious attempts to fulfill this objective is the book by John D'Emilio and Estelle Freedman (1988) titled *Intimate Matters: A History of Sexuality in America* in which they describe the sexual lives of ordinary Americans over the last nearly four centuries. They also analyze the various conceptualizations of sexuality and the way these formulations have influenced American society and culture. Other historians of the United States have focused on sexuality during specific periods of American history (Barker-Benfield 1976; Freedman 1982) or on specific sexual groups such as gays and lesbians (Katz 1976).

In another area of the arts, Carol Squires, whose academic specialty is photography, has published a volume titled, rather coyly, *Overexposed* (Squires 1999). Her book includes scholarly essays that accompany photographs of gay and lesbian relationships, fetishism, and exhibitionism. An example of the level of explicitness in Squires's work is a series of photographs labeled "harddick in Superman spandex." The photos in this series show a man in a Superman costume with his erect penis protruding through an opening at the crotch. In the field of art photography, Squires has found a niche that would almost certainly have been unacceptable in the academic world during the first half of the twentieth century. Today, however, her work is considered a contribution to scholarship.

These are just a few examples of the most prominent studies of sex and pornography now being routinely conducted in the humanities and the arts. Later in this chapter, where the focus is more directly on studies of pornography, we will examine a new subfield of the arts (in film studies) called *porn studies* (Williams 2004a).

### STUDIES OF SEX IN THE SOCIAL SCIENCES

After Kinsey published his two major reports on sexual behavior in the late 1940s and early 1950s, sex became a legitimate area for research in many of the social and behavioral sciences. But among the social sciences it was anthropology that had a head start on the others. Anthropologists, for unique historical reasons, began collecting data on sexual behavior long before sociologists and psychologists.

#### ANTHROPOLOGY AND THE STUDY OF SEX

Anthropology had its beginnings in the nineteenth century, first in Great Britain where it was a natural concomitant of British colonialism. After the British had established their control over societies in all parts of the world, but especially Africa and Asia, various scholars and adventurers traveled to those parts of the globe to study and describe the "native" cultures. Anthropology as a scientific discipline emerged out of investigations of these adventurers.

When studying these unfamiliar societies, anthropologists usually described the entire culture, including the sexual behavior of the people.

These descriptions were given fairly wide latitude by the elite and educated people of Britain, who were generally the only ones to read or hear about them. The normally restrictive watchdogs and censors of sexual material in Victorian and post-Victorian Britain were quite tolerant of these vivid sexual descriptions. In Foucaultian terms, their access to this "exotic" sexual knowledge may have contributed to British feelings of superiority and power over these "primitive" subjects and their "uncivilized" ways. Or, their tolerance may have emanated from the fact that the elites and intellectuals who had access to them were almost exclusively males. Whatever the reasons for their tolerance, it is certainly likely that these men found the exotic sexual customs titillating.

Anthropological research and scholarship soon spread to the United States where, even without an empire, scholars were greatly interested in studying the behaviors (including the sexual behaviors) of what was then called "primitive" culture. By 1951, when Ford and Beach published *Patterns of Sexual Behavior*, a comprehensive review of cross-cultural knowledge about sexual behavior, the authors were able to claim that their data came from "190 different societies . . . scattered around the world" (Ford and Beach 1951, 13). The various sections of their book reveal something of the comprehensiveness and detail of anthropological studies of sex: "The Nature of Coitus," "Types of Sexual Stimulation," "Circumstances of Coitus," "Attracting a Sex Partner," "Homosexual Behavior," and "Self-stimulation" (Ford and Beach 1951, 7).

Consider the section "Positions Assumed for Coitus" (Ford and Beach 1951, 32ff.). According to the studies of Kinsey, Ford and Beach noted, Americans overwhelmingly preferred sex with the woman lying on her back, the man above and facing her. When Kinsey conducted his studies in the late 1930s and early 1940s, 70 percent of Americans had never tried any other method of sexual intercourse. This method, commonly referred to as "the missionary" position, is preferred by the people of many societies around the world, but not all. For example, among the people of the western Pacific islands of Palau and Yap (both in the Carolines), couples preferred to have sex in a sitting position with the woman squatting over the man. Among the Kwakiutl Indians of the Pacific Northwest and the Masai of Africa, the preferred position for sexual intercourse has the man and woman lying side by side (Ford and Beach 1951). On the island of Truk, especially on those occasions when men and women might have a quick sexual encounter, they would often stand in a face-to-face position with the woman resting "her foot on the man's shoulder" (Ford and Beach 1951, 35).

Ford and Beach also described the rules of different societies regarding the appropriate partners for sexual coupling. Almost all societies have some form of mateship (or marriage), which provides long-term partners for sexual intercourse. Yet a surprising 40 percent of societies allowed for sexual liaisons outside of marriage. Among the Marquesans of the South Pacific, the Toda of India, and the Siriono of South America, men and women were expected to have sexual relations with people other than their spouses. The sexual partners in these liaisons were often the siblings of one's husband or wife.

Anthropologists have also reported on a number of societies in which sexual relationships were allowed between two men, or between men and boys. In 49 percent of the societies included in Ford and Beach's study, "homosexual activities of one sort or another were considered normal or socially acceptable" (Ford and Beach 1951, 137). The most common form of acceptable homosexuality occurred when a man dressed and acted like a woman (transvestism). But in a number of societies, hetero-sexual men, especially before marriage, engaged in anal intercourse, either with other men or with boys. Evans-Prichard (1970) found in his study of the Azande of the Southern Sudan that unmarried warriors had young boys who lived with them as personal aides. A boy would take care of the daily needs of his "husband," including the soldier's sexual needs. This Azande custom is strikingly similar to the customs of the ancient Greeks, in which men who were military officers or scholars had intercourse with young boys who served as their apprentices or students (Faceliere 1962; Foucault 1984/1985).[2]

Much of what we know about the influence of culture on sexual behavior has been provided by the cross-cultural studies of anthropolo-gists during the early years of the twentieth century. Other social sciences, as well as academic historians, generally stayed clear of the topic until the post-Kinsey years. A brief look at some of the other social sciences will reveal how widespread the study of sexual behavior has become today.

## SOCIOLOGICAL STUDIES OF SEX

Sociological studies of sexual attitudes and behavior began in the 1950s as a direct outgrowth of the Kinsey studies. Though Kinsey had opened the way for the "scientific" study of sex, sociologists and psychologists did not have the protection of being "true scientists." Furthermore, the United States in the 1950s was extremely conservative, both politically and cul-turally. Social scientists who undertook sex research needed to have con-siderable courage. Nonetheless, a few adventurous scholars rose to the challenge, usually conducting questionnaire and interview research and often using college students as their subjects (Christensen 1962; Ehrmann 1959; Reiss 1960).

The work of Ira Reiss is an important example of early sociological sex research among college students. While teaching at a Virginia college in the 1950s, Reiss gave a questionnaire to students at two colleges and two high schools, with one white and one black example of each institution. (Schools in Virginia were segregated at the time.) In 1959, Reiss moved to a college in New York where he again administered his questionnaire to students.

Reiss's primary interest was in students' attitudes about premarital sexual permissiveness. Students were asked whether they agreed or disagreed with a series of statements about various sexual activities. For example: "I believe that petting is acceptable for the male [or, for the female] before marriage if he [she] is engaged to be married." "I believe full sexual relations are acceptable for the male [or, the female] before marriage if he [she] is in love." Reiss used the responses to these and similar questions to construct a quantitative measure of permissiveness about premarital sexual behavior (Reiss 1967). The examples of items in Reiss's sexual permissiveness scale are quite tame by today's standards, but during the conservative 1950s, it took courage to venture even this far into sex research.

In the 1960s and 1970s, many more social researchers undertook studies of sexual behavior, publishing scholarly articles, writing books (including textbooks on sexual behavior), and presenting their research findings at scholarly conferences and, in some cases, through the mass media. Carlfred Broderick, a sociology professor at the University of Southern California, used his proximity to Hollywood to make it onto the Tonight Show with Johnny Carson, appearing on the show several times during the 1970s and 1980s as a self-proclaimed "sexologist."

Today, sociological and psychological scholarly journals routinely publish articles on sexual behavior, as do a number of multidisciplinary journals devoted specifically to sex. *The Journal of Sex Research* (started in 1963) and *Archives of Sexual Behavior* (started in 1971) are two leading examples.

An article from *The Journal of Sex Research* provides the flavor of what social scientists are likely to study. In 2000, Martin Barron and Michael Kimmel published "Sexual Violence in Three Pornographic Media: Toward a Sociological Explanation" (Barron and Kimmel 2000), in which they analyzed "sexually violent content" in a random sampling of skin and sex magazines, X-rated videos, and sexual stories appearing on the Usenet part of the Internet. Nearly forty magazines with sexual content were studied, ranging from mainstream publications to straight porno/hardcore. The research also included fifty videos and fifty sex stories from alt.sex.stories.

Barron and Kimmel used well-thought-out random sampling procedures to select the magazine stories, videos, and Internet stories they used for data. Their measurement of violent content was achieved by using five trained coders who applied a clearly defined coding system. They also used established statistical techniques to support their research methods and findings (Cohen's Kappa Coefficient to measure the reliability of coders and the Chi-square test of statistical significance to make inferences about differences between categories). The meticulous care taken by the researchers to describe their sampling and coding procedures illustrates how important it was for them to demonstrate a *scientific* methodology and thus give their research legitimacy.

A key finding of the Barron and Kimmel study was the progressive increase in violent content in sexual/pornographic materials from magazines to videos to the Internet. In interpreting their findings, the authors speculate that moving from magazines to the Internet represents an increasing "democratization" of pornography (i.e., the cost of production becomes less, the complexity of production becomes simpler, and the control of production becomes more diffuse). Nearly anyone with a computer can access the Internet and with sufficient motivation can produce pornography. The researchers further speculated that the Internet is male dominated, both in the production of sexual materials and in having an interest in viewing it. This male-dominant climate, they assert, is "The closest thing to the all-male locker room" in the pornography world (Barron and Kimmel 2000, 166). In this male-dominated environment, male authors compete with each other to produce the most violent, male-dominant sexual scenarios.

In addition to the Barron and Kimmel study, sociologists, psychologists, and other behavioral scientists are adding constantly to the body of knowledge about sexual behavior, sexual attitudes, and sexual norms. But at the same time, other individuals and groups are opposed to research on sex and often employ repressive measures to stop or thwart scientific research about sex.

## SOME PERSISTING PROBLEMS FOR SOCIAL SCIENTISTS STUDYING SEX

While it is now commonplace to study sexual behavior, researchers do still encounter obstacles to their research or criticisms of their findings.

Perhaps the most widely known sociological study of sexual behavior was reported in Laud Humphries's *Tearoom Trade: Impersonal Sex in Public Places* (1975). Humphries carried out his sociological observations in a restroom in a public park, where he acted as a "watch-queen" (a look-out charged with keeping an eye out for strangers or police officers). He also surreptitiously took down the license plate numbers of men who frequented the restroom and then later, in the capacity of a social research interviewer, visited the homes of these men in order to question them further.

The outcry against Humphries's research raged on a couple of fronts. Some social scientists objected to the invasion of personal privacy, since the men involved were not informed that they were the subjects of a sociological study of sexual behavior. Some members of the public considered the subject matter of Humphries's research too unpleasant and were especially upset by the revelation that some men who were living "normal" heterosexual lives were also engaging in sexual behavior with other men.

These objections have had the apparent effect of suppressing observational research on sexual behavior, since there have been relatively few similar studies in the years that followed Humphries's research. Most sex researchers rely on interviews and questionnaires, instead of observational studies. This is especially true of research of sexual behavior that runs counter to social norms or is illegal.

Even interview/questionnaire studies of sexual behavior sometimes encounter obstacles. In the 1990s, political opposition temporarily interrupted a major survey of the sexual behavior of American adults (Laumann, Gagnon, and Michael 1994). In 1987, largely in response to the increasing spread of the HIV virus and AIDS, the National Institutes of Health issued a call for research projects on adult sexual behavior in the United States. A number of prominent social scientists, located primarily at the University of Chicago, proposed to conduct a survey of twenty thousand randomly selected American adults. By survey research standards this was a very large sample, but a necessary one maintained the researchers if they were to make statistically sound conclusions for different segments of the population (e.g., young black women, older Hispanic males, etc.). The proposal was initially approved and funded by the National Institute of Child Health and Human Development.

In the early 1990s, however, then-Senator Jesse Helms of North Carolina began crusading to have the study killed. Senator Helms, supported by other conservative Senators, was adamantly opposed to the funding of sex research by the U.S. government. In 1991, the Senate cut off funding for the national survey of adult sexual behavior by a 66 to 34 vote (Laumann, Gagnon, and Michael 1994).

The researchers were then forced to rely on private groups and foundations for funding, requiring the research to be conducted on a much smaller scale than had originally been proposed. The final sample size was 3,432, instead of the 20,000 that would have provided a more useful and comprehensive sample.

The final reports of the study, and especially the book *The Social Organization of Sexuality: Sexual Practices in the United States* (Laumann et al. 1994), provided massive amounts of data on the sexual behavior of American adults. While the study was somewhat limited by the smaller-than-desired sample, it nonetheless gave valuable information about sexual behavior to social scientists, social policy makers, and to the general public.[3]

The attempt by the U.S. Senate during the 1990s to obstruct sexual research should not obscure the fundamental fact that today the scholarly study of sex is going on in virtually every relevant science or academic discipline. The results of sex research are widely reported, both in scholarly publications and in the mass media. The general public not only accepts the legitimacy of such studies, but also expects the results to be reported on radio and television, in newspapers, and in magazines.

When researchers focus their attention on the potential negative effects of *pornography*, as illustrated by the Barron and Kimmel research described earlier, or the research by Donnerstein and his associates that will be described later in this chapter, there is relatively little objection from either the public or politicians. However, when pornography is studied objectively, with no particular negative slant, acceptance is more limited. These obstacles have not deterred some scholars from approaching the study of pornography objectively, analyzing it simply as a form of communication (Cullen 2006).

## THE STUDY OF PORNOGRAPHY IN ACADEME

Linda Williams, a Professor of Film Studies at The University of California, Berkeley, is a pioneer in the scholarly study of pornography. Along with the work of two other film studies scholars, Constance Penley and Laura Kipnis, she can reasonably take credit for establishing and fostering the emerging field of porn studies (Williams 2004b). Williams has been instrumental in setting porn studies apart from previous academic and especially the antiporn feminist approaches to the study of pornography (Williams 2004a).

The study of pornography as a film genre grew out of Williams's earlier interest in "film bodies," which she describes as the study of "particular kinds of body movement and body spectacle [in different types of films]—musicals, horror films, low comedies, 'weepies'" (Williams 1989, xv). Williams, almost as an afterthought, decided to include pornographic films among the types of film to be studied.

Williams approached pornographic films with a set of views about the genre that she had garnered primarily from antiporn feminist critics (e.g., "literal voyeurism; sadism that punishes women for being sexual . . . ; fetishism" [Williams 1989, xvi]). When she actually started to view pornographic films, however, beginning with the earliest stag films[4] and going up to the pornographic works available in the 1980s, she discovered that the feminist stereotypes were not consistent with the evidence. This led her to change her primary focus to a much deeper and more extensive analysis of pornographic films. One result of this research was her ground-breaking and highly influential book *Hardcore: Power, Pleasure, and the "Frenzy of the Visible"* (Williams 1989).

In *HardCore*, Williams follows Michel Foucault's thesis that in contemporary society there is an incessant compulsion to speak about sex. This includes not just artistic, literary, cinematic, therapeutic, and social scientific discourse, but also the antipornography arguments of censors, moralists, and religionists. The latter groups oppose what they view as excessive amounts of sex in society, and are especially opposed to "deviant" forms of sex. But in so doing, they contribute to the continuing discourse about sex. Williams also cites Foucault's observation that all modes of sexual discourse provide "a machinery of power [that encroaches] further on bodies and their pleasures" (Williams 1999, 3). She adds: "Foucault thus offers, at least potentially, a way of conceptualizing power and pleasure within the history of discourses of sexuality" (Williams 1999, 3).

Williams's empirical observations have produced important substantive information regarding the assertion that pornography is a form of violence against women. She states bluntly that, while much has been written about pornographic violence against women, comparatively little has been written about the "actual texts" of pornographic films (Williams 1999, 29). Based on her observations of the texts, she maintains that pornographic films do not contain the level of violence against women that is often claimed by critics.

When *Hardcore* was published in 1999, most academic reviews were positive and did not question the seriousness of Williams's scholarship. Prior to publication she admits to having been apprehensive about how feminists, particularly those who were vehemently opposed to pornography, would respond to it. The antiporn feminist response was very limited, however. Williams wryly noted at the time, "anti-porn feminists ignored the book" (Williams 1999, ix).

After Williams's contribution to the legitimization of pornography as a subject for scholarly research, one important step remained to be taken in the academic world: teaching undergraduate and graduate courses with pornography as the subject matter. Williams waited until the spring of 1994 before offering her first upper-division undergraduate course on pornography.[5] The course was offered in the Film Studies department at the University of California, Irvine, "in the heart of conservative Orange County" (Williams 2004b, 12). Understandably apprehensive, Williams made it clear to prospective students that the course was an "experiment to determine whether the textual study of moving-image pornography had a place in the university curriculum" Williams 2004b, 12). Realizing that this was an experimental course, the students "were on especially good behavior" (Williams 2004b, 13). Initial enrollment in the class was high, with sixty students signing up to attend, but eventually the number settled at about thirty.

Williams made clear at the start that students would be seeing hardcore, sexually explicit films that would include gay male, lesbian, bisexual, straight, sadomasochistic and fetish pornography. The course syllabus contained the following boldface warning:

> Many of the films, videos, and images we will see in this class are bound to be offensive to some viewers. Please do not take this class unless you are willing to look closely at a wide variety of explicit, hard-core pornographic sexual representations and to discuss and write about them with the same kind of attention you would give to any other popular cultural form. (Williams 2004b, 14)

Williams also emphasized for prospective enrollees that the course would not be an especially easy one or simply an excuse to watch "dirty movies." The students viewed, discussed, and analyzed many pornographic films, including *Deep Throat*, *Behind the Green Door*, and *The Opening of Misty Beethoven*, but they were also required to read Williams's *Hardcore* book in its entirety (not an especially easy text), porn critic Catherine MacKinnon's *Only Words* (1993), parts of Michel Foucault's *History of Sexuality* (1978), twelve photocopied articles and "many" published essays (Williams 2004b, 13). Students were also asked to keep and turn in a journal, take a midterm examination, and write a final paper or prepare a project (Williams 2004b).

Williams still occasionally teaches the undergraduate course on pornography at Berkeley, where she also offers a graduate course on the subject. Her graduate-level course has resulted in published articles and book chapters by some of the participants (Williams 2004a). Many of her students and former students are now working on doctoral dissertations related in various ways to pornography.

## OTHER FILM STUDIES PORNOGRAPHY SCHOLARS

*New Yorker* journalist James Atlas claims that "higher learning has embraced pornography" (Atlas 1999). While that is probably an overstatement, pornography has certainly gained legitimacy, at least in the country's elite and more liberal academic institutions.

It is probably not a coincidence that at least two other pornography scholars, like Williams, are in Film Studies.

Constance Penley, whom Williams credits as being the first to teach pornography as a film genre, has also made at least a part of her scholarly reputation studying and teaching pornography. Penley, a Professor of Film Studies at the University of California, Santa Barbara has written and edited a number of books on film, including *Feminism and Film Theory* (Penley 1988), but her real mark on pornography studies was made by her provocatively titled article "Crackers and Whackers: The White Trashing of Porn," which originally appeared in Wray and Newitz's book *White Trash: Race and Gender in America* (1996) and has recently been republished in Williams's *Porn Studies* (2004a).

In this essay, Penley observes that many pornographic films (as well as pornography generally) implicitly scorn the conventional norms of the middle class. Penley also describes the tendency of pornographic films to ridicule male sexuality. The small penis and the limp penis after intercourse are found frequently in pornographic film humor.[6]

In the classic stag film, Penley observes, the limitations of male sexuality and the ineffectual male organ are often contrasted with the insatiable sexual potential of women (one orgasm for men, multiple orgasms for women). More significantly, women are in control of sex in much of film pornography and are portrayed as initiating sex and setting the terms for sexual encounters. In theoretical terms, women more often have sexual *agency* in pornography than do men (Penley 1997, 2004).

All of these subtexts of pornography, Penley claims, have been largely ignored by its critics. Feminist scholars have been especially inattentive to these elements of pornography because they have been fixated on the idea that pornography is primarily characterized by violence against women. Penley maintains: "it may be difficult to recognize that the tone of pornography—when one actually looks at it—is closer to *Hee Haw* than Nazi death camp fantasies" (Penley 2004, 314). To put it more simply, pornography is often based on humor, and as Penley points out, "the joke is usually on the man" (Penley 2004, 314). From stag films to current-day videos, pornography is much more likely to depict the sexual power of women than violence against women.

Like Williams, Penley has attained a position of considerable status in academe, though her analysis of films ranges beyond pornography and includes a book on science fiction movies (Penley 1997). Her academic appointments have taken her from the University of Illinois, to the University of Rochester, to the University of California, Santa Barbara, where she has served as the chair of the Department of Film Studies (1997–2001). She has attained the position of Full Professor and Director of the Center for Film, Television, and New Media at the University of California, Santa Barbara.

Another scholar who has gained at least part of her scholarly reputation through her study of pornography is Laura Kipnis, a Professor of Radio/Television/Film at Northwestern University. Kipnis's provocatively titled book, *Bound and Gagged: Pornography and the Politics of Fantasy in America* (Kipnis 1996) is one of the most frequently cited books on pornography.

Kipnis is a no-nonsense writer who uses case examples of pornography to illustrate the socio-cultural functions of the genre (Kipnis 1996). She urges her readers to:

> Abandon your prejudices about what kind of language is appropriate to serious philosophical inquiry, and you can see that within the staged, mythic world of pornography a number of philosophical questions are posed . . . questions concerning the social compact and the price of repression, questions about what men are (and aren't), what women are (and aren't), questions about how sexuality and gender roles are performed, about class, aesthetics, utopia, rebellion, power, desire, and commodification. (Kipnis 1996, viii)

Kipnis's list of questions may overpromise what a study of pornography can actually provide, but it certainly prepares her students for something beyond sexual titillation. They can also expect a rigorous intellectual experience.

Much like Williams and Penley, Kipnis is not interested in debating whether pornography should or should not exist. "It does exist," she explains, "and it's not going to go away. Why it exists, what it has to say, and who pornography is talking to, are more interesting questions than all these doomed, dreary attempts to debate it, regulate it, or protest it" (Kipnis 1996, x, xi).

An example from Kipnis's book *Bound and Gagged* demonstrates how she uses pornography to gain insight into society's workings. The case at hand is *fat pornography*. For those who have not explored the world of pornography, it may come as a surprise to learn that not all models found in pornographic magazines or videos, or on the Internet, have the ideal bodies found in *Playboy* or *Playgirl*. A few magazine titles suggest the genre's preferences for style and content: *Plumpers and Big Women*, *Jumbo Jezebel*, *Life in the Fat Lane*, and *Love's Savage Cupcake*. Some gay male magazines also cater to those who desire large or even fat sexual partners. Titles include: *Bulk Male*, *Husky*, and *Bustin Apart at the Seams* (Kipnis 1996, 94). The men featured in these gay male magazines are described as big "teddy bears," weighing 250 to 300 pounds, with barrel chests and lots of body hair.

Kipnis maintains that fat porn generally serves the same social function as pornography, that is, it allows people to see things that are normally hidden from public view. While fatness is widely ridiculed and reviled in our society, fat pornography provides a "celebration of fat, which defies the prevailing societal norms and social controls" (Kipnis 1996, 120). Kipnis concludes, "Fat is what our culture . . . doesn't want to look at. Pornography, in response, puts it on view. Fat pornography commemorates bodies that defy social norms, it solicits an erotic identification with bodies that are unresponsive to social control—with voracious, demanding, improper, non-upwardly mobile, socially transgressive bodies" (Kipnis 1996, 121). In addition to her analysis of fat porn, Kipnis also uses case examples of sadomasochism and transvestism, and an analysis of Larry Flynt's *Hustler* magazine, as ways of gaining insights into the workings of American society. She observes, "[W]e might . . . regard pornography as performing a social service: one of revealing these cultural sore spots, elucidating not only the connection between sex and the social but between our desires, our `selves,' and the casual everyday brutality of cultural conformity" (Kipnis 1996, 121). Kipnis has also established a considerable scholarly reputation beyond her study of pornography. She lists a wide variety of scholarly interests in her Northwestern University biography, including: "politics, body and psyche, with detours through aesthetics, love, Marx, adultery, scandal, Freud, and, of course, pornography." Her most recent books are *Against Love: A Polemic* (Kipnis 2003), which debunks the importance of love and marital fidelity, and *The Female Thing: Dirt, Sex, Envy, Vulnerability* (Kipnis 2006, in which she critically examines the conflict between feminism and femininity).

## A COMPREHENSIVE SCHOLARLY APPROACH
## TO THE STUDY OF PORNOGRAPHY

Unlike Williams, Penley, and Kipnis, Joseph W. Slade has taken a quite different approach to the study of pornography. A telecommunications professor at Ohio University in Athens, Ohio, Slade received his PhD in literature from New York University, and has published widely in the areas of literature, film, technology, and culture. But it is in the study of pornography (what he sometimes delicately calls "sexual representation") that he has made his reputation.

While writing a conventional literature dissertation on poet Edwin Markham during the 1960s, Slade became intrigued with what he rather formally calls "transgressive expression," specifically in the form of stag films, which were just starting to become "quasi-public" (Slade 2000b, xviii).[7]

Slade spent two summers doing research at the Kinsey Institute for research on Sex, Gender, and Reproduction, the nation's largest repository of sexual materials. The Kinsey collection contained approximately 1,200 stag films, both 8 and 16 mm. But Slade's research was not limited to the Kinsey collection. He estimated in 2000 that he had viewed more than 5,000 pornographic films or videos and has looked at as many as 150,000 pornographic photos (Slade 2000b, xviii).

In 2000, Professor Slade produced a massive compendium on pornography in the three volume publication, *Pornography and Sexual Representation: A Reference Guide* (Slade 2000b), complemented by a shorter volume, *Pornography in America: A Reference Handbook* (Slade 2000a). In these publications Slade has displayed an encyclopedic knowledge of pornography and sexual representation, covering nearly everything and everyone associated with American pornography. The areas covered include erotic art, erotic performers, erotic photography, dial-a-porn services, and much more. Almost nothing in the realm of sexual presentation and representation has escaped Slade's attention.

Unlike the scholarly work of Williams, Kipnis, and Penley, Slade approaches pornography in a less theoretical and more straightforward descriptive way. His objective is to describe, as comprehensively as possible, all pornographic works and all forms of sexual representation. His early work is largely limited to pornography in the United States, but recently he has moved toward a more international perspective (see Milter and Slade 2005). In 2004, he was selected to be the curator of an exhibit on stag films at the Museum of Sex in New York City.

An example of the comprehensiveness of Slade's work is his description of the enterprising career of Irving Klaw (1911–66), an early pioneer in the production of erotic materials whose career has been largely neglected by other scholars.

## The Pornography Career of Irving Klaw and His Sister Paula

Irving Klaw made his mark in the 1940s and 1950s, first by publishing magazines that featured Hollywood starlets in "pinup" poses (i.e., usually dressed in bathing suits), but later by offering magazines with photos featuring sexual fetishes.

In 1939, Klaw and his younger sister Paula opened a bookstore on 14th Street in lower Manhattan. The store was called "Movie Star News" and featured pinup photos of movie stars and starlets. Klaw first recognized the potential for more exotic products after "customers began asking for lingerie and bondage shots of their favorite Hollywood actresses" (Slade 2000a, 186). Klaw and his sister soon began photographing and filming young women, including some of the famous burlesque queens of the era (Lili St. Cyr and Tempest Storm, for example). By current-day standards, the photographs and 8-mm movies were relatively tame, with the models attired in "bathing suits, corsets, brassieres, satin panties, silk stockings, and high heels, all exaggerated as fetishes" (Slade 2000a, 187). Klaw was scrupulous about conforming to the standards of postal inspectors, making sure that "the fetish garments . . . conformed to the . . . amount of skin that could be exposed in the men's magazines" of the time (Museum of Sex 2002, 45). As a further precaution, Klaw also did not allow men to be shown with his women models.

One of Klaw's most famous "pinup" and fetish models was a striking brunette named Bettie Page, whose notoriety in the 1950s actually exceeded that of the Klaw's. Today, Bettie Page's photos—even those in which she was tied up with ropes, or shown spanking or being spanked by another woman—would not be considered pornographic (see Museum of Sex 2002, 47).[8]

Despite the comparative mildness of Klaw's photographs and movies, he was called before a Senate investigating committee in 1955, where Senator Estes Kefauver, the chairman of the committee, accused him of running a million dollar business in "obscenity" (Slade 2000a, 187). Witnesses appeared before the committee to testify that "watching the Klaws' movies would turn 'normal' juveniles into homosexuals" (Slade 2000a, 187). After the Senate hearings, Klaw moved his business to New Jersey, where he avoided further confrontations with the authorities until his arrest in 1963. At the time, he was terminally ill and agreed to "burn his entire stock of photos and films in exchange for having the charges dropped" (Slade 2000a, 187). The government agreed to his offer and he was released. Klaw died, and his sister Paula, who had secretly retained the master copies of all their photos and films, continued the business until her death thirty years later. Even in 2008 it is possible to find Bettie Page photographs that still have the Paula Klaw copyright in antique stores and flea markets.

## ACADEMIC CONFERENCES ON PORNOGRAPHY

Academic conferences legitimize scholarly topics because they bring together the leading experts in a field or a topic and give selected participants the opportunity to make speeches and present papers. These speeches and papers are then critiqued and discussed by other experts, as well as by audience members.

As an indication of the growing legitimacy of pornographic studies several conferences on pornography have been held at various college and university campuses (Jones 2000). In 1991, the History Department at the University of Pennsylvania sponsored a conference on "The Invention of Pornography." The scholarly papers presented at this conference were collected in Lynn Hunt's *The Invention of Pornography: Obscenity and the Origins of Modernity, 1500–1800* (Hunt 1993a).

A more contemporary approach to pornography occurred at "Exposed," a 1995 conference held at the University of California, Santa Cruz. The conference brought together pornography scholars and featured Annie Sprinkle, a porn star turned writer and lecturer, who showed some of her pornographic movies. Another conference on pornography titled "Revolting Behavior," was held at the State University of New York at New Paltz in 1997. This conference provoked one SUNY trustees to call for the resignation of the university president (Jones 2000).

An ostentatiously labeled conference on pornography was held in 1998 on the campus of California State University Northridge, near Los Angeles. This conference was called "The First Annual World Conference on Pornography," and was organized by faculty members at the Cal-State Northridge Center for Sex Research, in cooperation with representatives from the sex industry, and the Free Speech Coalition. The conference brought together "disparate groups in an attempt to provide an open forum for those who defend, research, and are intimately involved in the field of pornography" (Elias et al. 1999, 9).

The keynote speaker was Nadine Strossen, then president of the American Civil Liberties Union, and the author of *Defending Pornography: Free Speech, Sex, and the Fight for Women's Rights* (Strossen 1995). Strossen recounted a number of court cases in which the ACLU had defended individuals and groups charged with violating antipornography laws. She explained that these cases were "just the tip of a very large iceberg," and deplored the "consistent hostility to sexual expression" (Elias et al. 1999, 22).

Other papers presented at the conference represented a variety of topics, ranging from legal defenses of pornography to personalized reports by several actors and actresses in the pornography film industry. The following are just a few of the titles:

- My Years Defending *Playboy*
- America Unchained: Tattoos, Piercings, and Porn
- Topping from Below: Does Female Dominant Pornography Endorse the Rape of Women?
- What is Feminist Porn?
- Porn Wars on Campus
- A Serious Look at the Amazing Phenomenon of Erotic Comic Books
- Gay Porn/Queer Erotica
- The Forbidden Image: Child Pornography and the First Amendment
- Classical Roman Perspective on the Erotic, Obscenity, and Pornography

One session at the Northridge conference titled "All-Star Porn Panel" brought together more than twenty women and men who had appeared in pornographic films, including: Annie Sprinkle, Nina Hartley, Vanessa Del Rio, Veronica Hart, Sharon Mitchell, and Candida Royalle. The panelists described their experiences as actors in porn films and their reactions to the objectives of the conference. The moderator, porn actor Will Jarvis (a.k.a. Taliesin, the Bard), proudly emphasized the professional abilities of the members of the panel:

> I hope that if there is one thing you get from this conference [it] is that the actors and actresses . . . are all professional people. There are so many women and men who've tried to be in our business and can't. The women lay there like dead fish, and the men can't get erections. . . . Too many people have tried to do what we do and have not succeeded at it. (Elias et al. 1999, 448)

Female porn star Annie Sprinkle told the audience: "It's been so orgasmic being here. . . . This is my idea of a good time. I guess I've always been in a kind of perpetual pursuit of ecstasy and pleasure" (Elias et al. 1999, 452).

Fifty years ago (and probably more recently) it would have been impossible to hold a conference on pornography at any American college or university. Today, a conference on pornography, even one that includes a cluster of pornography stars, is acceptable (at least on some American campuses).

## WOMEN'S STUDIES AND PORNOGRAPHY

Many of the nation's colleges and universities have women's studies (sometimes called feminist studies) programs. Women's studies programs usually offer courses that point out the ways in which women are disadvantaged or subordinated, both in American society and most other societies of the world. Pornography is often identified as one of the ways in which women are subordinated.

A representative example of this perspective is offered by Ann Russo, a professor of women's studies at DePaul University, Chicago (Russo 1998). Russo begins by making the point that antipornography feminists have not been opposed to sexually explicit material, as such. Their attack has been on an industry that "contributes to pervasive social inequality and endemic sexual violence" (Russo 1998, 9). She says more fully: "[The] structure and dynamics of eroticized inequality, and the sexual mistreatment, abuse, and violence that occur in connection with [pornography's] production, distribution, and consumption," are the salient issues of the "feminist fight against pornography" (Russo 1998, 9).

### FEMINIST ARGUMENTS AGAINST PORNOGRAPHY

In academe, feminist scholars have made the connection between pornography and violence in two ways:

- The physical and emotional abuse suffered by women involved in the porn industry; and,
- The potential correlation between male consumption of pornography and actual acts of violence against women.

In the first case, women who participate in the making of pornography, especially in films and photographs, are said to be subjected to coercion and violence by their managers and handlers, who force them to engage in acts against their will (e.g., the Linda Lovelace story in Chapter 7). The very acts women must perform when making pornographic films and photographs are described as inherently violent (anal intercourse, the insertion of foreign objects into vaginas and anuses, fisting, having men ejaculate on their faces, etc.).

The second objection raised by feminists concerns the potential relationship between men's consumption of pornography and violent acts committed against women. Many feminist scholars have claimed that the absorption of violent sexual fantasies by men leads to acts of rape, battery, and torture of women, and possibly even murder (Dines, Jensen, and Russo 1998; Lederer 1980; Lederer and Delgado 1995). While such claims are often anecdotal or circumstantial, a few social scientists have conducted research to determine, using empirical evidence, whether pornography leads to aggression and violence against women.

Psychologist Edward Donnerstein and several of his research colleagues have been pioneers in experimental studies testing the hypothesis that pornography leads to violence against women (Malamuth and Donnerstein 1984; Donnerstein, Linz, and Penrod 1987; Green and Donnerstein 1998). Since the 1980s, Donnerstein has published over two hundred scientific journal articles and book chapters, authored or edited at least eight books, and received numerous research grants from funding agencies (Slade 2000a, 173).

Donnerstein's experimental research approach generally involved showing undergraduate males films with sexual and/or violent content. According to Slade, the researchers in Donnerstein's early experiments "did not find a significant relationship between exposure to *nonviolent* pornography and the tendency to view women as sex objects" (Slade 2000a, 173). From this, Donnerstein concluded that pornographic films only had negative effects on male viewers when sexual content was combined with violence. In his testimony before the Meese Commission (see Chapter 3), he reported that his research provided little evidence that viewing sex-only pornography leads to aggression or violence (Slade 2000a).

Some feminist academics have expressed conflicted views about the connection between pornography and violence against women. Gail Dines, a Professor of Sociology and Women's Studies at Wheelock College in Boston, described how she has lived between "two worlds" as she has tried to deal with pornography: the academic world and the world of an antipornography activist (Dines 1998, 163). As an academic Dines has increasingly accepted a "pro-pornography" position, asserting that she does not hold pornography responsible for "rape, battery, torture, and murder of women in the real world" (Dines 1998, 163).

As an antipornography activist, however, she has met "hundreds of women and men who have stories to tell about pornography and the devastating impact it has had on their lives" (Dines 1998, 163). Women often come to her after her lectures, eager to tell her "about what it is like to be coerced into making pornography by parents, brothers, uncles, boyfriends, husbands, and pimps" (Dines 1998, 163).

The personal conflicts described by Dines illustrate the situation faced by feminist scholars throughout academe. Feminist scholars have a commitment to intellectual inquiry that impels them to examine pornography as objectively and honestly as possible. At the same time, they cannot ignore the negative impact that pornography may have on the lives of women.

Conflicting viewpoints and competing evidence provide the raw material for discussion and debate in the academic world. These discussions and debates may begin in the classroom, but they more often extend to workshops, conferences, and scholarly meetings. These, in turn, lead to published articles and books. All of these scholarly activities add to the level of discourse about sex and pornography in the academic world.

Feminist scholars of all varieties—along with classicists, historians, art historians, social scientists, film critics, and other academics—have gained status and social power from their scholarship and research on sexual materials, erotica, and pornography. All of them derive their legitimacy from the rational-intellectual approach to the study of sexual behavior and sexual representations. Objective analysis of sexual matters has become an acceptable area of specialization in the arts and humanities, as well as the social and behavioral sciences. In today's hypersexual society, the academic world increasingly accepts and often rewards the professors who study (and teach courses about) sexual matters, erotica, and pornography.

## CHAPTER 6

# SEX THERAPY

## THE PROFESSION, THE BUSINESS, THE HUCKSTERS, AND THE SPAMMERS

Sigmund Freud (1856–1939) was born before the American Civil War, but he lived nearly four decades into the twentieth century. His life's work as a medical doctor who treated patients with psychological problems greatly affected the way people of Western societies came to view sex. It was Freud who first associated psychological well-being with sexuality. His ideas about sex were so revolutionary that it is no exaggeration to say that he was a *pioneer of sex.*

In his Viennese medical practice Freud became renowned for his work with patients who had mental disorders, some of which manifested themselves in physical ways. These physical abnormalities ranged from facial tics and stuttering to paralysis; the mental aberrations included everything from phobias to mental delusions. As Freud was treating these patients, he was also developing a general theory of the human psyche, and it was this theory that brought him to international prominence.[1]

Freud called his theory psychoanalysis, which involved treating patients by exploring their innermost thoughts and even their dreams. It was on the basis of his intensive sessions with patients that Freud derived his fundamental notions of sexual development. Freud asserted that normal sexual development goes through three stages: the oral, the anal, and the phallic. In the oral stage, the infant's lips are the key erogenous zone; in the anal stage, the anus is the erogenous zone; and in the phallic stage, the genitals are the principal erogenous zone. The oral stage begins in infancy; the phallic stage emerges at puberty. If a person remains fixated at the oral or anal stages of development, Freud believed various psychological and behavioral problems would be likely to manifest themselves.

Even today, cigarette smokers and compulsive eaters are often described as having "oral fixations," while people obsessed with cleanliness, orderliness, and possessiveness may be described as "anal compulsive."

While Freud's fundamental ideas about the human psyche continue to be influential today, many of his specific notions are widely discredited. A prominent example involves Freud's view of homosexuality, or what he called "inversion" (Brill 1938a, 554ff.). Freud viewed homosexuality as a mental illness, and until only a few decades ago, psychiatric diagnostic manuals persisted in treating it as such. Today that notion has been abandoned and, as a side effect, Freud's reputation has been tarnished.

In a similar way, Freud's views about females were deeply rooted in the patriarchal culture of nineteenth century Vienna. Sexism manifested itself in various ways in Freud's theorizing. A widely known—and now almost universally rejected—example is his assertion that all females have "penis envy," a belief that their own genital makeup is physically deficient in comparison with males (Brill 1938a, 595). In spite of the sexism and outdatedness of many of his theories, Freud's writings have contributed in an interesting way to the hypersexuality of contemporary society.

Most importantly, Freud used his psychoanalytic theory to bring sexual matters into the realm of *rational-intellectual discourse* (predating the work of Kinsey discussed in the previous chapter). Freud was such a prolific theorist that he often changed or modified his theories as new observations and experiences with patients inspired him. What is important for our discussion is not the "validity" of Freud's specific theories about sexuality, but the "importance" that he ascribed to sexuality. In his emphasis on the importance of sexuality in human development, Freud opened up a line of sexual discourse that continues to the present day.

Freud gave the medical and intellectual community a new way of thinking about and talking about sex. In the early decades of the twentieth century, his influence spread quickly among writers, scholars and intellectuals. In American academe, Freud's ideas were widely accepted and discussed in the fields of literature, drama, philosophy, history, anthropology, psychology, and sociology. Beyond the scholarly world, his sexually based concepts, such as *penis envy, the Oedipal Complex,* and *infant sexuality,* were often discussed by the literate public.

Additionally, a whole new type of sexual discourse was generated by those who were offended by Freud's ideas. Among his contemporaries, opposition came from the medical, religious, and political communities (Jones 2000; Torrey 1992). Again we are reminded of Foucault's observation that those who oppose or try to repress sexual discourse will inevitably increase the overall discourse about sex.

## SEX AND PSYCHOLOGICAL HEALTH

The impact of Freud's sexual theorizing has extended far beyond the cocktail party chatter about "anal compulsiveness" and "penis envy." When Freud successfully connected sexual development with psychological well-being he contributed a new legitimacy to sexual discourse in contemporary society. "In a normal sex life," he once famously wrote, "no neurosis is possible" (Brill 1938b, 15).

For Freud, traumatic sexual experiences, such as rape or incest, led to mental illnesses. In the last half of the twentieth century, while accepting the linkage between sex and the psyche, many sexual therapists have been more likely to turn Freud's ideas around—emphasizing the influence of psychological factors on sexual well-being. According to this view, sexual problems can be overcome by first addressing the psychological condition of the individual. To put this in concrete terms, today's fashionable sexual problems (impotence, frigidity, sexual addiction, pedophilic impulses, addiction to pornography) require psychological treatment. The sex therapy profession has emerged to meet that need.

## MASTERS AND JOHNSON:
## PIONEER SEX THERAPY RESEARCHERS

In the 1960s, physician William H. Masters and psychologist Virginia E. Johnson provided a new dimension to the discourse about sex in the United States. In contrast to Freud's contribution, these two researchers, whose names are now inextricably linked as *Masters and Johnson*,[2] brought the human physiology of sex back into play by doing what no scientists had done before: they observed, filmed, recorded, and measured couples having sexual intercourse, and individuals (both men and women) masturbating. The early 1960s were still very conservative times in American society, so Masters and Johnson truly deserve to be called sex pioneers.

In the course of their research, Masters and Johnson collected data on 382 females and 312 males, who provided more than 10,000 episodes of sexual activity (Masters, Johnson, and Kolodny 1994). Although some doctors and scholars had previews of the Masters and Johnson research through their publications of scholarly journal articles and presentations at professional meetings, most Americans did not know about their work until the publication of their book, *Human Sexual Response* (Masters and Johnson 1966).

The book was primarily a scientific report on the physiology of human sexual response, aimed at doctors and therapists and written in the style typically used by medical/science writers. The venerable publisher, Little,

Brown of Boston, initially printed only fifteen thousand copies, which would generally have been enough for the targeted audience. That number was entirely sold out prior to the announced publication date (Lehrman 1970). In the next four years more than three hundred thousand copies were sold and sales continued at a rate of two thousand to three thousand per month.

When the mass media reports of the Masters and Johnson research came out, most Americans were shocked at the audacity of what the researchers had done. Filming individuals masturbating and couples having sexual intercourse was offensive to many Americans. In an era when only stag films were showing men and women having sex, many thought Masters and Johnson were producing pornography.

In spite of these objections, the first Masters and Johnson book was not widely censored or banned. In part, this was due to the scientific writing style of the book; it was, after all described as "the physiology of human sexual response." One of the most well-publicized findings of Masters and Johnson was the observation that the "male sexual response cycle" differs from the "female sexual response cycle."[3] One result of this difference, and one that quickly made its way into public consciousness, was that "in physiologic terms, women have an infinitely greater orgasmic capacity than men do" (Masters, Johnson, and Kolodny 1994, 52). In simple terms, women can have multiple orgasms, men generally cannot.

Masters and Johnson's research was also given legitimacy because of its focus on identifying and suggesting treatments for common sexual dysfunctions: frigidity, inability to attain orgasms, painful sexual intercourse among women, impotence, and premature ejaculation among men (Masters and Johnson 1966).

Masters and Johnson addressed sexual problems more directly in their later publication *Human Sexual Inadequacy* (1970), which introduced *sex-surrogate therapy*, a method that involves a professional sexual partner who helps the patient with his or her problems. "In brief," wrote Masters and Johnson, along with their coauthor Kolodny, "a surrogate partner is a person who has been trained in the ins and outs of sex therapy and who temporarily becomes the paid partner of a sexually dysfunctional individual without a partner" (Masters, Johnson, and Kolodny 1994, 167). The sex surrogates used by Masters and Johnson in their clinical studies were most often females, who were helping males who had problems with impotence or premature ejaculation. In some instances, sex surrogates were employed to assist married men whose wives could not, or would not, participate.

One of the first women to come forward with an account of her experiences as a sex surrogate was Valerie X. Scott. In her book, *Surrogate Wife* (Scott 1971), she described her experiences as a sex surrogate with dozens of clients in the Masters and Johnson clinic. Scott's account is thoughtful and observant about her work as a sex surrogate, often explaining how she had sexual intercourse with clients, even though they might have been unpleasant or unappealing to her. Through her work, she claims, many of her clients (all of them male) were able to move toward a better accommodation to their sexual problems.

In their later writings, Masters, Johnson, and Kolodny retracted their initial earlier enthusiasm for sex surrogates, at least in part as a reaction to the HIV/AIDS scare of the 1980s (Masters, Johnson, and Kolodny 1985, 1994).[4] Even though Masters and Johnson later backed away from this form of therapy, sex surrogacy has continued to survive even without their imprimatur.

## SEX-SURROGATE THERAPY TODAY

Sex surrogates still practice their trade, at least on the West Coast and on the Internet. A professional organization called the International Professional Surrogates Association (IPSA) has officers, a code of ethics, a referral system, and a Web site (http://www.surrogatepartners.org). Vena Blanchard, a recent president of the Association and a senior trainer of sex surrogates, has devoted considerable effort to explaining and legitimizing the work of its members. In an interview with www.sexuality.org, she describes sex surrogacy as "a triadic" form of therapy, involving the therapist, the patient, and the sex surrogate (http://www.sexuality.org/vena99/html 1999, 1). Surrogate partner therapy, she explains, is not just a "mechanical" process. "[T]he therapist, client, and surrogate together are constantly reevaluating what's the most useful and appropriate" for the patient's problems (http://sexuality.org/vena99/html 1999, 2).

When sex surrogates describe their experiences in narrative form, their accounts often resemble pornographic fiction. Consider, for example, the following admission by contemporary sex surrogate Linda Poelzl: "As the work progresses, clothes come off and the touch becomes more sensual and then sexual" ("Keeping the 'Sex' in Sex: My Work as a Surrogate Partner," http://www.anythingthatmoves.com/ish19/therapist). Because these actions are offered as a part of sex therapy, they do have a degree of legitimacy for many Americans, making this form of sexual discourse generally acceptable.

## SEX THERAPY: THE PROFESSION AND BEYOND

In the rest of this chapter we will describe sex therapy in all of its many contemporary forms, from the most highly trained professional practitioners, to self-proclaimed sex therapists and "sex coaches" (the currently in-vogue title) (Britton 2005), to blatant hucksters and charlatans. All of these forms of sex therapy contribute to the current level of sexual discourse in American society, and thus to hypersexuality.

### PROFESSIONAL SEX THERAPISTS

The most legitimate sex therapists and counselors have earned academic and medical degrees and often have some form of certification. Florida is the only state that grants a license for sex therapists (as of June 2004); in that state individuals who already hold a license in another mental health field can earn a specialty license in sex therapy "by completing 120 hours of training and 20 hours of supervised clinical practice" (Feifer 2004, HE05). In other states, professional sex therapists typically receive certification from professional organizations associated with therapy, sex, or marriage, such as: The American Association of Sex Educators, Counselors & Therapists (AASECT); the American Academy of Clinical Sexologists (AACS); and the American Association for Marriage and Family Therapy (AAMFT).

Dr. Robert W. Birch is one such professional sex therapist. Now retired, Birch has written a concise introduction to sex therapy. "Sex Therapy is a professional and ethical treatment approach to the problems of sexual function and expression. . . . Sex therapy . . . is the focusing of specialized clinical skills on helping men and women as individuals and/or as couples to deal more effectively with their sexual expression (http://www.oralcaress/therapy).

Birch explains that sex therapists are nonjudgmental about the sex lives of their clients and respectful of values that clients do not wish to change. Sex therapists may suggest reading or viewing materials to their clients, or assignments, tasks, and experiences, as long as these do not conflict with the client's values. According to the ethical standards of sex therapists, clients should never be asked to disrobe or have sexual relations with the therapists; nor should they be treated stereotypically (as female, gay, or too old) (http://www.oralcaress/therapy).

Sex therapy from the perspectives of the major professional organizations listed earlier are almost always devoted to the sex problems of nonpathological people and not to the problems of sexual criminals, such as compulsive rapists, child molesters, exhibitionists, and incestuous predators. Although some sex therapists might work in prisons and mental hospitals, where they deal with people convicted of illegal activities or who exhibited psychotic behavior.

One preeminent sexual problem of "normal" individuals is the lack of desire for sex (Leiblum and Rosen 2000). In contemporary society most people believe they should have, indeed must have, a strong and consistent desire for sex. When this desire is lacking, they consider themselves inadequate, especially when they are in a marital relationship. Sex therapists routinely deal with this problem (Schnarch 2000; Pridal and LoPiccolo 2000).

Beyond the general problem of a lack of sexual desire, sex therapists have identified an array of other sexual disorders, some of which are specific to females, some to males, and some to both sexes.

One female disorder, in addition to the absence of sexual arousal, is the failure to achieve orgasm as a climactic experience of sex (*anorgasmia*). Another female sexual problem (also experienced by a few men) is *dyspareunia*. In the past, dyspareunia referred to "genital pain in either a male or a female before, during or after sexual intercourse . . . not caused by lack of lubrication" (Woody 1992, 37). A new conceptualization of dyspareunia, however, emphasizes that it is a pain disorder rather than a sexual disorder (Binik, Bergeron, and Khalife 2000). The specific female form of this problem is *vaginismus*: "involuntary spasm of the musculature of the outer third of the vagina that interferes with coitus" (Woody 1992, 37). As a result of this problem, some women have extreme vaginal pain during sexual intercourse. Many Americans first became aware of vaginismus when Joyce Maynard (1998) described in detail her sexual problems as a nineteen year old living with novelist J. D. Salinger, author of *Catcher in the Rye*. Maynard and Salinger were nearly unable to have vaginal intercourse because she found it extremely painful.

Male sexual disorders almost always involve problems related to the penis and ejaculation. The most common male sexual disorder is "erectile dysfunction" (Althof 2000; Rosen 2000), a euphemistic term for men who cannot achieve or maintain an erection during a sexual episode. Two other major sexual problems for men relate to ejaculation: premature ejaculation, in which the male ejaculates too soon after beginning sexual intercourse, and retarded ejaculation, in which the male ejaculates too late or not at all.

In recent years, another type of sexual dysfunction has entered the realm of popular public discourse through the sex therapy profession: *sexual addiction* (Earle and Earle 1995; Kafka 2000; Wincze 1995). While the meaning of sexual addiction has never been precisely defined, it is a term widely used by sex therapy professionals and is increasingly accepted by the public. One sex therapist has offered a somewhat grand medical description: "the disinhibited or exaggerated expression of human sexual arousal and appetitive behavior" (Kafka 2000, 472). In more everyday terms, sexual addicts experience higher levels of sexual desire than they feel they are able to accept, control, or manage (Nathan 1995, 356). "It is obvious to therapists who treat sexual problems," according to Wincze, "that there are individuals who have difficulty controlling their sexual behavior" (Wincze 1995, 381). Some sex therapists recommend that sex addicts enter a "Twelve-step approach, the program popularized by Alcoholics Anonymous. In this case, sex is regarded as the 'drug of choice'" (Kafka 2000, 471).

As we shall see later, sex therapists who subscribe to the addiction point of view do have their critics, including those who reject the facile labeling of various sexual behaviors as pathological. This debate within the therapeutic community is an instructive example of how sexual discourse has escalated in American society with the advent and growth of the sex therapy profession.

## SEX THERAPY THEORIES AND THERAPEUTIC APPROACHES

Professional sex therapists subscribe to a variety of psychological theories and therapeutic approaches in their treatment of patients and clients. Contemporary advocates of the traditional Freudian model still consider any form of sexual dysfunction to be deeply rooted in the psychological development of the individual patient's childhood experience. This treatment model is both intensive and extensive, with therapy often going on for years. While this model is not totally rejected by modern-day sex therapists, it has generally fallen out of favor among the contemporary therapists. Today the emphasis is more often on the client's current personal relationships—not his or her childhood experiences. The therapy is usually problem oriented and relatively limited in time (see the discussion of "brief therapy" that follows).

Many contemporary sex therapists employ a medical/physiological model, in which most sexual problems are considered to be physical in origin. Therefore, pharmaceuticals are the prescribed remedy. General medical practitioners are also more likely to resort to pharmaceutical modes of therapy when their patients have sexual problems.

## A NOTE ON BRIEF THERAPY

"Brief therapy" is a currently prominent form of sex therapy. It derived from the seminal work of anthropologist Gregory Bateson (1972) and psychologists Milton Erickson (Erickson 1967; Haley 1967) and Don Jackson (1961). Brief therapy, as the name implies, is pragmatic and short term. Its primary goal is to identify a patient's problem, find a way to reduce the problem or problem-producing behavior, and then, as soon as the patient is ready, end "professional help" (Green and Flemons 2004, xxiii).

Brief therapy does not subscribe to any special theoretical or medical approach, and its practitioners are especially reluctant to "pathologize" a patient's behavior (Green and Flemons 2004). Brief therapists shy away from labeling a patient as ill, pathological, or suffering from a disorder. Instead, they focus on the patient, what he or she says, and what needs to be done to reduce or eliminate the patient's problem (Green and Flemons 2004).

## CRITICS OF PROFESSIONAL SEX THERAPISTS

Professional sex therapists are not without their critics. Even among sex researchers, some have accused sex therapists of promoting medical labels for certain sexual dysfunctions. Therapists can then offer corrective measures. Reiss and Reiss (1990) have taken sex therapists to task for their tendency to label certain sexual behaviors as pathological or dysfunctional. Among the most prominent is the assertion that women who do not achieve orgasm during sexual intercourse, *unless they have had direct stimulation of the clitoris*, are *anorgasmic* (Reiss and Reiss 1990). The Reisses point out that the majority of women do not have orgasms when they have sexual intercourse, unless they or their partners directly stimulate the clitoris. The Reisses believe that labeling the majority of women as sexually pathological (*anorgasmic*) is both unfair and irrational.

Similar objections have been raised about current views claiming that some men are addicted to sex. When one looks at the historical record, many nineteenth century doctors labeled some women as sexual deviants, calling them *nymphomaniacs*, simply because they enjoyed sex (Barker-Benfield 1976; Groneman 2000). Today, men who have a high level of interest in sex may be called sex addicts (Earle and Earle 1995). A few men have labeled themselves as sex addicts in order to rationalize or excuse their sexual activities, especially when they have been unfaithful to their wives. As one example, the former major league baseball player Wade Boggs quickly sought refuge in the "sex addict" label after he was caught cheating on his wife.

Many antipornography voices apply the addiction label to men who show an interest in pornography. On antipornography Web sites, wives and girlfriends of "pornography addicts" describe the inattention or abuse they suffer when their partners are overly interested in pornographic videos or Web sites. Internet Web sites that seek to help men who are "addicted" to pornography offer a variety of therapeutic approaches to help them overcome their addiction. The therapies range from traditional twelve-step programs to Christian counseling.

While some of these criticisms may have validity, it is undoubtedly true that professionally trained sex therapists do help many people who have sexual problems. These may include victims of incest, sexual molestation, and rape, or they may simply be people whose socialization experiences have left them inhibited or fearful about sex.

From a more analytical perspective we should note that sex therapists also have a great deal of control over knowledge about sex in American society. Sex therapists and the media who report their work greatly influence what Americans think about sex today. As we will observe later, the influence of sex therapy on contemporary attitudes and behavior is not limited to the traditional professional community, but also includes the entertainment and commercial varieties of sex therapy.

## SEX THERAPY ON TELEVISION AND THE INTERNET

The traditional setting for sex therapy consists of a face-to-face meeting between therapist and patient, usually in a private practitioner's office. But sex therapy today has moved beyond the office and into the areas of television and the Internet.

One prominent example of sex therapists who have artfully blended their professional training with entertainment are Laura and Jennifer Berman. These two well-educated and highly entrepreneurial sex counselors are co-founders of The Berman Center, which they describe as "A specialized Health Center for Women—Focused on Female Sexual Health and Menopause Management" (http://www.bermancenter.com). Dr. Jennifer Berman has a medical degree from the Boston University School of Medicine with a specialty in urology. Laura Berman has a PhD from New York University with a specialty in Human Sexuality, Marriage, and Family Life. The Bermans have published in refereed scholarly journals, written chapters for books, and published their own book, *For Women Only: A Revolutionary Guide to Overcoming Sexual Dysfunction and Reclaiming Your Sex Life* (Berman, Berman, and Bumiller 2001).

The Berman Center is "dedicated to taking a natural, holistic approach to female sexual health and menopause management" (http://www.bermancenter.com). According to its promotional material, "Approximately 43 percent of American women suffer from sexual dysfunction. Specific problems may include couples conflicts, loss of intimacy, low libido, difficulties reaching orgasm, dryness, low sensation, and even pain." All of these problems are dealt with in a "premier health care facility with a beautiful, spa-like environment" (http://www.bermancenter.com).

The Berman sisters are ideally suited to bring their expertise to television and have done so successfully. The have their own series on the Discovery Health Channel, and have had special features on the Lifetime Channel. As guests they have appeared on "Good Morning America," "Oprah," and "Larry King Live." Their television presentations cover a variety of sexual topics, but especially topics important to women. A few examples of the topics they have addressed include: lackluster bedroom performance, hysterectomies, sex after breast cancer, troubles with thongs, unpleasant odors, and male semen. One of their television presentations was devoted to oral sex, which began by describing the results of a survey on the topic. Then, passersby on the street were questioned on a variety of related topics ("What is fellatio? What is cunnilingus?"). These questions were then addressed by a medical doctor, who went on to answer questions about oral sex from callers.

The Bermans treat their topics with seriousness, yet entertainingly. Their television presentations are part therapy, part education, and part entertainment. Through their television appearances and on the Internet they have added new openness to the sexual discourse in American society.

Alex Robboy is another well-educated sex therapist, with a Masters of Social Work and a Post-Masters Certificate in Marriage Counseling and Sex Therapy from the University of Pennsylvania. Robboy has also moved beyond the counseling room and especially to the Internet as a way of offering her services to the public (http://www.sextherapyinphiladelphia.com). Her clinical practice is in Philadelphia but her Web site gives her a vastly larger clientele and allows her to provide her philosophy and services. Her philosophy affirms that "sex is like dancing, it changes every time. It depends on culture, atmosphere and mood. Sometimes it is done alone, with a partner, or in a group. It can be fast and hard or slow and soft." (http://www.howtohavegoodsex.com).

On her Web site, Robboy offers links to her "favorite dating site," Match.com, and another site for people looking for sex, Adultfriendfinder. She also provides lists of her favorite sex toys and her favorite sex education books, including: *The Joy of Self Pleasuring, Sex Positions, Urge: Hot Secrets for Great Sex, 101 Grrreat Nights of Sex,* and *The Hot Guide for Safer Sex.*

Visitors to her Web site are invited to send e-mails with ideas or information about sex that they believe might benefit others. She also provides a newsletter featuring "sex tips," including: couple exercises, erotic stories, safer sex, techniques, and quizzes (http://www.howtohavegoodsex.com).

## SEX THERAPY AND ENTERTAINMENT: DR. RUTH AND BEYOND

The Berman sisters and Alex Robboy illustrate how sex therapy on television and the Internet can easily take on some of the characteristics of entertainment. The person who unquestionably pioneered the connection between sex therapy/advice and entertainment was Dr. Ruth Westheimer.

Dr. Westheimer has, for decades, been the nation's mass media expert on sex. Most adult Americans immediately recognize the name "Dr. Ruth" and associate her with sex. Dr. Ruth bills herself as a "psychosexual therapist" and claims to have pioneered the field of "media psychology," which presumably is the popular dissemination of psychology through the media of radio and television. Dr. Ruth holds a doctorate in education from Columbia University Teachers College, along with a Master's degree in sociology from the New School for Social Research. While these are respectable academic credentials, they have only a limited connection with sex or sex therapy. Her formal education on sexual matters came after a brief stint with Planned Parenthood, which, according to her Web site biography, "prompted her to further her education in human sexuality by studying under Dr. Helen Singer Kaplan," a renowned sex therapist, at New York Hospital-Cornell Medical Center (http://www.turnerlearning.com/newsroom/ontheroad/westheimer.html).

In 1980, Dr. Ruth started her media career with a 15-minute radio program, "Sexually Speaking," which aired on Sundays after midnight on WYNY-FM (NBC) in New York City. From that time on, her fame as an expert advisor on sexual matters has continued to grow in both the electronic media and in the literary world.

There are many reasons for Dr. Ruth's success, including her dedication to hard work and her single-minded focus on sex. Another reason for Dr. Ruth's wide acceptance has been her ability to combine a grandmotherly style (helped by a strong Middle-European accent) with frank, unblushing talk about sexual matters. Her unthreatening, reassuring persona has allowed her to say things about sex that could not have been said by many other radio or television personalities.

Over the many years of her career, Dr. Ruth has taught courses on sexuality at a number of major universities, written fifteen books and a syndicated column, appeared on innumerable radio and television shows, and produced videos on sex. Her first video was titled "Terrific Sex." Her two recent videos are part of the "Making Love Series" produced by Playboy, Inc. The titles of current videos are: "Arousal, Foreplay & Orgasm" and "Secrets for Greater Sensual Pleasure" (http://www .turnerlearning.com/newsroom/onthe road/westheimer.html). Never one to miss a marketing opportunity, Dr. Ruth has also put her name on the Dummies book series, authoring the book, *Sex for Dummies* (Westheimer 2005).

Dr. Ruth has probably been the most financially successful and widely recognized sex advisor of our time—her media and literary success has contributed greatly to the discourse about sex in American society. Further, her media celebrity and financial successes have encouraged many imitators or self-proclaimed "sexperts," who have also added to the variety and explicitness of sexual discourse in American society.

## AVA CADELL: "A NEW AND YOUNGER DR. RUTH"

*Cosmopolitan* magazine once described Ava Cadell as "one of America's leading Sexologists" (http://www.sexpert.com). On her Web site, Dr. Ava proudly proclaims that she has been called "The new and younger version of Dr. Ruth," and her biography does bear some striking similarities to her older and less glamorous predecessor. Born in Hungary, in the aftermath of the Hungarian Revolution, Cadell was sent to Austria where she was raised by nuns in an orphanage. By comparison, Dr. Ruth was born in Germany in 1928, but at the age of ten, in order to escape the Nazi regime, she was sent to an orphanage in Switzerland.

The young Ava Cadell (then called Ildiko Csath) was found in the orphanage by her grandmother and brought to Great Britain, where by age twenty-one she had started a career as a model, cover girl, and spokesperson for a leading cosmetics firm. During that period of her life, she became a familiar personality on British television and had roles in a number of European films. In 1982, in her mid-twenties, she went to Hollywood where she worked as a "Playboy spokesperson and hostess of 'Pillow Previews' on the Playboy Channel" (http://www.sexpert.com).

After leaving Playboy and working in the television/movie business for a few years, Cadell began the exploration of one of her "life's passions, SEX." She earned advanced degrees from two little-known educational institutions: a Doctorate of Philosophy in Human Behavior from Newport University and a Doctorate in Education in Human Sexuality from the Institute for Advanced Study in Human Sexuality in San Francisco (http://www.sexpert.com)—both of which lack the credentials of more highly respected institutions, such as Harvard, Stanford, and the University of California, Berkeley.[5] In addition to her double doctorate, Cadell reports that she is "A Board Certified Clinical Sexologist and Hypnotherapist, with a private counseling practice in Los Angeles" (http://www.sexpert.com).

More than a simple sex counseling therapist, Dr. Ava is also an ambitious entrepreneur with a strong presence on the Internet, where she has now established "Loveology University" and urges site visitors to become certified "Loveologists." She has published articles and books, appeared on almost every popular talk show of television and radio, and has been featured in magazine articles. She has also offered her availability as a public speaker and seminar participant. Her fee schedule as a keynote speaker or moderator begins at ten thousand dollars, but she will appear on a panel for seventy-five hundred dollars (http://www.avacadell.com).

## SEX THERAPY VIDEOS

"For $49.95, Your Sex Life Can Be Great!" Claims like this appear routinely in respectable American newspapers and magazines. This particular headline comes from an advertisement by the Sinclair Institute, one of the most prolific producers of sexual aids for individuals and couples. The ad has on occasion covered the entire back page of *The Washington Post* "Book World," a weekly book review publication. The ad might feature a formally dressed couple dancing face-to-face, accompanied by the headline: "After Years of Making Love the Same Old Way, Here's An Exciting New Beginning." The text of the ad extols "The BetterSex Video Series."

A similar advertisement has appeared in many other publications, including a supermarket women's magazine called *For Women First*. This magazine, obviously directed at women shoppers, and typically featuring articles on "healthy recipes," "holiday hairstyles," and "decorating ideas," features a sex-help ad with a headline that reads, "Sex Education for Me?" followed by the response, "Know-how is still the best aphrodisiac." The accompanying photograph shows a moderately attractive couple wrapped only in bath towels at the waist (the arms and hands of both the male and female strategically covering the woman's breasts). The overall image is sexy, but tasteful.

The advertising copy that accompanies this ad touts the three-volume BetterSex Video Series, which promises "erotic scenes of explicit sexual practices," that will "enhance sexual . . . pleasure." Those who purchase the tapes, for only $49.95, will be guided by "Dr. Judy Seifer, one of the country's most respected experts on sexuality." As an added bonus, purchasers will receive a "free twenty-minute video on oral sex" and "a brochure filled with videos and other adult products."

The videos, as promised, are sexually explicit. Several ordinary looking, though not unattractive, couples go through a gamut of sexual activities, including foreplay, sexual intercourse (in a variety of positions and settings), fellatio, cunnilingus, masturbation (both male and female), and anal intercourse. The sex scenes are introduced by Dr. Seifer and other sex therapists/sexologists, who contribute to an aura of reasonableness, expertise, and professionalism.[6] These professionals, all members of *Sexology Society of America* give advice, guidance, information, and vocabulary lessons ("fellatio, sometimes called a blow job, or giving head").

Purchasers of the BetterSex Video Series soon find their mailboxes filled with offers for other sexual aides. A typical catalog from the Sinclair Institute, which produces the BetterSex Video Series, is titled *Just for Lovers*. The cover of the catalog promises "Hot, New Products," specialized videos including "Unlock the Secrets of the G-Spot: The Ultimate O," and "Better Oral Sex Techniques." Also featured in this catalog is an ad for the "Bungee Swing, As Seen on HBO's Bettersex," which assures that: "Now anyone can be a sexual athlete." The accompanying photograph shows a smiling nude woman, suspended in a swing/harness, as her male companion stands between her legs, which she has draped over his shoulders. The advertising copy informs the reader that instructions for installing this sexual swing/harness, either in the ceiling or in a doorway, will be provided.

Also in the catalog are dildos of all shapes and sizes, assorted vibrators, and many other sex toys. Much of the catalog is devoted to photos and descriptions of X-rated videos, complete with a handy symbol guide showing the kinds of sex found in each film (e.g., "ideal for couples to watch together," "lesbian sex," "male/male sex," "high intensity sex scenes," "interracial sex," and "anal intercourse").

## More Products to Improve One's Sex Life

Have a problem with impotence? The most well-known product for impotence is Viagra, the first such drug approved by the Food and Drug Administration (Loe 2004). Pfizer markets Viagra and advertises it heavily on all media, including television. Former Senator and presidential candidate Robert Dole raised a few eyebrows, and prompted quite a number of jokes, when he appeared on television as a spokesman for

Viagra. Senator Dole even helped introduce to the public to the thera-peutic name for impotence: E. D. (short for erectile dysfunction). But Viagra is not just for older men. Raphael Palmeiro, a now retired major league baseball player and still a relatively young man, made several tele-vision commercials touting Viagra.

After the introduction of Viagra, other pharmaceutical companies quickly brought similar products to the market and launched their own advertising campaigns. The most prominent among these are Levitra (a product name that is clearly meant to suggest levitation) by Bayer Pharmaceuticals and Cialis produced by Lilly and Company. The televi-sion commercials for these products are sexually suggestive: "He's back to being the man he used to be" and "Will you be ready when she is?"

The television commercials for these products illustrate Foucault's observation that sexual discourse can emanate from a variety of sources. For instance, jokes about sexual impotence and male erections became acceptable topics for dinner table or cocktail party conversation among middle-class couples who can comfortably discus these commercials. A favorite source of humor is a Levitra commercial that includes the med-ical warning: "if you have an erection lasting for more than four hours, consult your physician."

## THE INTERNET AND ENHANCING SEXUAL LIFE

On the Internet the promotions for enhancing sexual life are more explicit than on television. "Hypnovision," for example, promises many different "adult" audiotapes, including "Get Hard/Stay Hard" (http://www.hypnovision.com/erection). These tapes are for both women and men. The theme of the Web site is "ARE YOU DARING ENOUGH TO TRY IT? MEN ARE YOU SUCCESSFUL WITH WOMEN? LADIES . . . WANT TO ATTRACT MEN AND DRIVE THEM WILD?"

The FDA-approved pharmaceuticals (Viagra, Levitra, and Cialis) have been followed quickly by other products that also promise to enhance the sex lives of men, as well as women. A Swedish soft drink originally called Nexite (changed from its original name to Niagra) (Frey 2001) claims to contain "South American herbs" and an "erotic recipe that jump-starts the female libido." The main ingredient is caffeine, but it also contains ginseng, damiana, and schizandra (Associated Press 2001).

Pinnacle, an advertising magazine distributed by the General Nutrition Corporation (GNC) and Great Earth Vitamin Stores, has two creatively named sex enhancers: "Horny Goat Weed" and "Monkeying Around." The Horny Goat Weed product reportedly comes from a plant of the same name, which is a key ingredient of the product. The manufacturer claims this product will "support . . . greater potency and performance!" Pinnacle's other sex-enhancement capsule, "Monkeying Around," is designed specifically for women. It contains "Monkey Ti Kuan Yin," oolong tea, zallouh root, and, according to the ad, "a bit of horny goat weed." Both products are sold as dietary supplements and do not need Food and Drug Administration approval. Generally, the scientific support for any claims made for these types of alleged sex enhancers is minimal or nonexistent.

One of the newer sex enhancement products on the market is called Viapren Strips. A conveniently packaged strip is simply placed under the tongue and according to the ad, "you'll be ready within minutes." Recommended for both "men and women, young and old," the advertising claim is for "increased libido, more frequent, longer-lasting sexual experiences, heightened sensitivity, more satisfaction for both of you."

## PERHAPS PENIS SIZE DOES MATTER

The longstanding cliché that the size of a man's penis is not important is apparently not believed by everyone. Pornography magazines have, for many years, featured back-of-the-magazine ads for "penis enlargement," but the penis-enlargement business has multiplied many times over with the advent of the Internet. A recent Yahoo search produced over seventy sites that offer some kind of help with penis enlargement.

The most popular Internet listing is Dr. Kaplan's Penis Enlargement Pump, which claims to provide an "FDA-Approved Medical Enlargement System." Dr Kaplan, the site reports, is "A graduate from the University of Chicago and Saybrook Institute in San Francisco, where he received his PhD in clinical psychology and human sexuality" (http://www.drjoelkaplan.com). The site offers an "Electrical Vacuum Pump," a "Trigger Hand Pump," a "Nipple Enlargement Pump" (apparently for women), and various other accessories.

Penile enlargement, nipple enlargement, and impotence solutions are just a small part of the extensive commercial realm of sex therapy. Through the Internet, books, magazines, newspapers, television, and radio, sex therapists, sexologists, sexperts, and sex coaches there is now an unending supply of information, advice, counseling, mechanisms, and materials that claim to aid people with the problems they have in their sexual lives.

Americans today want and expect to have satisfying sexual lives. When they are not satisfied with their sex lives, they firmly believe that something can be done about it. While most will seek medical advice from their physicians, they may also opt for a professional sex therapist, retain a sex coach, or turn to books, magazines, or television programs that offer advice, information, and products for addressing their sexual problems.

Sex therapy in all its forms and guises offers contemporary Americans a realm of discourse that hardly existed a half century ago. Freud, Masters and Johnson, professional sex therapy organizations and associations, educational curricula and programs, and the Internet have made an important contribution to our hypersexual society.

# SEX ON FILM

## STAG MOVIES, PORN FLICKS, HOLLYWOOD NC-17, AND VIDEOS/DVDS

On April 22, 2002, Ms. Linda Boreman, age fifty-three, of Denver, Colorado died as a result of injuries suffered in an automobile accident. Linda Boreman's death would probably not have attracted much attention, except that the world remembered her by a more well-known name: *Linda Lovelace*. Boreman's death was reported in obituaries in all major American and European newspapers—not under her given name but with the name she used as the famous star of the pornographic movie *Deep Throat*. *The Washington Post*, for example, featured her obituary under the large boldface headline "Linda Lovelace, Star of 'Deep Throat'" (*The Washington Post*, April 23, 2002, p. B6).

In the later years of her life, Linda Boreman claimed to hate the name Linda Lovelace. In one of the four books that she wrote about her life, Lovelace renounced her career as a pornographic film star: "My name is not Linda Lovelace. . . . If I had my way, the name Linda Lovelace would have vanished . . . and neither you nor I would ever hear it again. . . . But the world won't let Linda Lovelace rest in peace" (Lovelace with McGrady 1983, 9).

The actual facts of Lovelace's life story are difficult to determine, largely because of the varying accounts of her life and pornography career that she recounted in her different books. Her earliest books, *Inside Linda Lovelace* (Lovelace 1974a) and *The Intimate Diary of Linda Lovelace* (Lovelace 1974b), were published when she was still riding the crest of her pornographic celebrity and proudly describing her sexuality and sex exploits.

In one of her later books, *Ordeal*, published in the early 1980s, Lovelace offered an entirely new account of her entry into sex, prostitution, and pornography (Lovelace with McGrady 1983). She claims in this book that at the age of twenty-one she was violently dominated, exploited, and coerced into all types of sexual activity by her manager (and future husband) Chuck Traynor. According to Lovelace, it was Traynor who first provided her with addictive drugs and lured her into a pornographic career (Lovelace with McGrady 1983, 10).

In one early amateurish 8mm-film, Lovelace engaged in sex with a dog, which she says *Playboy* creator Hugh Hefner later acquired. Years later, after she had become famous and was staying with Traynor at the Playboy mansion, Hefner tried to persuade her to replicate the sex act with her pet dog Rufus. While she pretended to go along with Hefner's request, Lovelace reports that at the last minute she successfully thwarted the dog's efforts to penetrate her (Lovelace with McGrady 1983, 200–201).

The key event of Lovelace's life was the making of the movie *Deep Throat* in 1972. Originally titled "The Doctor Makes a Housecall," the movie featured Lovelace in the role of a visiting nurse. "My job was to go around and make people feel better," she later recalled. "Mostly men" (Lovelace with McGrady, *Ordeal*, 1983, 134). In the film, Lovelace is unable to experience an orgasm through normal sexual intercourse. A doctor, played by Harry Reems (who was soon to become a well-known male porn star in his own right), discovers that the nurse's clitoris is in her throat. Inspired by her physical abnormality, she provides oral sex (deep throat) to a variety of men (the doctor, the grocery delivery boy, and others) throughout the course of the movie.

*Deep Throat* has been proclaimed "the most famous and profitable smut movie in history" (http://www.joebobbriggs.com/drivein/2002/lindalovelace.html). The entire cost of production was twenty-three thousand dollars, a ridiculously small amount by movie-making standards even at that time. The entire movie lasted only sixty-two minutes, and while no one has ever judged it to be a work of cinematic art, it has become one of the most profitable films ever made. The profits started to come in immediately; by 1973, the box office gross was over 4 million dollars. It is now widely believed that the Mafia reaped most of *Deep Throat*'s profits, since one of its members bankrolled the filming. According to one report, the film may have produced as much as 600 million dollars in revenue since its original release in 1972 (Brown 2005), a handsome profit compared with the original investment of twenty-three thousand dollars. Lovelace, however, received almost none of that money for her performance in the film. Together, she and her husband/manager Chuck Traynor received a flat twelve hundred dollars for her contribution to the movie.

Lovelace benefited in other ways, however, as she acknowledged in her 1980 autobiography. She suddenly became a nationally famous celebrity. She was on the cover of *Esquire*, appeared nude in *Playboy*, was interviewed by *Penthouse*, and was the subject of stories in many other publications. She met the top names in show business, including Johnny Carson and Sammy Davis Jr. Together, she and Traynor eventually developed an intimate relationship with Davis and his wife Altovise. According to Lovelace, Davis favored the deep fellatio perfected by Lovelace in her celebrated films (Lovelace with McGrady 1983, 211).

After the publication of *Ordeal* in 1980, in which she renounced her pornographic past, Lovelace became a heroine of many American feminists, who saw her as a quintessential example of a woman who had been subjected to male oppression and violence, including her unwilling participation in the making of pornographic films. In the introduction to Lovelace's fourth autobiography, *Out of Bondage* (1986), feminist Gloria Steinem championed Lovelace's case as a victim of male violence who only made pornographic films because she was forced to do so by her husband and other men.[1]

### THE SIGNIFICANCE OF *DEEP THROAT* AND THE LIFE OF LINDA LOVELACE

The life of Linda Lovelace was both tragic and tawdry, but it also carried significant societal implications. Through her performance in *Deep Throat*, she became the personification of film pornography.[2] From a societal perspective, the film changed the American public's view of pornographic films. According to one movie aficionado:

> *Deep Throat* . . . changed America's sexual attitudes more than anything since the first Kinsey Report in 1948. . . . It super-charged the feminist movement. It gave the Mafia its most lucrative business since Prohibition. And it changed the nation's views of obscenity forever. (Briggs 2002, http://www.joebobbriggs.com/drivein/2002/lindalovelace.html)

While Briggs' assertions may be somewhat overstated, *Deep Throat* certainly had a substantial impact on America's attitudes toward pornography, making the genre acceptable to millions of people for the first time. Middle- and upper-class Americans were able to discuss pornography and perhaps even view some porno films. Even Jackie Kennedy Onassis is reported to have seen *Deep Throat* (Stephens 2003). Joseph Slade has employed the term "porn chic" to characterize the 1970s mass phenomenon of urban audiences who flocked to see *Deep Throat* and other porno films (Slade 2000a, 107).[3]

Though many Americans never saw *Deep Throat* they did know about it and they talked about it. The title of the film, *Deep Throat*, added to the American vocabulary and thus the sexual discourse of Americans. The term "deep throat" entered the language in many different ways and was almost immediately understood and used by the American public (Metcalf 2002). In 1973, Bob Woodward and Carl Bernstein, investigative reporters of *The Washington Post*, known for having exposed the Watergate scandal, used the label as a pseudonym for their key informant. Thanks to Lovelace and her role in the film, the allusion was immediately understandable to the reading public.[4]

The most recent mass-media restoration of Linda Lovelace and *Deep Throat* came in a 2005 NC-17-rated[5] documentary film titled *Inside Deep Throat*, produced by HBO. The documentary was interlaced with film clips from the 1970s and observations from current-day commentators who were explaining to today's audiences how *Deep Throat* came to be made and the impact it had on American society.

The success of *Deep Throat* was at least a partial result of the dramatic increases in *political democratization and personal liberty* that were sweeping across America during the 1960s and 1970s. By the time the film opened in 1972, the various court cases discussed in Chapter 2 had opened the doors for the distribution of pornographic materials of all kinds, including films. The Hollywood movie industry had broken the self-imposed restrictions it had imposed upon itself in the 1930s (more about this later in the chapter). By the time *Deep Throat* came on the scene, American moviegoers were already seeing films with some nudity and sexual content, though certainly nothing as explicitly pornographic as *Deep Throat*.

One countervailing event occurred in 1973 with the *Miller v. California* Supreme Court decision (see Chapter 2). This ruling did put something of a damper on film pornography distribution (Lane 2000, xvii). Fearing prosecution under the criterion of individual community standards, porno filmmakers were now more careful about where they distributed their films, wisely avoiding the legal confrontations that would inevitably result from distribution in Midwestern rural communities or in the Bible-Belt South. In many urban places, especially on the East and West Coasts, but also in other major cities across the country, it was still easy to find theaters showing "X-rated" films.

Two other factors proved to be influential in the production and distribution of pornographic films. First, once *Deep Throat* had been seen by millions of Americans, and tens of millions more Americans had learned about it and talked about it, it was no longer possible to "put this genie back in the bottle." *Deep Throat* and all it represented had become a part of American popular culture, and it remains there to this day.

Second, within a few years after *Deep Throat* had made its impact, two new technologies appeared that would not only keep the film pornography industry alive but actually cause it to thrive: the VCR and cable television. Before turning our attention to these and other developments in the film industry, we must first give a brief look at beginnings and early years of movie making in the United States. This will give us a more complete perspective on how sex came to be an important part of movies.

## SEX IN THE MOVIES

The movie industry has had two distinctly separate histories, especially in the way it has dealt with sexual materials. Both of these histories have, in their unique ways, led to the abundance of sexual material in today's mainstream movies and also the glut of pornographic films and videos.

For most Americans, the movie industry is characterized by films made by the major studios of the mainstream Hollywood movie industry. The longtime giants of Hollywood moviemaking have been Metro-Goldwyn-Mayer, Warner Brothers, 20th Century Fox, and Columbia Pictures. Second-generation Hollywood movie studios have included Walt Disney Pictures, Miramax, and Wonderworks. Today, some of these big names remain, but most have been absorbed by multinational conglomerates. Regardless of their corporate connections, and the emergence of independent studios, the traditional Hollywood movie industry still provides the movies that most Americans see in multiplexes across the country. The traditional Hollywood movie industry has had one history with regard to sexual material, while the pornography movie business has had a very different history.

The making of pornographic films had a shadier history through much of the first half of the twentieth century. Most importantly, a number of outlaw filmmakers produced and marketed what were called "stag films" or "blue movies" (Schlosser 2003), which were the forerunners of today's pornography film industry.

## FROM STAG FILMS TO PORN VIDEOS

Stag films came along in the early days of movie making and provide yet another reminder of the way new technologies almost always lead quickly to increased public access to sexual materials. Stag films were usually crudely made, with minimal story lines that were often as humorous as they were sexual. At a basic level these films were made to show naked women, frequently engaging in sexual intercourse or other sex acts with either men or women. Stag films had no artistic pretensions; they simply provided male viewers with moving pictures of female nudity and sexual activity.

Under the legal standards that prevailed during the first half of the twentieth century, stag films were clearly illegal. Stag films, after the 1920s, were mostly made by amateurs and distributed and shown chiefly by the producers themselves (Slade personal communication, 2005). Many "solid citizens" (almost always males) in the United States viewed this form of pornography during the first half of the twentieth century, usually at private screenings for members of organizations such as fraternities, service clubs, and athletic teams (Schlosser 2003).[6]

## THE ARRIVAL OF PORNOGRAPHIC FILMS

In the late 1960s and early 1970s, pornographic films started appearing in movie theaters, first on the East and West coasts and then later in other parts of the country. These were specialty theaters, open only to adults (Holliday 1999). Often these theaters were quite seedy and unattractive to the general public. To provide greater accessibility and anonymity, pornographic films were sometimes shown at drive-in theaters, many devoted exclusively to erotic and pornographic films. In addition to *Deep Throat*, other pornographic classics of the era included *The Devil and Miss Jones*, *The Opening of Misty Beethoven*, and *Behind the Green Door*.[7]

These early days of the pornographic movie business eventually expanded to today's billion-dollar porno film industry (Lane 2000; Faludi 1995, 1999). The videos and DVDs now produced by the porn-film industry have a very different audience from the old-time stag films. Today's sex videos are more likely to be viewed in living rooms, bedrooms, and hotel rooms than in dingy, dark, street theaters. Pornographic films are no longer in the nether world of "dirty old men in raincoats" as was once the cultural cliché.

## THE PORNOGRAPHIC FILM INDUSTRY

Thousands of pornographic films are produced each year in the United States. The majority of these (an estimated ten thousand each year) are made in the suburban community of Chatsworth, California located in the San Fernando Valley, north of Los Angeles (Faludi 1995, 1999; Lane 2000; Milter and Slade 2005).

Makers of porn films need only some basic technical equipment, a setting, and a few women and men who will engage in sex acts before the camera (Gittler 1999). Countless young women and men make their way to California every year with the dream of making it in the movie business. Some may see the porn-film business as a stepping-stone to mainstream movies, but others simply see pornographic films as an easy way to make big money (Faludi 1999; Gittler 1999).

A few of the early stars of pornographic movies have been able to carve out longer-lasting careers in pornography. For example, Marilyn Chambers, the star of *Behind the Green Door*, and countless other films, continues to sell her old films on the Internet. Others have parlayed their porno-film careers into sex-related fields. Nina Hartley has become a kind of sexual guru, making instructional films on how to give good oral sex and perform other sex acts. Annie Sprinkle, an early porn star, has transformed herself into a performance artist and writer. Photographs of her performances now hang in museums around the country.

Annie Sprinkle's recent book, *Annie Sprinkle: Post-Porn Modernist: My 25 Years as a Multimedia Whore* (Sprinkle 1998), is largely comprised of old photographs and illustrations from her pornography career. While Sprinkle proclaims that she is a "post-porn modernist," her book offers little that could be considered culturally significant. Instead, the reader is treated to old publicity photographs of her early career in burlesque and porn magazines, including photos of her vagina being penetrated by various objects or of her urinating (an obvious reference to her professional name).

Traci Lords is one of the few porn film stars who did succeed in making the transition from pornography films to mainstream films and television (Lords 2003). Lords notoriously performed in pornographic movies when she was between the ages of fifteen and eighteen! In her autobiography, she describes how she was introduced to the world of still-photo pornography at age fifteen with the assistance of her informal stepfather, a man who had already sexually abused her. An exceptionally beautiful young woman, Lords was soon noticed by pornographic filmmakers who immediately featured her in their films. She made more than one hundred X-rated movies while still underage. Everything came to a halt in 1986 when Lords, then eighteen years old, was arrested by the Los Angeles police for being under the influence of cocaine, a *de rigueur* recreational substance for people in the pornographic filmmaking business at the time.

When it came to light that Lords had made most of her sexually explicit films while still underage, there were major repercussions. The Meese Commission used her history in porno films to demonstrate the moral corruption of the pornography business. A United States statute was subsequently passed that declared: "a pornography producer or distributor is required to check two forms of identification for each model or actor, and to maintain copies of each person's identification in the company's records" (Lane 2000, 126).

This statute, while it was written to harass the makers of porn videos, had the unintended consequence of making them more rigorous about their record keeping and accounting, matters about which the porn industry had previously been notoriously lax (Slade 1999, 242–43). Today it is standard practice in the porn film business to pose actresses holding their driver's licenses before any filming occurs (Gittler 1999).

Traci Lords's first step away from the porn industry was but a half step: an appearance in the John Waters movie, *Cry Baby*.[8] She then went on to appear in a few B-movies (*Virtuosity* and *Mortal Combat*) and has since had parts in a variety of television programs (*Melrose Place*, *First Wave*, *MacGyver*, *Roseanne*, and *Black Scorpion* (Lane 2000; http://bookmark.weht.net/WEHT/Traci_Lords).

Only a small percentage of the women who have appeared in pornographic movies (and even fewer men) have gone on to achieve long-term success in the entertainment industry. The vast majority of young people who find their way into porn films do sex work for a while and then disappear. One young aspiring actress told interviewer Ian Gittler: "I'm not doing fuck films anymore. . . . I got a part in an independent feature. They're going to show it at Cannes. . . . Anyway, after doing fifty videos the thrill is gone. Three months in this business is long enough." (Gittler 1999, 30).

A current-day porn actress who has ridden high on the wave of success is Jenna Jameson, who earns as much as 1 million dollars a year (http://cbsnews.com/stories/2003/60minutes/main585049.shtml) and has a number-two ranking among the top fifty porn stars. Her many films include *Hollywood Orgies*, *Briana Loves Jenna*, *The Masseuse*, *Bella Loves Jenna*, *Girls Only*, and *Deep Inside Jenna* (a title that was surely inspired by *Deep Throat*).[9] Jameson has also published a best-selling (eleven weeks on the *New York Times* best seller list) autobiographical book, *How to Make Love Like a Porn Star: A Cautionary Tale* (Strauss and Jameson 2004), further contributing to her fame and respectability.

Jameson's films are only a tiny part of the many hundreds of readily available X-rated videos. Today porn films can be obtained through cable/satellite television, the Internet, the few remaining Mom & Pop video stores, flea markets, and, of course, any store that features "adult" in its name. (A William Hamilton cartoon of the 1980s depicted a nine-year-old girl explaining to her girlfriend as they walked past an adult book store, "Adult means dirty.")

The titles of porn films offer an abundance of punning and sopho-moric humor. A few examples reveal both the attempts at humor and the diversity of the subject matter: *Farmers Daughters Do Beverley Hills* (a reflection of a porno classic *Debbie Does Dallas*), *Baby Sitters Gone Bad, Once Upon a Secretary, Bad Wives, Bobby Sox*, and a new Debbie revival, *Debbie Does Dallas: The Next Generation*. In the gay and lesbian genre, typical titles include: *Playing with the Coach's Balls, Plowmaster*, and *Dykes of Hazzard*. The list could go on endlessly; one Internet Web site advertises more than three thousand titles.

In recent years, the separate paths of Hollywood and pornography films have moved closer together, but it took several decades for this to happen. Sexuality in Hollywood mainstream movies has had a very dif-ferent path than the one taken by its pornographic cousin.

## MAINSTREAM MOVIES AND SEX

In the earliest years of commercial moviemaking in the United States, many film producers and directors took an anything-goes attitude. The new technology provided early filmmakers with a new way of offering sexual and pornographic materials. The very name, "motion pictures," said it all. Sexual acts involve all kinds of action, and motion pictures could now capture and display the action that photographs could not. David F. Friedman, then chairman of the Adult Film Association of America is said to have remarked, "five minutes after the motion picture camera was perfected there was probably a naked woman posing in front of same" (Holliday 1999, 342). An exaggeration perhaps, but not that far from the truth. An extant 1896 French short film, titled *Les Bain*, features an actress named Louise Willy taking off her clothes (O'Toole 1998).

During the first decades of the twentieth century, a few filmmakers on the fringes of Hollywood began making "nudie" films. These soon moved beyond crude short films and started adding minimal story lines. One classic example is the 1924 *The Casting Couch*, which told a quintessen-tial Hollywood story. In order to get a movie part the aspiring actress must please the producer doing the casting. This situation leads, of course, to scenes in which the young woman is disrobed and seduced by the powerful movie mogul.

But in the late 1920s, Hollywood filmmakers (at least those at the major studios) abruptly abandoned the wide-open attitude toward sex in their films. By the early 1930s, the leaders of the film industry accepted a strict code of ethics that effectively eliminated almost any activity on screen that was even slightly sexual, including any sexually suggestive language. This self-imposed censorship by the film industry was one of the most effective restrictions on the sexual content of art and speech in the twentieth century. The self-imposed Hollywood censorship of movies lasted nearly three decades. The restrictive rules imposed on American movies in this era are so ludicrous and humorous that they deserve recounting.

## THE HOLLYWOOD SELF-IMPOSED HAYS CODE

In the 1920s, Hollywood was shaken by a series of scandals associated with prominent film stars. These scandals involved stars having sex with teenage girls, murder, drugs, and notorious marital breakups (Norman 2007). A number of the Hollywood films during that era also contained scenes of violence and nudity, and these too led to public outrage and calls for censorship.

It was the job of Will Hays, then president of the Motion Picture Producers and Distributors of America, to establish controls on the film industry. While Hays's name is often associated with the censorship of American movies, his early efforts were ineffectual. Most observers agree that the major behind-the-scenes influence on the self-censorship of the movie industry was the Catholic Church. In the words of one critic of the Catholic Church and its censorship of sexual material: "After World War I, Irish-oriented American Catholics began taking over the leadership in anti-obscenity militancy. . . . Catholic organizations such as the National Office for Decent Literature and [in 1933] the Legion of Decency became the nation's most militant and effective defender of morals and censorship" (quoted in Jones 2000, 547). When the Legion of Decency came into being it started publishing the names of movies that were considered by Catholic authorities to be objectionable to Church doctrine. Catholic adherents were prohibited from attending the films that were so blacklisted.

In the meantime, the film industry, under Hays's direction, established its own code of ethics in 1930 (Farhi 2004). Formally called The Motion Picture Production Code (often simply The Hays Code), it defined the "do's and don'ts" for filmmakers and distributors. These restrictions became particularly effective in 1934 when Joseph Breen was brought to Hollywood to head the Production Code Administration.

By today's standards, the Hays Code was amusingly restrictive. The guiding principle of the Hays Code was: "No picture shall be produced that will lower the moral standards of those who see it." The Code focused primarily on two key areas: crime and sex. In the area of crime, for example, no film presentation should move the audience toward "sympathy with the crime as against law and justice" (http://www.artsreformation.com).

The film industry has been surprisingly faithful to the principle that criminals, murderers, and other villains must get their comeuppance at the end of the movie. The audience may sympathize with Thelma and Louise through the entire movie of the same name, but in the end they must go flying off to their deaths into the Grand Canyon.

But it was sex that was most restricted by the Motion Picture Production Code. The following are some of the Code's explicit references to sexuality:

"The sanctity of the institution of marriage and the home shall be upheld. Pictures shall not infer [sic] that low forms of sex relationship are the accepted or common thing."

"Adultery . . . must not be explicitly treated, or justified, or treated attractively."

"Scenes of Passion . . . should not be introduced when not essential to the plot. . . . Excessive and lustful kissing, lustful embraces, suggestive postures and gestures, are not to be shown. In general, passion should be so treated that these scenes do not stimulate the lower and baser element."

"Seduction or rape . . . should never be more than suggested, and only when essential for the plot, and even then should never be shown by explicit method. They are never the proper subject for comedy."

"Sexual perversion [a reference to homosexuality] or any inference to it is forbidden."

"White slavery [a dated and implicitly racist euphemism for prostitution] shall not be treated."

"Miscegenation [an explicit reference to sex relationships between the white and black races] is forbidden."

The Code also prohibited film presentations of "sex hygiene," "venereal diseases," and "childbirth. While all of these subjects might have been societally beneficial, film executives were anxious to "head off government control of movies." They were willing to make every possible accommodation in order to avoid governmentally imposed restrictions (Briggs 2003, 36; Schaefer 1999).

The prohibition of sex hygiene films was prompted by a spate of movies made in the early years of the film industry (around World War I). These films often focused on the dangers of syphilis and gonorrhea—so much so that in the trade they were referred to as "clap operas" (Briggs 2003, 35). Sex hygiene movies purported to educate the public about the biology of sex and the problems associated with sex. The makers and distributors may have been sincerely interested in providing parents and young adults with knowledge and information (and even moral lessons) about sex and sexual diseases, but they may also simply have been interested in attracting audiences who wanted to see sexual material.

Despite the prohibitions of the Hollywood Code, sex-hygiene films continued to be produced through the 1930s and 1940s by what one film authority has called "the outlaw studios." The outlaw studios included the producers of "stag films," but also the sex-hygiene films that were able to reach a larger and more mainstream audience of American moviegoers.

One of the most famous sex-hygiene movies was titled "Mom and Dad," which appeared in 1945 and was shown in theaters throughout the United States for almost two decades (Briggs 2003; Carlson 2003). The promotional genius behind this film was Kroger Babb, who generously dubbed himself, "America's Fearless Young Showman" (Briggs 2003, 32). "Mom and Dad" has been called "America's most successful exploitation flick" (Carlson 2003, C9), though there have certainly been many contenders for that dubious honor in the ensuing half century.

In its heyday, "Mom and Dad" was touted as "the Motion Picture that "DARES DISCUSS AND EXPLAIN SEX AS NEVER BEFORE SEEN AND HEARD" (Carlson 2003, C9). The movie told the story of a sweet and innocent teenage girl who becomes pregnant after a brief romance with a dashing young military pilot, who soon thereafter dies in an airplane crash. The girl's parents, the "Mom and Dad" of the film's title, eventually help their daughter through this ordeal, though the mother is somewhat villainized because she had failed to discuss sex with her teenage daughter. Viewed as a cautionary tale, this family melodrama offered a parenting lesson for the moms and dads in the audience.

The sex that had "never before been seen and heard" consisted of thrown-in film footage of a baby being born—making this a revolutionary piece of film for a general audience. As an added bit of sex hygiene the movie also provided close-ups of venereal disease sores—implying these too might have been the products of illegitimate sex.

Several publicity stunts were used to attract audiences to "Mom and Dad." The film was always advertised as an "adults-only" movie, which at that time, as now, suggested sexual material. The standard for adulthood was surprisingly lenient for this film, since high school age youngsters were admitted if they were accompanied by a parent. However, males and females of whatever age were not allowed to see the movie together. Women were allowed to see the matinee presentations, while men could attend the evening showing.

In theaters where the film was shown, the promoters stationed two women who posed as nurses, though their credentials were limited to the uniforms they wore. As a further-legitimizing element, an "eminent sexual hygiene commentator" named "Elliot Forbes" was on hand for each showing. Midway through the film, the screen projection stopped and Elliot Forbes gave a 20-minute lecture on "the need for openness in sex education," along with observations on "the morality of the times, the biology of the body, and what the community [could] do to avoid the ruination of its youth" (Briggs 2003, 33). Since the movie was shown all over the country, there were several Elliot Forbeses. Over the course of the film's run at least twenty-six different actors appeared on theater stages, all of whom had been hired to put on a performance for the audience.

The movie "Mom and Dad" was made in only six days, but it grossed an estimated 100 million dollars in showings throughout the country over a period of twenty-three years. Public enthusiasm for this film convinced Hollywood that the movie viewers were ready to see sexual material on the screen. It would still be a few years, however, before the major Hollywood studios would venture into the sexual realm. When Hollywood did finally open the door to more sex in its movies, the objective was entertainment, and the motive was to make profits, not to provide education.

## BREAKING THE HAYS CODE

In 1952, the Supreme Court reversed a 1915 ruling and declared that motion pictures were protected by the First Amendment. But even before this ruling some filmmakers were starting to challenge the sexual restrictions imposed by the Motion Picture Production Code.

One of the earliest Hollywood films to challenge the Code was *The Outlaw*, which introduced actress Jane Russell to the American public. Although the film was made in 1941, it was only briefly released in 1943 and again in 1946 before its general release in 1950. In many American communities local censors were able to keep the movie off the screens until the 1960s (http://www.briansdriveintheatre.com).

*The Outlaw* was produced, and partially directed by Howard Hughes, the multi-talented, multi-millionaire, who eventually became an ultra-weird recluse.[10] The movie was little more than a fictitious episode in the life of the western bad boy Jesse James, but the film was expertly promoted by Hughes. When it finally reached the general audience in 1950, Americans everywhere understood that the movie was not really about Jesse James; it was about sex. More specifically, it was about Jane Russell's breasts. People throughout the country flocked to see the movie, even though it had no explicit sex scenes, only a suggestive scene in which Russell's character allows the wounded and feverish Jesse James to join her in bed (this gesture was ostensibly for the therapeutic value that contact with her would bring). As a result of this solicitous care, James passed through his health crisis during the night and went on to kill another day.

Another early breach of the Hays Code came in 1953 with the release of Otto Preminger's *The Moon Is Blue*. By today's standards this film would be considered a sweet romantic comedy, but in the 1950s it caused a furor and was even banned in some regions of the country. Why? Because the story line was about a young virgin (played by Maggie McNamara) and the two young men played by William Holden and David Niven who were determined to make her a nonvirgin. The film was considered particularly risque, and possibly in violation of the Hays Code, because the word "virgin" was actually spoken by the actors.

### RUSS MEYER BRINGS FEMALE NUDITY TO AMERICAN MOVIES

Russ Meyer brought female nudity to movies in much the same style as Hugh Hefner did with *Playboy*. It is probably not a coincidence that Meyer, early in his career, worked as a *Playboy* photographer, where he photographed two early sexpots of that era: Jayne Mansfield and Mamie Van Doren (Bernstein 2004; Slade 2000a).

In 1959, Meyer wrote, produced, and directed *The Immoral Mr. Teas*, a film that gave him instant notoriety and set the course for the rest of his movie-making life.[11] The simple plot of *Mr. Teas* provided a pretext for showing young starlets with bare breasts and behinds. Meyer employed a former army buddy named Bill Teas to play the role of a door-to-door salesman. After receiving anesthesia from his dentist, Mr. Teas sees, or at least thinks he sees, every woman he meets in the nude. Not surprisingly, almost all the women who answer the door for Teas' door-to-door calls just happen to have oversize breasts and rounded derrieres.

*Mr. Teas* was a great financial success. Filmed in four days at the unbelievably low cost of twenty-four thousand dollars, it was distributed at art theaters and a few other theaters not influenced by the Hollywood movie industry. The film netted a million dollar profit, which bankrolled much of the rest of Meyer's filmmaking career (Bernstein 2004; Williams 1999).

Some of Meyers' later movies (including *Faster Pussycat, Kill, Kill*) mixed violence with sex, ensuring that his films would appeal to many more millions of moviegoers. But blatant sex, in the form of naked female bodies, was always the primary feature of his films.[12]

Many imitators followed Meyers's successes, producing a genre known as "fleshpot films." Roger Ebert, the noted film critic and also a friend and collaborator of Meyer, made the following comment regarding the presentation of women in Meyer's movies: "Meyer is almost unique in the world of popular eroticism in seeing women not as passive victims but as aggressive sexual beings who demand that their needs be met" (Bernstein 2004, B4).

## MAINSTREAM HOLLYWOOD CHALLENGES THE HAYS CODE

In the 1960s, mainstream Hollywood film producers started to challenge the Hays Code more directly. In 1965 *The Pawnbroker*, a serious and highly praised film directed by Sidney Lumet and starring Rod Steiger and Geraldine Fitzgerald, was released. In the one scene that directly challenged the Code, a young African-American woman stood in front of Rod Steiger, the pawnbroker, and slowly unbuttoned her blouse, revealing her breasts. Millions of Americans went to see the film and critics loved it (Scheuer 1985, 535).

During the 1960s, foreign films were also making their way into urban American theaters. Movies made in France, Italy, Sweden, and other Scandinavian countries offered much more sexual material and nudity than American-made movies of that era.

It was at about this time that the French actress Brigitte Bardot became a worldwide symbol of female sexuality in films. She made her debut in director Roger Vadim's 1957 film, *And God Created Woman*, a movie that made her an instant sex star. Bardot followed her first movie with a long list of generally mediocre films that unrelentingly featured her nudity and sexuality. In the United States, moviegoers sought out Bardot's films in the foreign-film and art theaters, perhaps not as much for her acting ability as for the promise of sex on the screen.

In 1967, the Swedish film *I Am Curious Yellow* gained great notoriety and enormous ticket sales, again mostly for its sexual content. The film's actors were often shown naked and filmed having sex in all sorts of places, including, most memorably, a tree.

During the late 1960s, Hollywood moviemakers were very much aware that a "sexual revolution" was sweeping through American culture. Sexual activities of all types were not just being accepted, they were celebrated. Filmmakers could see that sex in movies would be increasingly profitable. In this more tolerant atmosphere, the Hays Code was soon broken with impunity.

In 1972, Hollywood icon Marlon Brando appeared in director Bernardo Bertolucci's *Last Tango in Paris*, which had sexual scenes the intensity of which had never been seen before in an American film. While the movie did not have explicit sex (e.g., female and male genitalia, penetration), the sexual scenes were nonetheless vivid and erotic. In one especially noteworthy and taboo-breaking scene, Brando and the young female actress, Maria Schneider, were shown having what appeared to be anal intercourse. At the beginning of the scene, Brando asks his partner for butter as a prelude to their sex. Even Linda Lovelace in a *Playboy* interview (and this was before she became negative about pornography) pronounced the movie "disgusting" (Lane 2000, 87).

Thirty years after *Last Tango*, Bertolucci directed a film titled "Dreamers," which reveals how far we have come since 1972. The plot of *Dreamers* revolves exclusively around three teenagers in 1968 Paris. Two of the three are twins, a female and a male, while the third is an American male student who is visiting France. The film takes place in the apartment of the twins' parents, who have conveniently left on holiday. The three young people are shown in full-frontal nudity and in an incestuous relationship involving the twins (Denby 2004a; Thomson 2004).

Full-frontal female nudity now occurs frequently in Hollywood movies, though it is still rare for male actors' genitals to be seen on screen. *Time* magazine has noted that male nudity is now becoming a part of American films ("Full Disclosure: More Actors Share Their [Private] Parts," *Time*, August 30, 2004, p. 71). In one of the movies included in the story (the biographical film about Alfred Kinsey described in Chapter 5), actor Peter Sarsgaard appears completely nude, though the star Liam Neeson does not.[13] The 2007 movie *Walk Hard: The Dewey Cox Story* featuring John C. Reilly has a number of scenes in which Reilly, as the aptly named Dewey Cox, is shown frontally nude (Denby 2008).

## ANDY WARHOL AND THE RISE OF UNDERGROUND FILMS

The 1960s marked the beginning of another genre of film that was very different from traditional Hollywood fare: experimental or underground

films. Sex was often a part of these films, but they were not generally considered pornographic or exploitation films. Underground films were
often made in New York City, where the most publicly known creator
was the pop-artist of that era Andy Warhol (Watson 2003).

Warhol made his initial, and most lasting, reputation with his art-
works. The most famous were his silk screenings of Campbell's soup cans,
Brillo boxes, Marilyn Monroe, Jackie Kennedy, and Mao Zedong helped
to create the subfield of contemporary art called "pop-art."

After establishing his reputation in painting and printmaking, Warhol
increasingly turned his attention to making films. His films, especially the
early ones, largely featured the photogenic people who crowded into his
artistic headquarters in downtown Manhattan (known as the "Factory"),
using no script or plot line and only a stationary camera. As the largely
passive, de facto director, Warhol randomly instructed his "actors" to
take off some of their clothing or engage in some other activity.

Warhol's films often had nudity, both male and female, but sexual
activity was more likely to be implied or simulated. Sexual activity in
Warhol films was just as likely to be homosexual as heterosexual, since
many of his preferred actors were gay, lesbian, or bisexual.

One example of a Warhol movie with suggestive sexual content was
the mid-sixties *My Hustler*, filmed on Fire Island. The film's principal
character was a nonactor who was found shortly before shooting (while
hitchhiking) and given the screen name Paul America. In his personal life,
"Paul America was good-looking and sexually available" (Watson 2003,
234), which meant the young Adonis had sexual relationships with both
men and women in the Warhol coterie. *The Hustler* loosely portrayed the
competition between a young beach hustler (played by America) and an
over-the-hill hustler. While the film had no explicit sex, nakedness and
implied sex abounded.

Warhol's underground films and those of other experimental filmmakers were not widely distributed in the United States, but they did
receive attention in the New York cultural scene. Major American
newspapers, as well as some national magazines such as *Time* and
*Newsweek*, sometimes reviewed the films, occasionally giving them
mild praise. The films were generally tolerated, in spite of the nudity
and sexual suggestiveness.

A major exception to the general tolerance involved Warhol's last
movie, *Blue Movie* (Watson 2003). *Blue Movie* was based on a very simple concept: filming a man and a woman *before, during, and after* sexual
intercourse. Typical of his style, Warhol simply brought two attractive
actors together to play the principal parts. As a matter of fact, the two had

previously been lovers in their personal lives. Warhol filmed three reels: their talk in bed leading up to sex, their sexual banter and sexual activity which culminated in sexual intercourse, and their after-sex talk while sharing a meal. The film was done in a naturalistic style, much closer to the way in which real people have sex than would normally be expected in a pornographic film.

In July of 1969 *Blue Movie* opened at the Garrick Theatre in New York City. After eleven days, the New York City police confiscated the film, and on September 17, a three-judge panel declared it to be pornographic under existing law. It met all three criteria that the Supreme Court had established: "it aroused prurient interest; it offended community standards; and it had no redeeming social value" (Watson 2003, 394).

The underground film business, as exemplified by Warhol's productions, had only limited direct impact on American culture, primarily because only a few of the films were shown to large audiences. (*Chelsea Girls* had the widest distribution.) Indirectly, however, underground films contributed to the larger revolution in sexual standards and behavior that was going on in American society, particularly through the largely positive coverage by many reviewers in the mainstream media.

Andy Warhol may not have been a great filmmaker, but his sex films became a part of what Americans in that era read about and talked about. Whether they were supportive of or opposed the films, the reviews and discussions they provoked added to the sexual discourse of American society.

## FROM *AMERICAN GRAFFITI* TO *AMERICAN PIE*, AND BEYOND

In 1973, a teenage rite-of-passage movie, *American Graffiti*, swept the country. The film has become a classic and continues to appear routinely on cable/satellite television. *American Graffiti* tells the story of a group of graduating high school students enjoying their last weekend night of the summer before heading off to college or other parts of the adult world.

The movie chronicles some typical teenage hijinks, mostly involving cruising and racing cars, playing pranks on the local police, and hanging out at the local drive-in restaurant. The boy-girl relations of *American Graffiti* involve late-night, last-chance attempts at romance.

Actual sex is only hinted at; there is necking and adolescent groping, but no nudity or simulated sexual intercourse. Even though the film was made in the early 1970s at the height of the sexual revolution, its sexual content was only a muted version of the anything-goes moral zeitgeist. On American movie screens teenagers were not yet engaging in sex.

Things had changed dramatically by 1999, however, when the movie *American Pie* arrived in the nation's theaters with a title that was intentionally evocative of *American Graffiti*. David Weitz, the director of *American Pie* admitted somewhat coyly, "I liked the idea that our movie had a title similar to *American Graffiti*." "The idea of male intimacy is something that underlies the film," Weitz continued, "When we were trying to conceptualize the sex aspect, it was that these guys were now going to separate and move on and not really be such close friends anymore. So instead of thinking about it, they're obsessing about sex" (http://www.preview-online.com/july august/feature).

Just as in *American Graffiti*, the story of *American Pie* features a group of four male graduating high school seniors who are headed for their final prom. Each of the boys vows that he will lose his virginity before the night is over. One can imagine how the film might have been pitched to a potential producer: "It's basically a remake of *American Graffiti*; except in this version, the guys all get laid."

*American Pie* is unremittingly focused on sex. The movie opens with a scene of male masturbation, one of several masturbation scenes in the movie. In one of the film's hot bedroom scenes, the girl is so sexually provocative and eager for sex that the boy (Jason Biggs) ejaculates involuntarily before he gets to the real thing, while at the same time the complete episode is broadcast on the Internet for the entire neighborhood to watch.

The movie includes a number of scenes in which the boys discuss their understandings of sex and sexual intercourse, including discussions of a dubious teenage-male contention that having sex with a female gives a sensation much like penetrating a warm apple pie. The leading male character literally tests the hypothesis after he finds a warm apple pie in his mother's kitchen and succumbs to the temptation to have sex with it.

Had *American Pie* been released in the early 1970s (at the time of *American Graffiti*), the explicit sexual dialogue would have shocked theater audiences, and censors would have emerged from all quarters in towns and cities throughout the country to condemn the film. But today, *American Pie*, and its successors, *American Pie II*, *American Marriage*, and *The Naked Mile*, are all viewed as lighthearted, though sometimes sexually titillating, comedies—and not particularly shocking.

## THE FATE OF X-RATED FILMS

What has become of traditional X-rated films in today's more sexually permissive society? In major metropolitan areas it is nearly impossible to find a theater showing X-rated (hard-core pornography) films. A few urban theaters feature marquees that recall the X-rated theaters of the 1970s and 1980s, but these are usually connected with strip clubs. For example, The Lusty Lady theaters, in San Francisco and Seattle, do offer sex movies for their customers, but in the form of videos that more closely resemble "peep show" shorts than feature films. Clients view the videos in private booths or as a backdrop for the naked dancing women.[14]

The few X-rated theaters that can still be found, feature titles such as: *Just Over 18*, *Fresh Meat No. 11*, *Nurses*, and *Smooth Ride*. These films or videos are produced by the porn-film industry and are aimed primarily at VCR and DVD showings. Pornographic movie houses are the victims of new technology; most are nearly extinct today, put out of business by the advent of VCR and DVD players, and satellite/cable television.

## THE MOVIE RATING SYSTEM

Under the prevailing American movie rating system, the X-rated movie no longer exists. The current rating system for American movies grew out of a self-imposed system that went into effect in 1968 and has its own special categories. This system was created by the Motion Picture Association of America and the National Association of Theatre Owners. The purpose, according to the Web site for today's movie industry, is to "provide parents with advance information on films, enabling parents to make judgments on movies they want or do not want their children to see" (http://www.filmratings.com). The subtext of this statement is the reluctance of moviemakers and theatre owners to be subjected to community objections and potential legal actions for the movies they produce and distribute. For approximately thirty years, this self-rating system has managed to avoid further censorship, even though the films have become more explicit about sex, more profane and vulgar in language, and more violent.

The current rating system, adopted in 1980, includes the following categories:

- G—General Audiences,
- PG—Parental Guidance Suggested,
- PG-13—Parents Strongly Cautioned,
- R—Restricted (anyone under seventeen must be accompanied by a parent or an adult guardian),
- NC-17—No one seventeen or younger will be admitted.

When the rating system was first introduced, filmmakers generally tried to avoid the R rating because they feared the loss of the teenage market. Today, however, R and PG-13 ratings are generally believed to increase ticket sales (Bogart 2005). The only category that still reduces the attendance of teenagers is NC-17, where teenagers are turned away at the box office.

For this reason, the majority of all Hollywood releases today are either PG-13 or R rated. PG-13 movies have moved steadily toward more explicit sexual material, more vivid sexual language, and more violence (Mundy 2003). Directors have learned how to slip in just enough sexual material, vulgar language, and violence to make PG-13 films titillating and exciting without crossing the line that keeps teenagers from buying tickets (or their parents from purchasing tickets for them). Sexual activity is implied by innuendo, euphemistic language (e.g., *The Spy Who Shagged Me*), and off-screen action. In *Ace Ventura, Pet Detective* (PG-13), Jim Carrey's character recovers a lost parrot for an attractive, young female customer, who asks, "Shall I pay you, or would you like me to take your pants off instead?" As Carrey contorts his plastic face to milk the line for a laugh, the young woman drops to her knees, implying that she is giving him oral sex (Mundy 2003, 27). In another scene, Carrey announces, "I'd lose thirty pounds porking his wife." Today's teenagers and preteens probably have little difficulty interpreting the meaning of "porking" in this context (Mundy 2003, 28); it obviously has nothing to with pigs or pork chops.

Movie reviewer Nell Minnow, who reviews almost all PG-13 movies in her columns, has expressed concern that preteens and teenagers will develop erroneous views about adult life from the movies, assuming that "adult life consists mostly of recreational sex, recreationally arguing, and recreationally beating up mindless sluts" (Mundy 2003, 29).

## FROM *BEACH BLANKET BINGO* TO *GIRLS GONE WILD*

Another way of revealing the degree to which films have become more sexually explicit over the years is by comparing the "beach/bikini/spring break" films of the 1960s with those made today. Two classic 1960s films in this genre were *Bikini Beach*, and *Beach Blanket Bingo* (1965), both of which starred Frankie Avalon (a teenage singing heartthrob at the time) and Annette Funicello (a shapely, former Disney Mouseketeer). In these films, which were aimed primarily at teenage and young-adult audiences, the sex was limited to displays of nubile young women cavorting on California beaches in their bikinis. At the time, such scenes were considered to be somewhat daring, but within acceptable limits for most Americans.

The "spring break" movie in that era was similarly innocent. The most prominent example was *Where the Boys Are* (1960), which promised to reveal to American audiences "what college girls and boys do in Fort Lauderdale while on vacation." The action included "song, comedy, and drama" (Scheuer 1985, 753), with plenty of romance, but no sex.

By contrast, today's films about the beach and spring break are blatantly sexual. *The Real Cancun*, for example, was an R-rated beach movie that was shown in theaters throughout the country. One reviewer called *The Real Cancun* an "extended version of every episode of MTV's "Real World 1-12" (Wiltz 2003, C1), and, in fact, the producers of *The Real Cancun*, also made "Real World."

*The Real Cancun* had no famous or even unknown actors. The simple strategy of the moviemakers, inspired by reality TV, was to select sixteen young men and women who were strangers to each other, transport them to Cancun and put them up in a posh hotel where they were videotaped at all hours of the day and night. Everything that happens there is exhaustively and sometimes embarrassingly captured on film, including drinking, profanity, sexual displays (including an obligatory wet-T-shirt contest), and sexual activity (shown semimodestly under a blanket). *The Real Cancun* is radically different from the 1960s movie version of spring break in Fort Lauderdale.

A somewhat more realistic spring-break movie is the well-publicized and ongoing video series *Girls Gone Wild*. The DVDs and VCRs of *Girls Gone Wild*, which now number up to one hundred, feature girls who are not actresses but who enjoy partying and are willing to show various parts of their bodies in the heat of the moment. The signature setting of *Girls Gone Wild* is spring break on the beaches of Florida or other southern climes, but the camera crews also show up at Mardi Gras, college parties, and sports bars (Levy 2004).

The marketing genius behind *Girls Gone Wild* is a thirty-something entrepreneur named Joseph Francis. In 1999 Francis started showing up at the popular spring-break locales and Mardi Gras parties with a small camera crew. He reportedly financed his enterprise by maxing out his credit cards. In just four years, the enormous sales of *Girls Gone Wild* videotapes and related products (T-shirts, caps, posters, etc.) made Francis's empire worth a reported 100 million dollars (Smalley 2003). According to *Newsweek*, Francis is thinking about starting a nationwide chain of restaurants, along the lines of Hooters.

Along with his success, Francis has also encountered some serious legal troubles. In 2003, authorities in Panama City, Florida, charged him with "racketeering, obscenity, and conspiracy to use a child in a sexual performance" (Smalley 2003, 35). Among the charges were allegations that underage girls were filmed nude and encouraged by Francis and his colleagues to masturbate and engage in other sexual acts. These acts apparently occurred in a private setting (perhaps the condominium rented by Francis and his movie company Mantra), not in public on the beach. If convicted of these charges, Francis could possibly be sentenced to prison time. Civil suits have also been filed against Francis by parents of fifteen- and sixteen-year-old girls, who were allegedly filmed by him and his associates, either nude or engaging in sexual acts.

Between 2004 and 2006 Joe Francis and his company Mantra Films, Inc. pleaded guilty to various federal charges for which he has been fined several million dollars. Other charges against Francis and Mantra are still pending.

Despite Francis's nagging legal problems, he has single-handedly produced a pornographic trope—"Girls Gone Wild"—that is almost as recognizable today as "Debbie Does Dallas" in the porno movie world. With these three short words, Francis became a multimillionaire before the age of thirty, and in the process added a new concept to the sexual lexicon of the United States—and thanks to the Internet, the rest of the world as well.

## THE AVAILABILITY OF SEX IN MOVIES, ON DVDS AND VIDEOS TODAY

Today, movies no longer face the harsh constraints of Hollywood censors, either in theaters or on DVDs and videos. The pornographic film industry alone puts out thousands videos and DVDs every year, with little external resistance. The result is that Americans today can see movies in their local theaters that have erotic sex scenes, or they can rent or buy videos and DVDs that show either soft-core or hard-core sex. Moving-image sex and pornography is now available for almost every American who wishes to see it.

This abundant source of sexual material and pornography has opened up vast new areas of discourse about sex in American society. Any literate American who pays even the slightest attention to popular culture will understand what "deep throat" means, or what a reference to butter means in connection with Last Tango in Paris, or what it means for Debbie to "do" Dallas, or the real meaning of *American Pie*. These terms, allusions, and references have now all become a part of the language, the sexual discourse, of most Americans, including those who find the abundance of sex and pornography in films objectionable

CHAPTER 8

# RADIO AND TELEVISION
## FROM CAUTIOUS BEGINNINGS TO SHOCK JOCKS AND ANYTHING-GOES CABLE AND SATELLITE TELEVISION

In many of the preceding chapters, specific individuals have played critically important roles that have led to America's hypersexual society. The history of radio and television, especially the early history, did not have a specific individual who had such influence. In the case of radio and television, the major influence has been a nearly anonymous five-person group of federal government appointees: The Federal Communications Commission (FCC).

Since 1927, the radio airwaves have been controlled by this commission (first called the Federal Radio Commission). Later, with the advent of television, the FCC has controlled both radio and television. The Commission is charged with monitoring radio and television broadcasts on the publicly owned airwaves, and most importantly it grants licenses to individual broadcasting stations. Commission members are especially sensitive to the fact that radio and television programs go directly into the homes of Americans—unlike traditional movies, which people could only see after choosing to buy a ticket.

The FCC as a censoring body is not a paper tiger. It is a very powerful force, as the Infinity and Clear Channel radio networks learned when the FCC cracked down on Howard Stern's radio program and as CBS television learned when it was fined for the Superbowl half time show when one of Janet Jackson's breasts was momentarily shown.

The five people on the FCC can levy heavy fines and in recent years they have shown an increasing willingness to do so. It is also important to note that it is the United States Congress that sets the levels of these fines.

In 2006, the Congress passed and President George W. Bush signed a bill that increased the maximum penalty to 325,000 dollars for radio and television broadcasts that the FCC considers indecent. On the occasion of signing this bill President Bush said that broadcasters "too often pushed the bounds of decency" (Baker 2006, A6). He went on to say, "The language is becoming courser during the times when children will be seeing television" (Baker 2006, A6) And he added, "People are saying, 'We're tired of it, and we expect the government to do something about it'" (Baker 2006, A6).

The FCC can mete out an even more serious punishment than fines. If the FCC believes that particular broadcasters are not conforming to expected standards, it can revoke their licenses. In the words of one broadcasting executive, "'You lose your license, that's the death penalty'" (Frey 2004, C8).

The FCC is required by law to review all complaints that come in from listeners—both individuals and organized groups. When the members of religious or political organizations are urged to submit complaints they can force the FCC to review specific radio or television shows.[1]

The content of radio broadcasts has, from its beginnings, been highly constrained by these government controls. When television came along it too fell cautiously into line. In addition, television networks were influenced by the self-censorship of the movie industry described in the last chapter. Over the years, television has been more successful than radio in breaking away from governmental restrictions on sexual materials, but both radio and television had nearly pristine content for decades after their appearance in the American media world. A brief look at the history of sexual material on these media will provide insight into the part radio and television play in today's hypersexual society.

## THE ABSENCE OF SEXUAL MATERIAL ON EARLY RADIO

The first American radio broadcast occurred on Christmas Eve, 1906—it was limited to a short talk and a violin interlude (Nachman 1998). Slowly during the 1920s, but then quickly in the 1930s, commercial radio broadcasts spread across the United States. During the first three decades of commercial radio, and continuing well into the 1960s, radio was nearly free of sexual material. The only exceptions were a few double entendres that some comedians were able to sneak past the network censors.

Mid-twentieth century comedian Bob Hope was noted for pushing the boundaries of sexual acceptance, beginning with his radio program and continuing later on his television broadcasts. One historian of radio claims that "Bob Hope was America's most famous dirty comic"

(Nachman 1998, 141). Hope's material on both radio and television was tame by current-day standards.[2]

Other major radio comedians during the early era of radio, such as Jack Benny and Fred Allen, rarely touched on anything sexual. Edgar Bergen (Candice Bergen's father), through his ventriloquist dummy Charlie McCarthy, would often have Charlie make wisecracks about girls, but the material was not much more than a leering sexism.

### RADIO SOAP OPERAS—AS PURE AS IVORY SOAP

Soap operas were an important part of radio programming in its early years. These programs generally ran during the afternoon hours and were primarily aimed at women in the home. Laundry and cosmetic soap manufacturers were often the sponsors, thus the name soap operas. While these dramas were built around every aspect of personal and family life they rarely strayed onto the topic of sex. As one example, a popular drama of the day was called *The Romance of Helen Trent*.

The leading character of this program was Helen Trent, a thirty-fivish divorcee who remained ageless and sexually pure for the twenty-seven years the program stayed on the air. Her long-time boyfriend Gil relentlessly pursued her, but never once was there an episode in which they had sex or sex was even implied (Nachman 1998, 374). By the standards of today's soap operas, this was an incredible period of abstinence.

The extreme sexual restrictiveness of early radio is illustrated by an incident that occurred on a long-running family serial (not quite a soap opera) called *One Man's Family*. This radio program portrayed an upper-middle class family that was a model of propriety. In a low-key style, the problems and concerns of this San Francisco extended family went on for years, with never a mention of sex. Yet, on one occasion, a listener complained to the president of NBC about an episode that had two of the program's characters carrying on a conversation *in bed*. The listener found this offensive and took the time to write a complaining letter.

One might suppose that a high-level network executive would have ignored such a trivial complaint. Instead, the NBC executive wrote a letter to the writer and director of the series, asking angrily "How far is this sex trend in *One Man's Family* going to go?" (Nachman 1998, 396). The letter went on to say, "I hope you will discontinue this type of presentation before we are asked to do so by our New York office if not [by] the Federal Communications Commission" (Nachman 1998, 396). This example reveals how sensitive radio executives were to both the public's complaints about sexual material and to the federal government agency, the FCC, that controlled radio broadcasting.

Radio broadcasts continued to follow these restrictive policies about sex for decades thereafter. The reason is revealed in the *One Man's Family* example in which a single listener might find some material, no matter how sexually innocuous, objectionable and network executives would take the objection seriously. Of course, when large numbers of listeners made similar complaints the matter was taken even more seriously.

The fear of radio executives was that the federal government, through the FCC, would impose penalties or possibly rescind licenses. Later in this chapter we will take a closer look at the way the government, through the FCC and the Congress, continues to impose censorship on radio and broadcast television.

But first we will see how radio has moved beyond its early years and is now dealing with sexual materials more aggressively. Two areas of radio broadcasting have seriously challenged government censorship: "shock-jock" disk jockeys and music lyrics. In both areas the censors, both governmental and private citizens (or groups), have had some success in restricting radio content. The career of radio shock jock Howard Stern provides a vivid example of someone who has pushed the limits of sexual (and just plain crude) material on his radio broadcasts. He has paid some price for doing so, but he has also become a multimillionaire in the process.

### HOWARD STERN—THE ULTIMATE SHOCK JOCK

Howard Stern has spent his entire adult life, beginning when he was a college student, in radio. He now also has a television show on cable/satellite, but this program is not much more than a videotape of his radio show. Radio is, by Stern's own repeated claim, *his life*.

Stern was born in 1954 in Jackson Heights, New York to middle-class parents who were well enough off to send him to Boston University where he did very well academically. He graduated with a 3.8 grade average according to a Web site biography (http://www.imdb.com/name/nmooo1769/bio), even though he has candidly admitted that during his college years he was fond of taking drugs—quaaludes being his favorite (Stern 1995).

While in college, Stern worked at the university's radio station, where as part of a student group he helped to create a special series. The key to the series was that students would confess their most serious sin. But the show lasted only one episode before it was pulled by the university administration. This was a harbinger of Stern's later radio career where he frequently encountered objections from management (and the government) and threats to take him off the air.

After graduating from college Stern took a job as a disk jockey at a small three-thousand-watt radio station in Briarcliff Manor, New York. From there he moved quickly up the hierarchy of radio markets, first to Washington, DC, and then to WNBC in New York City. He obviously attracted large audiences in these major markets, but he was at the same time battling station executives about what he was saying on the air.

Stern has written two books that chronicle, in a haphazard manner, his life and his radio career. The first of these books, *Private Parts* (Stern 1993), which was later made into a feature-length film, covers the early stages of his career. Stern's second book *Miss America* (Stern 1995) continues his autobiographical account, along with his observations about popular-culture events and well-known people.[3] Both of these books are print versions of Stern's inimitable style: scatological language, an obsession with sex, embarrassing self-revelations, and attacks on anyone he dislikes or who is in some way vulnerable. What Stern has said about his radio broadcasts is also true of his books, "compassion never enters into my world when I'm doing my radio show" (Stern 1995, 113).

As part of his self-revelation Stern continues to put on the printed page much of the material he has already offered on his radio show. He opened his second book by describing how he often spent his free time (when his then-wife was out of the house) looking for pornography on the Internet and masturbating. Stern called it "Cybersurfing for Vagina" (Stern 1995, 2–3).

Stern went on in this book to describe his young-adult bouts with obsessive-compulsive disorder, his continuing fantasies about the women with whom he would like to have sex, his often cruel and insensitive treatment of his radio-show coworkers, and his run for governor of New York, among other topics.

Stern has proved himself to be the quintessential "shock jock," and though he has many imitators he stands at the top with regard to both income and celebrity/notoriety. In the late 1990s, Stern signed a five-year contract for 100 million dollars, putting him at that time in the highly rarefied company of conservative political talk show host Rush Limbaugh. As for fame, *Forbes Magazine* once named Stern among the one hundred most powerful celebrities in the United States (http://www.imdb.com/name/nmooo1769/bio).

Stern immodestly describes his success on radio as coming from his singular talent: "I'm *extraordinary* at one thing—and that's radio. I'm not just good at it, I'm the *best* at it" (Stern 1995, 257). He takes special pride in one particular contribution he made to radio: "I invented saying PENIS and VAGINA on the radio, and I'll go to my grave proud of that accomplishment" (Stern 1995, 258).[4] As an incidental related point, Stern has built part of his radio persona around his repeated claim that he has an extraordinarily *small* penis.

It is universally agreed that Howard Stern's program is relentlessly tasteless and vulgar. Anything having to do with sexual body parts or body functions is routine material for Stern. Ethnic, racial, and religious groups are likely to be labeled with stereotypic descriptions. Making fun of people with disabilities is a standard part of Stern's repertoire. On one occasion he did a fifteen-minute bit on the Miss America who was hearing impaired. His observation: "I can't offend her because she can't hear my jokes anyway" (Stern 1995, 137). In recent years, Stern has turned more and more often to bringing young women on his show who are willing to take off their clothes—on radio, of course, their actions can only be described by Stern, but on his television show they can be seen (though breasts and pubic areas are pixeled).

Stern's main obsession, about which he talks incessantly, is sex. Any guest who agrees to be interviewed on his show is likely to be asked intrusive questions about his or her sex life. After the 2004 Olympics, Stern had gold-medal swimmer Amanda Beard on his show and he took the occasion to comment repeatedly on her great body, especially her "wonderful ass," and to ask, among other things if she shaved her pubic hair. In his usual style, Stern also asked Beard if she would have sex with him if he and his current girlfriend were to split up. Beard allowed that he was attractive, but fended off the question.

Hollywood actor Alec Baldwin once appeared on Stern's show, and though Baldwin's primary objective was to promote his new movie, Stern, by his own admission, wanted only to know what it was like to have sex with Baldwin's then-wife Kim Basinger. Stern also asked Baldwin, relevant to nothing that had preceded it: "Hey, did Kim ever have sex with a black man?" He went on to ask: "You ever handcuff her to the bed? I'd like to handcuff your wife to a bed. Did you last a long time the first time you nailed Kim?" After these and other questions, Stern fantasized on air about what he would do with Kim Basinger if he had her in bed: "spread eagled," "nine-and-a-half tongues," "If I can't satisfy you with what's in my pants, I'll use one of Alec's cigars," and so on (Stern 1995, 421).

Infinity Broadcasting was Stern's employer during his final years on broadcast radio, but this network has been severely fined for things Stern said on air. According to Stern's 1995 book, the FCC fined Infinity Broadcasting 1.7 million dollars. Among the offending topics Stern talked about were: a conversation with his radio sidekick Robin Quivers about the relative merits of shaving vs. waxing pubic hair; expressions of disgust about Pee Wee Herman masturbating at a porno movie; and in a tele-phone conversation with his wife, before their divorce, Stern told her that he took a can of tuna to bed when she was not there so he wouldn't know she was gone (Stern 1995).

Stern ran into serious trouble with the FCC in 2004, when major fines were levied against the two key companies that distributed his show. In early 2004, Clear Channel officials, apparently anticipating that the FCC was about to crack down on Stern's program, suspended him for an on-air incident they considered vulgar (Frey 2004, C1). The company found Stern's questions offensive when he was interviewing Rick Salomon, the man who had been videotaped having sex with Paris Hilton. This video-tape had already been widely distributed on the Internet and Stern was curious about the sexual life of Paris Hilton. Stern asked his usual ques-tions, such as whether or not Salomon had engaged in anal sex with Paris Hilton.

It was in mid-2004 that Stern, and especially the companies with whom he had contracts, were fined by the FCC. Clear Channel Communications, one of the two broadcasting chains that carried Stern's radio show on six stations, was fined 495,000 dollars for "individual utterances" that Stern made about oral sex on a show broadcast a year ear-lier. In the wake of this FCC fine, Clear Channel severed all ties with Stern (Frey 2004, C1).

Infinity Broadcasting (owned by Viacom), Stern's other distributor, was under threat of large FCC fines and giving indications that it might not renew Stern's contract when it was to expire in January 2006. Even though Stern was bringing in 100 million dollars a year in advertising rev-enue the fines were getting high enough to offset the income (Ahrens 2004).

In October 2004, before Infinity could fire him, Stern announced that he had signed a 500-million-dollar deal with SIRIUS Satellite Radio (Kurtz and Ahrens 2004). Broadcasting on satellite radio would free Stern from governmental censorship, just as cable and satellite television had been freed.

Howard Stern's style as a shock jock has been emulated by disk jock-eys around the country. As just one example, "Opie and Anthony" (Gregg Hughes and Anthony Cumia, respectively) have had a turbulent, though also profitable, radio career (emanating from Boston, New York, and now satellite radio). Among their many notorious stunts was a contest for real-life couples who would be willing to have sex in notable public places. This contest reached the limits of public acceptance when a Virginia couple had sex in the vestibule of St. Patrick's cathedral in New

York City. These goings-on were reported live on the Opie and Anthony show by a program observer, but it led to their firing in 2002. Since then, these two shock jocks have returned to both satellite radio and broadcast radio (http://en.wikipedia.org/wiki/Opie_and_Anthony).[5]

Shock jocks around the country continue to be some of the major challengers to the restrictions on sexual materials on radio. As shock jocks continue to test the limits of acceptability they are often immensely popular among radio listeners, even though they always operate under the threat of serious fines by the FCC (or of being fired by their stations or broadcasting companies).

### SEXUALLY ORIENTED MUSIC LYRICS ON BROADCAST RADIO

Tipper Gore, the wife of then-Senator Al Gore, and the man who nearly won the presidency of the United States in 2000, received considerable public attention in 1985 when she appeared before a Senate Investigating Committee where she chastised the music industry for what she considered the offensive and immoral lyrics of much popular music. The objectionable lyrics were not simply about sex, although sex was particularly threatening to parents and adults who feared it would have a corrupting effect on young people.[6]

As a result of the threats of governmental censorship and boycotts by organized groups, the U.S. recording industry in 1990 introduced Parent Advisory labels for CDs and tapes. These were to identify music that contained explicit lyrics, including depictions of sex and violence (http://www.mediaawareness/english/parents/music/inappropriate/explicit_lyrics.cfm).

The Parental Advisory labels have not eliminated sex and violence from popular music though they may have reduced the amount of such music heard on radio. Popular music today is permeated with lyrics that refer to sex, both directly and by various euphemisms. One has only to listen to, among many other choices, the recent albums/CDs of Lil' Kim[7], 50 Cent, Pink, Princess Superstar, Kool Keith, Peaches, DJ Assault, Eminem, or even alt-rock's Liz Phair, to find sexual material.

Teenagers and preteens may not be able to hear all of this music on radio, but much of it can be found on cable and satellite television, or it can be purchased on CDs or DVDs. Record spinners on broadcast radio continue to be cautious about what they put on the air because watchdogs in the public and government are on guard.

## SEXUAL MATERIAL ON TELEVISION DURING THE EARLY YEARS

In the 1950s, the early years of television, network executives dealt with sex in a very gingerly manner. The TV moguls of that era were very aware of the power of the FCC and were also undoubtedly influenced by the code of ethics (the Hays Code) that still controlled the movie industry. In 1951 the National Association of Radio and Television Broadcasters established its own voluntary Code of Ethics. Under the rules of the Code, sex was a forbidden topic. Much like in the movies, a man and woman could not be shown in bed together. Even married couples slept in twin beds. Off-color jokes, profanity, and words relating to sexuality were forbidden. The television Code of Ethics banned "such views of performers as emphasize anatomical details indecently" (Chunovic 2000, 19). Television broadcasters were also warned that "the use of locations closely associated with sexual life or with sexual sin must be governed by good taste or delicacy." While these carefully formulated restrictions may have left some room for interpretation, they were clearly designed to keep writers, directors, and producers in line.

A much more explicit rule of the early television Code of Ethics was one relating to illicit sex, which was never to be. Illicit sex in the 1950s meant any sex that was treated favorably outside the bonds of marriage. By way of seeing how much change has occurred since then, we might ask how many of the most popular broadcast television shows today—sitcoms, hour-long dramas, soap operas, other daytime shows, as well as late-night programs—could survive without having some depiction of nonmarital sex? The obvious answer is, not many.

Also prohibited on early television were any scenes showing sex crimes and "abnormalities." Sex crimes referred most obviously to rape, but the word "abnormalities" in the 1950s was understood to be a code word for homosexuality.

Even with the television Code of Ethics in place, complaints started coming in to Congress and the FCC about indecency on television. The early complaints were often about women performers who were showing too much skin and performing in a way that was considered suggestive and offensive. The United States House of Representatives passed a resolution calling for a "full and complete investigation and study to determine the extent to which radio and television programs contain immoral or offensive material" (Chunovic 2000, 30).

It was in the 1950s that an Arkansas Congressman with the improbable name of Ezekiel Chandler Gathers chaired a hearing that investigated the issue of immoral and offensive material on television. Congressman Gathers opened the proceedings by announcing that he had seen a television program showing a "grass-skirted young woman and a thinly clad gentleman dancing the hootchy-kootchy." The dance ended, he said, with the "attractive young lady shaking all the way down to the floor, landing on her hands. . . . My children saw that and I could not get it turned off to save my life" (Chunovic 2000, 26).

Congressman Gathers's hearing also focused special attention on one of the most talked about and blatantly sexual personalities of early television. Her name was Dagmar, and she was not so much a personality as a body. A former showgirl, Dagmar was ideally suited for television appearances. She was a statuesque (5' 9") beauty who usually appeared on television wearing evening gowns that offered enough décolletage to give evidence of her forty-inch bust.

Congressman Gathers's committee hearings scared the television networks into being very careful about how much female anatomy they displayed on screen, a fear that lasted into the 1960s.

American television in the 1960s did start, in a limited way, to break out of the restraints of sexual censorship. One notable example was a primetime soap opera called *Peyton Place*, which was based on a steamy novel of the same name by Grace Metalious described in Chapter 4 (Metalious 1956). Since millions of Americans had read the book, the very title suggested sexuality and sexual escapades. Within the limits of the times, some episodes of *Peyton Place* did have sexually suggestive dialogue. Extramarital relations were a mainstay of the plot lines, though most of the sex was off screen and thus left to the viewer's imagination.

Even displays of female anatomy continued to be severely limited on 1960s American television. As an example, a popular sitcom of the mid-1960s, called *I Dream of Jeannie*, starred Barbara Eden in the role of a two-thousand-year-old genie (but still looking youthfully beautiful). Jeannie's costume involved harem pants, a headdress, and a short Bolero jacket. However, a censorship issue raged about whether or not Jeannie's bare midriff, and specifically her navel, could be shown on television. Network officials ruled that her naval could not be shown.

Later in the 1960s, as the flower-child generation began to bloom, some of the restrictions regarding female bodies started to fall. Rowan and Martin's *Laugh In*, a popular late-60s variety show, often had dancers and female actresses clad in bikinis. Goldie Hawn, then in the early years of her career, was one of the ingénues who proudly displayed her belly button. The female bodies and the sometimes-risque humor of *Laugh In* were part of television's response to the early stages of the society's sexual revolution. The public, in the spirit of the times, accepted *Laugh In* on television. Even the then-President of the United States, Richard M.

Nixon, made a brief videotaped appearance on the show. Nixon's appearance was only about a decade after Congressman Gathers complained about grass-skirted and thinly clad dancers on television doing the "hootchy-kootchy."

Sex on television quickly followed the cultural and legal breakthroughs of the late 1960s and early 1970s. Almost all major types of television programming moved toward more sexual material. To see where we stand today we will begin with the staple of prime-time broadcast television, the situation comedy.

## SEX ON THE SITCOMS

In 1971, a new and different sitcom came to American television. Premiering on CBS, it was called *All in the Family*. This program was not devoted to sex, but it did try to draw attention to a wide variety of social issues, sex being among them. Different episodes of *All in the Family* dealt with racism, anti-Semitism, politics, war, male-female relations, marriage, and so on. The style of show was to make television audiences confront the realities of social life, most of which had previously been invisible on primetime comedy shows. Impotence and homosexuality were just two of the heretofore prohibited topics this program addressed. *All in the Family* did not show blatant sex, but it certainly added to public discourse about sexual matters that had hardly ever been spoken of in "polite company."

Throughout the 1970s and into the 1980s new sitcoms such as *M\*A\*S\*H* (1972–83) and *Three's Company* came on the scene, both of which had sexual suggestiveness, and at least in the case of *M\*A\*S\*H*, a few sex scenes and even a bit of nudity. *Three's Company* more often took a "smirky" attitude toward sex and contented itself with showing Suzanne Somers wrapped in a towel or bouncing around in a "tight top and shorts" (Chunovic 2000, 79).

But sex came to sitcoms in a big way with the Fox network show *Married with Children* (Chunovic 2000). This sitcom, which had sex as a major theme, ran for a decade (from 1987 to 1997) and broke almost all previous taboos related to sex. This sitcom became the most popular Fox network show and shaped television's future, even though many critics were offended by its crudeness and blatant sexism. One critic characterized this program as "immensely influential . . . not only because it extended the reach of what was permissible for over-the-air TV, but because its no-taste humor was genuinely funny" (Chunovic 2000, 114). It was funny, and it made money.

*Married with Children* was built around Al and Peg Bundy the discontented married parents of Kelly and Bud. The daughter Kelly, played by Christina Applegate, was a sexy and suggestively promiscuous teenage daughter,[8] while the son Bud was an eager but sexually frustrated preteen son. The sexual material took several different forms over the life of the show. Among them was Al looking at or talking about his pornography magazines, especially the fictitious *Big 'Uns*. Also, Al's job at a shoe store gave him the opportunity to ogle the shapely women customers.

Peg on the other hand was regularly pestering Al to have sex, or alternately complaining about how sexually inadequate he was. Kelly, the attractive teenager, was frequently going out or coming back from a date, and then naively revealing that sex was part of the action. For his part, younger brother Bud, was usually making jibes at Kelly about being a slut or revealing that he was lusting after girls and women he could not win.

Not surprisingly, *Married with Children* attracted the attention of major censorship groups in the 1980s. The Reverend Donald Wildmon, who headed both the Christian Leaders for Responsible Television and the American Family Association, vigorously castigated the program and the Fox network. A private citizen, Terry Rakolta, mother of four, initiated a boycott against Coca Cola for sponsoring the program. The soft drink company knuckled under and withdrew its sponsorship of the show (Chunovic 2000, 116). Despite these efforts at censorship, *Married with Children* ran for much longer than the typical life span of even the most successful sitcoms. *Married with Children* clearly helped to change television's view of sexual content and broadcast television has never looked back.

The television industry during the 1980s gradually withdrew censorship of its programs. The three major television networks, ABC, CBS, and NBC, stopped reviewing their shows, as did the Fox network after its successful run of *Married with Children*.

During the early 1990s, the previously mentioned anti-smut crusader Reverend Donald Wildmon made the claim that in one year the three major television networks broadcast more than ten thousand sexual "incidents" during prime time. Moreover, according to Wildmon, the overwhelming majority of these sexual incidents were outside "the sacrament bonds" (U.S. News and World Report 1992). In more statistical terms, according to Wildmon's count, network television presented fourteen outside-of-marriage sex incidents for every one within marriage (U.S. News and World Report 1992).

Once television had made the sexual breakthrough of the 1980s, and more importantly when cable, and later satellite, television gained a place in most American homes, sex became commonplace on home screens. This was certainly true of daytime television, especially soap operas and talk shows.

## DAYTIME TELEVISION

With regard to sex, soap operas have come a long way since the radio days of *The Romance of Helen Trent* and *One Man's Family*. Only one of the radio originals (*Guiding Light*) successfully made the transition to television for the long term. The original *Guiding Light*, as its name suggests, had a somber, even semi-sacred quality, but not so in its twenty-first-century television version. Much like all the other current-day soap operas,[9] the plot lines of today's *Guiding Light* have a full share of sex and violence. This is not to say that romance and family relationships are not still a part of the stories, but within these contexts sex and sexuality are omnipresent.

As a first clue to the sexuality of modern-day soap operas we have only to see the lead actors and actresses. The stars today are mostly young, attractive, and ostentatiously sexual (see any issue of *Soap Opera Weekly*). Passionate love scenes are now standard fare on today's television soap operas. The sexual activity ranges from deep kissing to passionate stroking and caressing, and often the beginning stages of sexual intercourse before the fadeout. A 2004 episode of *General Hospital* had a sex scene that went beyond the limits of the network arbiters. The female actress in that scene, Lesli Kay, knew immediately when she saw the broadcast that some of the sex had been cut from the show. She said, "When I watched the scene, I realized they cut it. . . . They cut the whole part where Lorenzo [King] put Lisa [Kay] down on the desk" (*Soap Opera Weekly* 2004, 8). The program did show Kay ripping off King's black tank top and his pulling down her bra straps, but at the point where she wrapped her legs around his body the scene faded out.

Soap operas today are no longer the homespun, familistic, sometimes romantic shows of radio and early television. Romance is still a mainstay of most of today's soaps, and though violence sometimes intrudes, sexual behavior and sexuality are now an important part of most stories.

### DAYTIME TALK SHOWS

The producers and hosts of daytime talk shows are under relentless pressure to fill their five-days-a-week schedules. As American society has moved toward greater sexual openness, television talk show hosts recognized that sex had broad and persistent audience appeal (Grindstaff 2002).

Even though some of these daytime talk shows have come and gone, the hosts of these shows—Maury Povich, Sally Jessy Raphael, Montel Williams, Rikki Lake, Jenny Jones, Jerry Springer, and many others—quickly learned that sex sells. Even Oprah Winfrey, the ultimate television entrepreneur, did for a time jump into the fray of exotic sex topics, but she soon withdrew and returned to the topics with which she is most comfortable (i.e., educational and moralistic themes and topics—AIDS and how to prevent it, teenage pregnancy, relationship counseling, and inspiring books).

But the more flamboyant talk show hosts, the ones who did not shy away from any topic no matter how tasteless, have pushed sexual topics relentlessly and to the limits. The more bizarre the sexual behavior, the more likely viewers are to watch the program. These shows specialize in bringing on guests who will bare their personal lives, no matter how embarrassing. Many topics challenge credulity: mothers and daughters who have had sex with the same man; fathers and sons who have had sex with the same woman; sisters who have had sex (and so on through all possible combinations and permutations).

Every other imaginable subject related to sex has been covered at one time or another on the daytime talk shows: rape (both victims and perpetrators), pedophilia, homosexuality, sexual fetishes (including sadomasochism and bondage), incest, cross-dressing, transvestitism, impotence and frigidity, sexual addictions, nymphomania, prostitution (females, males, and teenagers), and more.

Since no sexual topic is off limits for television's daytime talk shows, public discourse about sexual topics has greatly expanded. Senator Joseph Lieberman, reflecting on television talk show content in moral terms, has observed, "These talk shows really take the abnormal and make it acceptable, and in doing so degrade the culture" (Kurtz 1995, C8).

## SEX ON PRIMETIME BROADCAST TELEVISION

Sex is now found routinely on primetime broadcast television shows, even during the previously sacrosanct "family hour" between 8:00 to 9:00 P.M. The Henry J. Kaiser Family Foundation conducts a biennial survey of sexual material on television and has documented the amount and type of sex on TV. The biennial reports from this survey are based on carefully drawn samples of all programs (except newscasts, sports events, and children's shows) and provide some of the best available information about sex on television. The Kaiser Foundation is relatively objective in its research and reporting, since it has no strong bias except for a continuing concern about health, especially the health of young people.

According to the 2005 biennial report of the Kaiser Family Foundation, 77 percent of primetime television shows have some sexual content (Kaiser Family Foundation Report, Executive Summary, 2005).[10] This percentage is significantly greater than that found in the 1998 study, when it was 67 percent. The percentage of sex on primetime shows has also risen since the 2003 report when it was 71 percent.

In 2005, among the major genres of television programs, both daytime and primetime, movies had the highest percentage with some sexual content, 92 percent. Sitcoms, drama series, and soap operas have nearly equal amounts of sexual content with 87 percent, 87 percent, and 85 percent respectively. Seventy percent of news magazines have sexual content, while 67 percent of talk shows do. Reality shows[11] had, by far, the lowest percentage with sexual content, 28 percent (Kaiser Family Foundation Report, Executive Summary, 2005, 6).

The researchers focused special attention on the top twenty programs most frequently watched by teenagers, aged twelve to seventeen. They found the percentage of teenage programs with at least some sexual content especially high. Compared with the overall average of 64 percent, 83 percent of teenage programs had some sexual content.

In the 2003 study, a new trend that did appear was an increase in the number of programs that included a message about the risks and responsibilities associated with having sex. This trend should not be exaggerated since the percentage of such shows is still only 10 percent (Kaiser Family Foundation Report, Executive Summary, 2005, 7).

Increases in television risk-and-responsibilities messages are making another contribution to the total volume of sexual discourse in American society. In fact, as these studies of television programming demonstrate, sex on TV is primarily talk, or what the researchers call "sexual dialogue" (Kunkel et al. 2003, 8). Television programming has approximately twice as much talk about sex as it has sexual behavior. But sexual discourse is just as much a contributor to the hypersexualization of society as depictions of sexual behavior.

## BREAKING SEX TABOOS ON PRIMETIME/BROADCAST TV

During the last fifteen years almost every sexual taboo about what can be said or shown on television has been broken. Many breaches have occurred on primetime broadcast television, but if not there, then on late-night programs. And whatever taboos may have remained have been broken on cable and satellite television, but more about that later.

The realm of forbidden words on television and radio was famously challenged by comedian George Carlin when he built a routine around

"The Seven Dirty Words You Can't Say on Radio or Television." They hardly need repeating, but for the record Carlin identified the forbidden words as, *shit, piss, fuck, cunt, cocksucker, motherfucker,* and *tits.* In one manner or another these words have now been spoken on television (including the Carlin routine itself).

The f-word has been especially interesting because it has moved into the general public vocabulary (Achenbach 2006). At the same time, the word fuck has surreptitiously crept into much dialogue on television, through an array of euphemisms. In its adjectival form it is not uncommon to hear on television "freaking or freakin'," "fricking or fricken'," "frigging or friggin.'"[12] But the actual utterance of the word fuck, or some variation thereof, has occasionally been uttered on broadcast television. A much-publicized incident occurred at the Golden Globe awards shows where U-2's Bono blurted out, "This is really, really fucking brilliant." This led to an initial ruling by the FCC, which held that "fucking" when used as an adjective, was acceptable on television. But "fucking" used in a sexual context was not. This FCC Solomon-like decision was later rescinded, so for the moment the f-word straight is not acceptable in any grammatical form.

Another incident on an awards show offered some similar strong language. This time at the Billboard Awards, Nicole Richie, one of the stars (along with Paris Hilton) of *The Simple Life*—a semi-reality program that depicted the experiences of two city-girl celebrities down on the farm—uttered a double-barreled fusillade of forbidden words. Richie said, "Why do they call it the 'Simple Life?' Have you ever tried to get cow shit out of a Prada purse? It's not so fucking simple" (http://www.sfgate.com, 2004).

The commonplace public use of the f-word was illustrated when Vice President Cheney, on the floor of the United States Senate, said it in anger and loud enough for bystanders to hear. Cheney was angry at Democratic Senator Patrick Leahy of Vermont, who had made a critical comment about the Halliburton corporation, a company that Cheney had headed before becoming Vice President. When Leahy walked up to Cheney and offered an innocuous greeting, Cheney blurted out, "Fuck you" (or perhaps it was "Fuck off," since witnesses do not agree). In either case, the word was heard and with the required ellipses and bleepings, was reported on all the major news media of the country.

Over the years on the after-primetime *Saturday Night Live*, actors have on some occasions inadvertently uttered the f-word. However, because of the show's broadcast time and the fact that the word was not built into the script there was little public outcry or network fuss. While on the subject of *Saturday Night Live*, it needs to be said that this program has succeeded in breaking down taboos against many forms of sexual material, as well as other topics considered off-limits for television. Actor Tom Hanks, recalls hosting the show when "The Penis Song" was dropped from the program at the last minute (a not unusual occurrence for *Saturday Night Live*). But only a few weeks later, "The Penis Song," did make the show, certainly breaking new ground for broadcast television (Shales and Miller 2002, 407).

Still on the *Saturday Night Live* show and the topic of penises, the show once had a skit taking off on President Clinton and his sexual adventures with Monica Lewinsky. In this skit, an actor playing a President Clinton type has a young woman come into his office and duck under his desk while he is on the phone. The Clinton-like actor comments that he is not used to thinking while his "wang is being mouthed." Aside from the sexual event of fellatio, the use of the word "wang" for penis is just one of many euphemisms that are used on television today. Among the other substitutes are: dong, schlong, Mr. Johnson, and many others.

Another sexual word that has made it on television programs is fellatio. In 1999, the ABC network show *The Practice*, had the word "blowjob" in one of its scripts. The censors at that time made them substitute the more formal fellatio (Chunovic 2000, 153). But the word "blowjob" has by now made it to television, if not on broadcast TV, then at least on HBO. In an episode of *Sex and the City* Carrie quizzed a young woman admirer about her claim to being a total virgin. Carrie asks, "No blowjobs, no handjobs?" "Nope," says the young woman. Carrie's expression is one of bemused incredulity. We will have more to say about *Sex and the City*, as well as another hit HBO show *The Sopranos* later.

Turning from words to sexual action on television, network shows are more likely to skate around the edges of sexual behavior rather than show it directly. As one example, consider the female orgasm. On primetime television shows it is not the orgasm directly, but the *fake orgasm* that has frequently been put on view. The 1989 movie *When Harry Met Sally* introduced the American public to the idea that women might sometimes (often?) fake orgasms[13], if the situation calls for it.[14] In the movie, Sally (Meg Ryan) demonstrates to Harry (Billy Crystal) how a woman can easily produce a convincing fake orgasm, which she does with all the requisite heavy breathing, moaning, and facial contortions. After the *When Harry Met Sally* film, television writers quickly saw the humorous possibilities of the fake orgasm. It was sex, though not really sex, and it could be shown on primetime television. Its humor rested on the idea that women can easily deceive ego-driven, and sexually anxious men. As an added advantage, the fake orgasm gave female actors an opportunity to pull off virtuoso performances.

One of the most impressive television fake orgasms was acted out by Elaine (Julia Louis-Dreyfus) on the *Seinfeld* show. Sitting in the familiar booth at the coffee shop Elaine amazed Jerry, George, and Kramer by first owning up to doing fake orgasms (even with Jerry) and then reproducing the facial expressions and vocal sounds of her fake job. Not to be outdone, Kramer then claimed that he too had faked an orgasm, though he left the details to the viewer's imagination.

The fake orgasm has been used in a number of other television programs, including *Mad about You, Friends, Ally McBeal,* and *Sex and the City.* Today, the fake-orgasm trope has become such a familiar part of American popular culture that it needs no special introduction or explanation when script writers use it.

The *Seinfeld* show also brought masturbation into American living rooms. In one of their most famous shows, Jerry, George, Elaine, and Kramer make a bet about who could go the longest without masturbating. The actual word was never used but it was implied by the opening scene in which George confessed that his mother came home unexpectedly and caught him doing "that" with one of his mother's *Glamour* magazines. It matters little who won the bet, the important point is that *Seinfeld* made viewers laugh at the topic of adult masturbation.

Gay sex came to television with some very popular situation comedies. Ellen Degeneres broke the ice when she famously kissed Laura Dern on her sitcom *Ellen*. While Ellen and Laura did not engage in actual sex, the viewers could easily assume that sex followed the passionate kiss after the fade out.

The most successful gay-oriented sitcom, one that made gay sex the *raison-detre* of the entire series was *Will and Grace*. The premise of the show was that Will and Grace, though they may previously have had a romantic relationship while in college, were now sharing an apartment in New York. Will is now openly gay; Grace is not. Again in this sitcom, gay sex is never actually shown, but it was always present, by innuendo, double entendres, and much of the humor of the show.

These are but a few of the sexual breakthrough moments of broadcast television. Many primetime shows, both sitcoms and hour-long dramas, have provided audiences with scenes of nudity and sex. *NYPD Blue* led the way in its first program, when a New York detective ends up in the bedroom of one of his female colleagues. In 2004, *NYPD Blue*, nearing the last program of the series, still provided the cautionary note that "adult nudity" may be shown. This is but one of the many hour-long dramas on today's primetime television that have incorporated sex into their story lines.

## SEX ON CABLE/SATELLITE

Cable television came to America gradually after some tentative beginnings in the 1950s. In its early years, cable television was often most successful in remote areas of the country where the reception of broadcast television was poor and limited. Early cable TV was largely devoted to educational programs and local sports, but in the 1980s satellite technology moved up a step with extremely large satellite disks—these were about the size of a Volkswagen Beetle. It was only in the 1990s that cable television blossomed and satellite television was revolutionized by the development of the small dish-like receivers. With this technological development, sexual material became readily available to tens of millions of Americans.

Via cable or satellite television, music videos, comedy programs, movies, dramatic series, and talk shows have made sex routinely available on television. For viewers who are willing to pay additional fees, more sexually oriented channels are also available (The Playboy channel, for example).

### SEX AND THE CITY AND BEYOND

Perhaps no television show on cable/satellite television has been as sexually titillating as the HBO sitcom *Sex and the City*. This show had millions of avid viewers, and although the series has ended it has continued to be popular in syndication.[15] In addition to enormous fan support, the show received critical acclaim, and won numerous awards from the television industry.

*Sex and the City* featured four thirty-something unmarried women who live independent, and semi-glamorous lives in New York City. They were nearly always dressed in knockout clothes (unless they were supposed to be in a grungy mood) and because of the well-written scripts their conversations were studded with zingers, sophisticated observations, and one-liners (usually about men or sex). Carrie (Sarah Jessica Parker) was the commentator and the questioning observer of every episode, this because she played the role of a newspaper columnist who wrote about relationships and sex. Samantha (Kim Cattrall) was the most persistently devoted to sex, including, if the situation arose, sex with another woman. Miranda (Cynthia Nixon) was the lawyer trying to make partner (thus intelligent), but she was also a down-to-earth and practical woman. Charlotte (Kristin Davis) was the most naive and prudish of the group, which often made her the butt of others' jokes.

Despite the name of the series, *Sex and the City* was far from hard-core pornography, though it did occasionally range into soft-core. Much of the show was devoted to talk, or sexual discourse, rather than action, and the action, when it was shown, was often filmed with a blurred focus, or showed from behind the actors. Another concession to modesty was that the women were often seen in bed wearing negligees, slips, or, highly unrealistically, bras and panties. Even the male actors sometimes left the bed wearing their shorts.

Despite these conventional television modesties, *Sex and the City* offered enough sex to live up to its name—especially in words, but also in nudity and some action. In one of the early episodes of the series, Samantha was shown riding on top of her partner, while encouraging him by saying: "Fuck me, fuck me you hot stud." It was also Samantha who ultimately met her greatest sexual challenge when she picked up a partner who had an extremely large penis. Even though she first thought this was her sexual ideal, she finally backed off. Her ultimate line was "Can we just be friends?"

All of the other main characters had their time in bed, or wherever: Carrie had most of her on-screen sex with her true love, simply called "Big" (again for how well endowed he was, not for his height or weight). But she also had other romances, especially with the reluctant hunk named Adam whom she tried valiantly to seduce. Miranda, who eventually hooked up with her steady guy Steve, in one episode learned that she had the sexually transmitted disease Chlamydia. She therefore had to call and inform all of her previous sexual partners. To her surprise the number of former lovers came to forty-two.

Even the upright and uptight Charlotte had her occasional bed time in the series. In one episode Charlotte revealed to her friends that her boyfriend, during his orgasm, says repeatedly, "You fucking whore," "You fucking bitch." She was shocked, but her friends were blasé' about this revelation, apparently considering it a normal part of some male orgasms.

*Sex and the City* did not shy away from the f-word or almost any other kind of scatology/profanity. In one otherwise innocuous and brief sub-plot, Miranda and her boyfriend Steve bicker about his practicing to shoot a basketball (he was preparing for a midcourse shot during halftime at a New York Knicks' game). In the three or four minutes of screen time devoted to this issue the two of them used the word "fucking," or some variation thereof, no less than nine times.

On the subject of the language used on *Sex and the City*, in one episode Samantha has an affair with a handsome African-American celebrity. In the after-sex conversation with her friends, several references were made to "big black cock." This potentially racist, or at least politically incorrect, dialogue was racially balanced by three references to Samantha's "white pussy." Just to provide further balance by gender, Samantha at one point in this show referred to the "black ass" of her boyfriend's sister. This episode of *Sex and the City* illustrates how the show's producers were not afraid to challenge cultural taboos about sex and, in this case, racial stereotypes.

## THE SOPRANOS

A second extremely successful cable/satellite television show (ratings, critical praise, and awards) was HBO's *The Sopranos*, which ended its final season in 2007. Sex was not the primary raison dêtre, of this show. It was primarily focused on the criminal and family life of Tony Soprano (James Gadolfini). Given Tony's criminal and social environment, which includes a strip club that served as a backdrop for many scenes, it is not surprising that nudity, obscenities/profanities, and violence were commonplace. The f-word was used incessantly, but so also were many other previously forbidden words (e.g., "an ignorant cunt," or "you prick").

Sexual action occurred only on some episodes of *The Sopranos*, but when it did it clearly reached into the soft-core genre. Tony had more than one mistress during the course of the series and the sex scenes were often heated and explicit. On one occasion Tony's Russian mistress tried unsuccessfully to give him oral sex, but he couldn't get an erection because of the Prozac he had taken (Chunovic 2000).

One television observer has characterized both the violence and the sex on *The Sopranos* as "quick, brutish, and authentic" (Chunovic 2000, 158). On occasion, sex on *The Sopranos* was more playful. In one episode Tony brought a nurse (actually a stripper from his club) to care for a sick friend in the hospital. The "girl in the too-tight nurse's uniform" does a little bump and grind and shrugs out of her nurse's costume. Topless, nipples erect, wearing only a thong, she licks the sick man's neck. "Time for your sponge bath," she says (Chunovic 2000, 159). A similar scene occurred on a show when one of Tony's friends was released from prison. Tony generously provided a couple of his strippers who gave the ex-con an erotic dual welcome.

Beyond the popular *Sex and the City* and *The Sopranos* (both now in reruns) cable/satellite television has offered and continues to present many other programs and films featuring sex. HBO has offered *Real Sex*, a journalistic/sociological documentary about sex in all its variations, augmented by on-the-street interviews asking probing questions such as,

"What is your favorite intercourse position?" or "Which type of oral sex do the two of you like best?" The Cinema movie channel has a late-evening show called *The Best Sex Ever*, which builds episodes around fictional call-ins to a radio show hostess. The caller narrates a best-ever sexual experience, which the actors then dramatize. The sexual action involves female nudity, some full frontal, and soft-core sexual acts. Comedy Central has had *The Man Show*, which featured locker-room/ fraternity-house humor about women and sex (plus vulgar scatological material). *South Park*, the adult cartoon features small-children characters saying extremely adult things.[16]

In 2007, comedian Bob Saget, did an hour-long comedy routine on HBO that was universally judged to be one of the crudest and most sex-laden shows ever seen on television (Shales 2007).[17] In addition to the incessant use of the f-word, Saget joked about lusting after the young girl-friends of his daughters, voyeurism, and other sexual topics. Saget also had one of the crudest contributions to the video *The Aristocrats*. This is a video version of a long-standing inside joke among comedians, in which each tells the filthiest version of the joke he or she can come up with (comedians George Carlin, Sarah Silverman, Jason Alexander, Whoopi Goldberg, Jon Stewart and many, many others contributed bits to this video).

The list of television shows that present (or have presented) sexual material is extensive, but some of the best known include Fox's *The X Show*, MTV's *Real World*, *The Blame Game*, and *Road Rules*, and USA's *Strip Poker*. While some of these sexually oriented shows have come and gone (at least into syndication, e.g., *Personals* and *Studs*), they continue to be followed by similar or even more-daringly sexual shows.

On any given day, cable/satellite television provides a menu of sexual programs and videos that may be purchased on the premier channels (for ten to fifteen dollars). A few examples of the available titles provide sufficient information to reveal the sexual topics than can be seen on cable/satellite television for anyone willing to pay the nominal cost: *Naughty Amateur Home Videos*, *Playboy's Sexy Girls Next Door*, *Lovers Spell: Sensual Magic*, *Naughty Young Latin Lovers*, *Young Ripe Mellons: Real and Perky*, *The Lesbo Condo*, *Men Not Required*, *Asian Sex Academy*, *Sex in the Desert*, and *Sex Forever*.

Radio and television were two of the major technological communication creations of the twentieth century. As such they both had the promise of bringing sexual materials and pornography to the American public, just as many other earlier technological advances had done. But contrary to our argument in Chapter 2 that technological advances are quick to bring sexual materials and pornography to the population, both radio and television were slow to fulfill that prediction.

Because radio is provided to the public on governmentally controlled airwaves, and because it goes without cost into every home that has a radio, it has always been subject to threats of government censorship. Many broadcast radio stations have challenged governmental controls, especially those with shock jocks and popular music lyrics, but radio continues to be somewhat timid about sexual material.

However, more recent technological advances are likely to break through the limitations of the government on radio broadcasting. Satellite radio is making its entry into broadcasting and since it is beyond the bounds of the government-controlled airwaves, and subscribers have to pay for the privilege of hearing it, the threat of governmental censorship is nearly impossible. If satellite radio proves to be a successful economic enterprise, there will be no limits on the sexual content of radio.

Television had a similar slow start in the introduction of sexual material. Broadcast television only gradually challenged the sexual standards of the network censors, but since the breakthroughs of the 1970s, television programs have continued to test the limits of acceptability. As with radio, the FCC continues to be a threat to television programmers. However, even with the monetary penalties hanging over broadcast television, daytime television, both soap operas and talk shows, prime time sitcoms, and especially late-night entertainment and movies continue to contest the older sexual standards. Most importantly, the technological introduction of cable and satellite television has made the censorship of sexual material almost impossible.

Despite continuing attempts by the government and special interest groups to limit sexual material on radio and television, both mediums are making major contributions to the hypersexuality of American society.

## CHAPTER 9

# SEX ON THE INTERNET
## UNLIMITED AND UNCONTROLLED

In November 2000, a San Jose, California, judge ruled that Stephen Cohen of Tijuana, Mexico should pay 65 million dollars in damages for stealing something from Gary Kremen of San Francisco, California. The stolen object was obviously something of great value, but what? An ocean-going yacht? A Boeing 707? A shopping mall? A stock market portfolio? In fact, it was only six letters, divided in half by a dot: sex.com.

In the early 1990s, Kremen cleverly anticipated that certain Web site domain names would someday be valuable (O'Brien 2004). In addition to sex.com, he also registered jobs.com, housing.com and other potentially lucrative domain names. Even though Kremen had the foresight to register sex.com, he did nothing with it. In the mid-1990s, Stephen Cohen forged a document that gave him ownership of sex.com, which he used to create a pornography Web site from which he earned millions of dollars. When Kremen learned of it he filed suit and after a three-year court battle the Web site was returned to Kremen and he was awarded the 65 million dollars—40 million dollars in actual damages and 25 million dollars in punitive damages.[1]

In the years before Kremen regained control of sex.com, Cohen earned five hundred thousand dollars a month by selling banner ads for actual online pornography sites. Kremen proved to be a less successful manager of sex.com than Cohen, however, firing employees and attorneys right and left, filing various lawsuits, and generally neglecting the business because of his drug use. At the same time, competition in the Internet porn business was also increasing. Even so, in 2003, sex.com still provided Kremen with a monthly revenue of three hundred thousand dollars, largely drawn from advertisers for other porn sites (twenty-three hundred of them) and sixty linked search engines from around the world.[2]

The details of Gary Kremen's battle to regain control of the sex.com domain name reveal just how lucrative pornography is on the Internet. Even though the management skills of Kremen left much to be desired, this Web site is apparently still able to bring in more than 3.5 million dollars a year.

## Computer Technology and Pornography

Computer technology came to American society around the middle of the twentieth century. During the first few decades of computers (all of which were what we now call "mainframe" computers) they were primarily used by the military, universities, and business/industry. Personal computers were not widely available until the late 1970s, and it was another decade before the Internet came on the scene. No one can doubt that the Internet opened the way for the abundance of sexual material and pornography in American society.

As we have seen before, new communication technologies generally result in the availability of sexual materials (including erotica and pornography) to larger and larger audiences. The availability of sexual materials is further enhanced when large numbers of people have the political freedom and economic wherewithal to take advantage of the new technology.

By the 1990s, millions of Americans became able, with the click of a mouse, to gain access to all types of sexual materials on their home computers. Pornography Web sites quickly became the most frequently visited and most profitable sites, and they continue to be so today.

With regard to political democratization/personal liberty, the nature of the Internet has made it nearly impossible for the government to limit sexual materials or pornography, no matter how extreme (the one major exception is pornography that involves children or adolescents under the age of eighteen). Any American who owns a personal computer and has access to the Internet can read and view sexual and pornographic materials, as long as these materials are not prohibited by child pornography laws.

Economic development and personal affluence have also played an important role in the increasing capacity of computer technology to bring sexual material and pornography to Americans. In the earliest years of personal computers (the 1970s and 1980s), only a limited number of Americans could afford this new technology, but computers quickly became less expensive and thus more broadly available throughout the population. As they were decreasing in price, computers were also becoming more powerful. Today, the majority of Americans own computers, and most users can also afford access to the Internet. Another technological development that has given even more access to the Internet is the cell phone. With the Apple iPhone and its counterparts, Americans can check the Internet wherever and whenever they want.

## SEXUAL MATERIAL AND PORNOGRAPHY ON THE INTERNET

Sex and pornography on the Internet are too abundant and rapidly changing to be described completely. At best, the abundance of online sexual materials can only be presented in a snapshot fashion. Following are some working categories to illustrate the amount and variety of sexual material and pornography on the Internet:

1. Standard pornography Web sites (including Web sites catering to special sexual tastes);
2. Nudity and sex aimed at attracting viewers (even when a product or service is not primarily sexual);
3. Sexual information, sex education, and sexual products;
4. Interpersonal communications about sex (chat rooms and emails).
5. Blogs, YouTube, MySpace, Facebook, and other personal Web sites.

## STANDARD PORNOGRAPHY WEB SITES

Pornography Web sites have become fairly standardized on the Internet. Even a novice can quickly learn to navigate the vast array of pornographic sites. A step-by-step search for pornography on the Internet might include the following:

Finding Pornography Web sites. The first step in a search for pornography is to select any one of the available Internet search engines (Google, Yahoo, etc). Next, enter any sexual or sexually suggestive word or phrase (sex, pornography, voyeurism, kinky sex, or any one of many vulgar sexual terms). This step will yield dozens (often hundreds) of pornography Web sites.

Not only is it easy to find pornography Web sites—it is nearly impossible to avoid them. Suppose, for example, one wants to get statistical data on teenage sexual activity, based on the most recent social-scientific research. No matter which key words one enters (teenage sex, adolescent sexual activity, etc.), the few relevant informational Web sites are overwhelmed by pornographic sites ("barely-legal teen sex pics," "teen erotica club," etc.). Paid advertisements also frequently appear on the side of the screen, offering pornographic sites featuring young models. While it is easy enough to ignore the individual sites, it is impossible to ignore the ubiquity of sex on the Internet.

*A Typical Pornographic Web Site.* An overwhelming percentage of pornographic Web sites are aimed at heterosexual males.[3] Typical pornographic sites feature one or more images of naked or nearly naked women, often engaged in sexual acts. Each site includes a generous supply of "fine print," usually boilerplate material declaring that "adult material" is to be found on the site and asking visitors to affirm that they are eighteen years or older before entering.

A particularly cautious Web site (http://www.blondflasher.com) begins with the usual required affirmation, "I swear/affirm that as of this moment, I am a legal adult, at least 18 YEARS OF AGE and able view sexually explicate [*sic*] material according to my local laws," followed by a much more elaborate statement about who is not authorized to download the material from the site, including those who are, "under the age of eighteen years, are offended by such materials, offended by any of the following words." The list of words that follows includes every conceivable word or phrase that is even remotely associated with sex. These range from predictable entries such as, bisexual, dildo, Lolita, threesomes, and many others, to more perplexing entries (Acapulco, basketball, conferencing, hockey, passwords, sports cars, and water). The apparent purpose of the extensive list is to provide a "fair warning" about the content of the site to minors or to anyone who might object to the information and images that it provides. Most pornographic sites do not go to such extremes, however, offering only *pro forma* warnings and disclaimers, usually in ultra-small print.

After these perfunctory warnings and disclaimers, the visitor is next invited either to "Exit" or "Enter" the site. Upon entering a pornographic Web site, the visitor is typically presented with a number of options. Visitors who have already paid a membership fee may go directly to the category "Members." Others can generally choose from various categories, such as "Free Photos," "Preview," or "Join." If the viewer chooses to preview the site, he[4] will usually get a sampling of the photographs of the featured person or performers. These sample photographs provide ample nudity, though sometimes the models' pubic areas and nipples are demurely covered with starbursts or pixels. More often, the preview photographs present a variety of sexual images, sometimes including hardcore sex, in which couples are engaged in sexual intercourse, fellatio, and sometimes cunnilingus. Hardcore sex may also include "kinky," "bizarre," and "exotic" sex, including anal intercourse, sadomasochism, bondage, "fisting," "water sports," "sex toys," and "bestiality."

Many pornography Web sites also offer video clips of sexual displays and sexual activity as an introductory enticement. These clips usually last for less than a minute and provide only a sample of what will be seen after paying the membership fee. As a result of these video "teasers," vast amounts of pornographic material can be viewed on the Internet today without paying membership fees, providing credit card numbers, or giving any other identifying information—a fact that any computer-savvy teenager, for example, will quickly recognize.

A visit to a Web site (pornographic or otherwise) almost always provides "links" to other related sites—with one porno site leading to the next, which leads to the next, and so on. Many pornographic sites have a selection category called "Friends," a code word for links to sites with similar sexual material (not a reference to the television sitcom).

Other links feature blinking, flashing, or other attention-getting Internet ads, designed to entice the viewer to enter a new site. Such ads frequently provide "Indexes" (or listings) of available pornographic sites around a given theme. Following is a brief excerpt from one such index, which purports to feature "amateurs," a term frequently used to suggest that the women depicted are not professional exotic dancers, pornography models, or pornography video actresses.[5]

| | |
|---|---|
| **** | Ginny Blond, bi-sexual "girl next door": shares her secrets. SMOKIN! |
| ** | Kathy Sexy ass brunette with a body that can kill most men! She's a SEX MACHINE |
| ** | Nicki Sexy Asian/American radiologist gets naked on the Web just for her boyfriend |
| **** | Sierra Hot young tattooed trailer-park chick! Loves to suck and fuck |
| *** | Page Sexy 24-year-old secretary with nice buns! Nice KOOCHIE and nice TITS! |

This index, which is only one of the many such indexes to be found on the Internet, lists at least three hundred Web sites, each with additional links to other similar sites.

Pornographic sites often display a list of the types of sex they have to offer. Following are only a few of the hard core and crudely explicit (also relentlessly sexist) labels provided by one such site (http://www.cum .freepornhoster.com/index2.html):

Asian slut     Asian girls

| | |
|---|---|
| Panty soak | Cum filled panties |
| Transsexual | Fat and aged women |
| Foxy ebony babes | Hardcore gay sex |
| Chicks with cocks | Shemale whores |
| Fat huge older girls | Boobs & ass |
| Big tits and booty | Male & male sex acts |

The list goes on and on, often redundantly so, but is aimed at attracting every conceivable sexual interest.

## NARRATIVE PORNOGRAPHY WEB SITES

A number of pornographic sites today use narrative story lines to present sexual photos and videos. One classic narrative, called the casting couch, had its origins in the movie industry (see Chapter 7). The casting couch scenario is built around an aspiring actress who meets with a movie executive who may want to cast her in a movie. Inevitably, the movie mogul asks to see the young woman without her clothes and then asks her to "audition" on the "couch" in his office. This often-told Hollywood story has now been transformed into an Internet porno genre. A current example (www.tonyscastingcouch.com) promises "160 girls" who have had sex with Tony as a part of their interviews with him.

Among the earliest and apparently most successful (judged both by their continuing presence on the Internet and the number of imitators) of the narrative pornography sites are www.mikesapartment.com and www.bangbus.com.

Mike's apartment is ostensibly an apartment in Amsterdam. According to the plot line, an "apartment for rent" ad has been placed in the newspaper. When interested young women arrive, they are greeted at the door by an unseen male and an already running video camera. The invariably young and reasonably attractive female respondents have most likely been recruited from escort services, strip clubs, or are aspiring models or actresses.

In a typical scenario, a young woman arrives at the apartment innocently inquiring about the ad. After having been shown around and finding the apartment acceptable, she is told that the rent is free if she agrees to engage in sexual acts. The woman always agrees to the terms offered, sometimes hesitantly, whereupon she is filmed while undressing and having sex with one of the men in the apartment—usually sexual intercourse, fellatio, or both. Or the young woman may simply masturbate for the camera. The viewer is expected to suspend rational judgment and accept the idea that almost any young woman looking for an apartment would readily agree to be filmed having sex, in exchange for free rent.[6]

Another early entry among the narrative porno sites is www.bangbus .com. In the story line, a couple of guys cruise the streets of a city (perhaps Miami) in a van or minibus looking for girls. They find young women on the streets (walking or waiting for a bus), in shopping malls, or in other public places. The women are enticed to enter the "bus," usually by offers of money, and asked if they are willing to be videotaped. Once on board the women soon take off their clothes and proceed to have sex (usually sexual intercourse and fellatio) with one or more of the males. All the live action is videotaped for the site.

This site is blatantly misogynistic. The women are called "stupid," "sluts," "whores," and other sexist labels. After being filmed, the woman is sometimes dumped out of the bus without receiving the money she has been promised—adding to both the alleged reality of the narrative and the exploitative nature of the vignette.

The success of the bangbus is confirmed by the site's numerous imitators and spin-offs, including www.thenastybus.com, in which a converted yellow school bus provides the place of the sexual action, and www.bangboat.com, in which everything occurs on a semi-luxury boat.

An even-cruder addition to the narrative pornography genre is www.gangbangsquad.com. The site's photographs and videos feature a young woman engaged in sexual acts with four men simultaneously. "How much would it cost," asks the site's tagline, "to get your average slut off the street to gangbang four dudes? Every week we answer that burning question and show you the hard-core video action." In the site's images and videos, the woman may be giving oral sex to one man, giving a hand job to another, and at the same time being penetrated both vaginally and anally by two other men. Currently, this Web site offers its members episodes with more than eighty different young women, each having sex with four men, with new photos and videos added each week.

While no one has investigated the validity of the claims made by the narrative pornography sites, the photographs and videos appear to be staged and feature young women who have almost certainly agreed in advance to engage in various sexual acts. And they are probably paid for doing so. These sites are designed to excite the fantasies of men who view women as sexual commodities.

## PERSONALIZED PORNOGRAPHY WEB SITES

Many women, and some couples, have created sexual and pornographic Web sites as a way of establishing personal recognition. At the mild end of the spectrum are women who set up video cameras in their homes or apartments, through which they provide Internet viewers with 24/7 videos of their everyday activities. The earliest versions of these were most likely to show partially or completely undressed young women and, sometimes, though rarely, sexual activity. Since the early sites were free, the primary motive was to draw attention to oneself, and not financial profit.

Today, however, almost all sites of this type have some financial aspect. www.cutewebcamgirl.com, for example, features a young woman named Tina, who claims to be living with her parents in Miami and assures the viewer: "Me, my sister and all members/users on this site are 18+ years of age." Tina is shown in a number of photographs wearing jeans or cut-offs, a skimpy halter top, tank top, or bra. She accentuates her cuteness and innocence by wearing her hair in long pigtails.

"I'm single," says the site invitingly, "and I'd love to show you my tight body . . . My webcam is almost always on, even if I'm not there, you may find my sister online." Tina offers to chat with subscribers, introduce them to "lots of cute girls," and help them re-create their sexual fantasies, no matter how explicit (http://www.cutewebcamgirl.com). It is not uncommon for young women who establish these sites to receive gifts or cash from their admirers. *Elle* magazine recently called attention to a Web site with the name "Myfreeimplants.com." This site features women who want to have breast implants. Men who are interested in this project may send the woman an e-mail for $1.20 per message. One dollar goes to the woman the other twenty cents goes to the Web site (Carlson 2007).

Other personal sites focus much more directly on explicit sex. www.audreylive.com, for example, features a young woman who claims to be nineteen, but who presents herself in clothes, haircuts, and glasses that make her look more like sixteen. The site provides subscribers with a streaming video cam with "live shows," "cock sucking," "kinky toys," and "hardcore vids," as well as opportunities for lives chats and responses to specific requests from subscribers.

Several other personal Web sites have attained a more professional status, in that the participants are well-known in the pornography world. (Among the most venerable of these are Jen 'n Dave and cum2oasis).

Jen and Dave are two very ordinary-looking people who have made a career of posting nude and sexual photographs of themselves online. While they are now married, early in the early years of the Web site they were not. While Jen, who serves as the site's primary attraction, would hardly be described as attractive or shapely, she has nonetheless posed for hundreds, if not thousands of sexual photographs. Her photographs

SEX ON THE INTERNET

include partial or full nudity, masturbation (by hand or with vibrators and dildos), exhibitionism in public places, sex with other women (many of whom also have pornography sites), and heterosexual sex (oral, anal, vaginal), both with her husband Dave and other partners.

To personalize their site, Jen and Dave describe their personal histories, their marriage, and their everyday activities. They report on the pornography conferences they attend, the parties they sponsor, and their trips to Mardi Gras and various vacation spas. They also provide site visitors with their itinerary for upcoming months, inviting fans to see them in person.

Another successful personal Web site, www.cum2oasis.com, features Oasis, who promotes herself as "a complete slut." She sponsors and appears at events where she takes off her clothes, gives fellatio, and has sex with men she has only just met. To increase her appeal, Oasis describes her transition from a shy, conventional young woman to "a complete slut" who proudly keeps a running account of the number of men with whom she has had sex and the number of blowjobs she has given. Paraphrasing the familiar McDonalds advertising mantra ("more than 1 billion served"), Oasis claims to have "fucked" over 190 and "sucked" over 400.

Jen and Dave and Oasis are among the most successful personalized porno sites on the Internet, but many others have followed their lead. An interesting feature of Internet porn sites—and one that defies conventional business principles—is the willingness of site owners to provide users with links to competitive sites. It's hard to imagine McDonald's announcing to its customers, "If you don't find what you want here, let us provide the addresses of the nearest Wendy's, Burger King, or Taco Bell."

## NAKED CELEBRITIES ON THE INTERNET

Americans are endlessly fascinated by the private lives of celebrities, as confirmed by the continuing popularity of *People Magazine*, *Us*, and their imitators. The Internet has brought a new dimension to celebrity watching—viewing photographs and videos of celebrities in the nude or engaged in sexual activities.[7] Some of these photographs or video images were taken deliberately, as part of a commercial film or photo shoot. Others were taken in private and then leaked to the media by former lovers or associates, either out of vindictiveness or greed. Others are the result of youthful indiscretion, before the celebrity achieved fame (as an example, nude photographs of a young Dr. Laura Schlesinger, the conservative advice giver, can be found on the Internet).

Today, anyone who has a computer and access to the Internet can easily see Pamela Anderson and Tommy Lee having sex on their boat. Or, see the ice skater Tonya Harding having sex on her wedding night. Or, watch publicity-hungry Paris Hilton having sex with her ex-boyfriend Rick Salomon. These are but a few, and the most famous, of the many people who have let their sex video tapes slip into the public realm on the Internet.

Many celebrity photographs were snapped surreptitiously by paparazzi, using zoom lenses and other techniques. In almost all cases, the celebrities had no idea they were being photographed in private settings: swimming, sunbathing, interacting with lovers, etc. Famous nude celebrity photographs have been taken of Jackie Kennedy Onassis (displayed in *Hustler Magazine*), Princess Diana, Sarah Fergeson, and a number of Hollywood stars. A prominent example of a site specializing in celebrity photos in the nude or partially naked is www.celebs31.home.ro/chantelle_michell.

## SPECIAL SEXUAL INTERESTS ON THE INTERNET

The Internet is an especially prolific source of information for individuals who want to explore or engage in special sexual interests. These include sites that describe and illustrate unusual and on occasion illegal sexual practices.

For example, a number of Internet sites are devoted to the world of "swingers." This term originated in the 1970s and generally referred to sexually liberated couples interested in having sexual experiences with outsiders: other couples, other women, or, in some cases, other men.

One index site, http://www.swingers100.com, offers the "Top 100 Web sites for Swingers," including short descriptions of sites that promise to put visitors in touch with like-minded people. The following three examples are purported to be among the "top 5 sites." They are: The Swingers Board (with "thousands of ads, java chat, swinger stories, advice & more"); SwingWorld.Net (with "free ads for singers, gays and lesbians, erotic stories, and much more"); and SwingerAds.com (more than fifty thousand free ads with pictures").

### SEXUAL FETISH WEB SITES

"Everything is fetish fodder," claims George Gurley, who has explored the realm of unusual sexual tastes. He goes on to say, "I can't think of anything in this world that couldn't be sexualized by somebody" (Gurley 2001, 186). The book *Deviant Desires: Incredibly Strange Sex*, Katherine Gates (2000) makes much the same point.

A person with an unusual sexual fetish who lives in a small or moderate-sized community will probably find it difficult to connect with someone who has the same sexual obsession. But on the Internet it is easy to find Web sites that cater to any sexual fetish, no matter how fantastic or grotesque. Even pornography stores, which sell all manner of sexual magazines, videos, books, and paraphernalia, may not cater to the most bizarre sexual tastes. The Internet allows a person with a special sexual fetish to search through thousands of available sites to locate the fetish of choice. Internet users can also make contact with other users who might want to chat about their unusual sexual interests. A selective look at just a few sexual fetish sites on the Internet will illustrate the point.

*Adults Who Want to Be Babies.* The Internet magazine *Salon.com*, published an article titled, "Fetish Nation" (http://www.salon.com/feature/1998/07cov_02feature3.html), describing how Carol Lloyd visited two devotees of this most unusual fetish: *adults who want to be babies.* This unusual fetish is well documented among the clientele of sex workers who specialize in female dominance (McClintock 1993). In England, individuals who want to behave like babies are called "babyists."

Lloyd interviewed "Baby Tommy" and his partner "Marky," both middle-aged men who live north of San Francisco on Mt. Tamalpais. Two decades ago, Baby Tommy started an organization called "Diaper-Pail Friends," which today has its own Web site (http://www.dpf.com) and thirteen thousand members. Adult men who are interested in this fetish (apparently this is a nearly exclusive male fetish) get pleasure from wearing diapers, being treated like babies, and even practicing incontinence. "They host parties all over the nation, which allow [them] to make friends, wet their pants, and change each other's diapers" (http://www.salon.com/feature/1998/07cov_02feature3.html).

The Diaper Pail Friends' Web site offers links to other pages that visitors may also want to explore, but the first page provides an "Overview and Introduction" of the "diaper pail" organization. Another page invites visitors to "Make Friends," while other pages provide information on conferences, chat rooms, parties, clubs, and "Our Store." The "Store" peddles diapers, pants, clothing, videos, audios, and stories (http://www.dpf.com).

Adults-who-want-to-be-babies (abbreviated as "Abies" by the in-group) have already moved beyond the Internet world and into the arena of popular American culture through the Jerry Springer show. For this television appearance Baby Tommy did his best to enlist females who would appear on the show, but lamented the difficulty of finding "sane female Abies" (http://www.salon.com).

*Furries and Plushies.* Another fetish group involves "furries" or (less commonly) "plushies" (Gurley 2001), self-designated labels for people (very often but not always gay males) who are sexually turned on by possessing, seeing, and being dressed as furry stuffed animals. "Furries" and "plushies" have their own special organizations with conferences, Internet chat rooms, and sites that offer products for their special needs.

At their conferences, the attendees often dress up in furry animal costumes and may also engage in sexual activities with other conferees.[8] Some individuals may also engage in sexual relations with life-size, stuffed furry animals (Gurley 2001). These large stuffed animals can easily be purchased on the Internet. "This webpage," announces one popular site, "is for anyone into collecting, cuddling, or intimacy with plushies (stuffed animals)" (www.fangwolf.com). Another site offers stuffed animals with oversized male erections (www.ercollection.com). The stuffed animals, which have been given humorous, sexually suggestive names ("Randy" the raccoon, "Slowpoke" the turtle, "Bendover" the Rover dog), are pictured on the site.

*Smoking Women.* Another sexual fantasy involves women who smoke. On one Web site, women smokers are effusively described as "Women Who Swallow Thick, Creamy, Billows of White Smoke." The site's preview photographs feature naked women smoking cigars and cigarettes, often blowing out plumes of smoke. Paying members are promised "1,000s of Smoking Pics," "Live Smoking with Chat," and "Hours of Erotic Videos" (www.sexysmokers.com).

The sexual appeal of women smoking dates back to the nineteenth century, but became especially prominent in the early years of the twentieth century when cigarettes became popular and were a symbol of daring and liberated women. A collection of vintage photographs of naked or nearly naked smoking women has been published under the title, "*Feu D'amour: Seductive Smoke* (Taschen 1994).

*Pregnant and Lactating Women.* When film star Demi Moore appeared naked and immensely pregnant on the cover of *Vanity Fair* in September 1991, her photograph captured the attention of the American media and the public, reinforcing the cliché: "A woman is never more beautiful than when she is pregnant." The magazine's sophisticated editors were surely aware that, for a small but select audience, the Moore photograph would have more than just shock value; it would also have sexual appeal. Judging by the abundance of pregnancy fetish sites on the Internet, pregnant women with enlarged breasts are indeed sexually stimulating for many men. Just two of many sites of this genre are www.pregnantbang.com and www.preggoplayground.com. Preggo" and "Preggy" are the code words for Web sites that feature photos and videos of women who are usually enormously pregnant. These pornographic sites show pregnant women completely naked with legs spread and, in some cases, having sexual or anal intercourse.

The Internet also provides sites like www.massivemilkers.com and www.hotterxxx.com/sexylactating, where lactating women are shown squirting milk out of their usually enlarged breasts. Sometimes the squirting is done for the benefit of the camera; other times the milk is squirted in a cup or glass; and sometimes it is squirted in the face or mouth of another person (males and females). A surprising number of sites show photos of women using breast pumps, a device usually employed by new mothers when they want to save breast milk for their babies.

## A Note on the Sexism of Sexual Fantasies and Fetishes on the Internet

The Internet is a technology that provides millions of men (and some women) with access to pictures and words that feed their sexual fantasies and fetishes. At no other time in history have such a large number of people been able to experience or simply explore the extremes of sexual fantasy. Today, individuals with almost any imaginable sexual taste or obsession can indulge their interests on the Internet

Following the example of the Marquis de Sade, sexual fetishes have frequently involved the humiliation and degradation of women. That is certainly true of many Internet pornography sites. However, Internet sites that feature kinky and bizarre sex do not always and only degrade women; many simply appeal to men's sexual fantasies about various features and behaviors of women (smoking, high heels, pregnancy and lactation). Other fetishes—such as furry stuffed animals or "babyism"—have little or nothing to do with women.

## Attention-Getting Nudity and Sex on the Internet

The makers of automobile parts (and virtually every other consumer product) have known for decades that nudity and sex sell products, even products that are completely unrelated to sex (Reichert 2003). Most American males know that the back rooms of service stations and car repair shops very often feature calendars and posters of scantily clad or nude women. They are there advertising auto parts or other services related to cars. Whether or not sex and nudity sells auto parts, such pictures do catch the attention of males who frequent these places of business. And so it is with the Internet. If someone has a product to sell, or simply wants to draw attention to a product, nudity (almost exclusively female nudity) is an effective tool—both on and off the Internet. Regarding the Internet, a few examples will illustrate the point.

*The Naked Novelist.* Aspiring British novelist, Carol Muskoron decided to use sex as a way of promoting her literary ambitions (Weeks 2001b). Muskoron saw a television feature about female strippers who were advancing their careers by appearing on Internet sites. This inspired her to ask: Why not create a personal Web site called The Naked Novelist (www.nakednovelist.com)? Muskoron's Web site follows in the footsteps of many other webcam sites, with a video camera recording her every activity, but on this site, the emphasis is on her writing. It would, no doubt, be exceptionally boring to watch a writer sitting at the keyboard for endless hours, but in this case Muskoron composes in the nude, or nearly so. "It's a literary site," she explains, "The whole idea is stripping literature down to its bare essentials" (Weeks 2001b, C3). Despite the belabored double entendre, Muskoron insists that hers is "not a porn site."

*News in the Nude.* Female nudity on U.S. broadcast television lags behind a number of European countries, where it is commonplace. In Europe, even routine television news broadcasts sometimes feature naked women. A Russian news program called *The Naked Truth*, which can be seen on the Internet, features an attractive young female newswoman who delivers the news of the day while taking off her clothes, item by item, until she is nude. Even when the news is uninteresting, male viewers are likely to stay tuned for the final items (of news and clothing).

Naked women can also be seen presenting the latest stock quotations on http://www.marketwrapunwrapped.com. The site, originating in Australia, features young women who present the day's market news while naked. A spokesman for this site promises, "not only do you get your stock reports for less than the cost of a daily newspaper, but it gets read to you by 'absolutely gorgeous' newsreaders with nothing on" (http://cooltech.iafrica.com).

Naked novelists, newscasters, and stock market reporters, as well as other women actively engaged, are now routinely found on the Internet. It is only a matter of time until other enterprising businesses and activities introduce their own nude attractions (e.g., nude artists, nude sculptors, nude chefs, nude real estate agents, nude physical fitness trainers, etc.). The Internet is ideal for exploiting the attention-getting potential of the nude body, since it offers a way of marketing and advertising sexual images that cannot be easily controlled or censored.

## SEXUAL INFORMATION, EDUCATION, AND
## SEX PRODUCTS ON THE INTERNET

The field of sex therapy as we saw in Chapter 6 has been quick to take advantage of opportunities provided by the Internet. It is nearly impossible today to avoid the intrusion of SPAM e-mails, advertisements, and pop-ups that insist on enhancing one's sex life. Among the most ubiquitous are the offers for penis and breast enlargement, along with a variety of other sexual aids and devices.

But the Internet also offers the Web sites of organizations that are devoted to providing sexual information and education. One of the most venerable of these organizations is the Sex Information and Education Council of the United States (commonly known as SIECUS). While this organization predates the Internet by many decades, its Web site (http://www.siecus.com) offers information on subjects ranging from sex education to sexual pleasure.

SIECUS has always been committed to promoting sexuality education, advocating for sexual and reproductive rights, and fighting against sexual misinformation, sex censorship and discrimination associated with gender, age, or sexual orientation (http://siecus.org/policy/index.html). While SIECUS was the target of many attacks by conservative critics during the middle years of the twentieth century, today it is more aptly called a moderate voice in the cacophony of sexual discourse in American society.

The Society for Human Sexuality (http://www. sexuality.org) is also devoted to sexual education and information, but with a more distinct emphasis on the enjoyment of sex. This Seattle-based organization describes itself as "a social and educational organization whose purpose [it] is to promote understanding and appreciation for the many forms of adult intimate relationships and consensual sexual expression." The Society describes itself on the Internet as expanding sexual expression and experience. It does so by sponsoring a wide variety of activities related to sex, including workshops on erotic dance and erotic talk, as well as a seminar on how to host erotic events. This organization does not appear to have a significant profit motive, which is unusual, because many individuals and organizations on the Internet do want to sell their products even while they provide sexual education and information.

Betty Dodson's www.bettydodson.com, for example, offers females information about sex and sexual products designed primarily for them.[9] Dodson has had a successful career advocating and promoting masturbation for women, though she has recently expanded her attention to the masturbation of couples. On her Web site, Dodson explains that she "is devoted to liberating masturbation, erotic sex education and promoting sexual diversity." Her best selling book, *Sex for One: The Joy of Selfloving* (Dodson 1996), which she originally self-published in 1974 under the title *Liberating Masturbation*, has been her mainstay. Her more recent book, *Orgasm for Two: The Joy of Partnersex* (2002), explores the possibilities of mutual masturbation for couples.

More than just a vehicle for selling her books, Dodson's site also provides links to "Betty's Sex Shop," which features videos, vibrators, and barbells (for strengthening vaginal muscles). Other features include "Orgasms: First/Better," "Genital Art Gallery," "Sex for One Genitals," "Joy of Masturbation," and "Hot Sex Links."

Joani Blank's www.goodvibes.com also promotes masturbation for women. Blank describes herself as a sex therapist and educator. In 1977, she became "dismayed by the lack of resources for women seeking accurate sex information and good quality sex toys." To meet these needs, Blank established Good Vibrations, a retail store in San Francisco, dedicated to providing a "clean alternative to conventional `adult' bookstores."

Blank now operates a number of Good Vibrations retail stores in the San Francisco area, along with a mail-order catalog marketed through the Internet. In 1987, she incorporated under the name Open Enterprises Cooperative, Inc., which she describes as "a worker-owned, women-owned cooperative providing access to accurate sex information and sex toys, books and videos." Access to these materials is provided through retail stores, a call center, and publishing companies. The aim of the corporation is "to promote healthy attitudes about sex" (www.goodvibes.com).

Materials advertised on the goodvibes Web site include: the book *I Am My Lover: Women Pleasure Themselves* (1997) and the video *Carol Queen's Great Vibrations: A Consumer Guide to Vibrators*. The blurb for the video proclaims: "the irrepressible Ms. Queen talks about and demonstrates the use of more than a dozen different kinds of vibrators. Reassuring and helpful to new users, lively and enhancing for others" (www.joaniblank.com/sexuality.html).

Good Vibrations also offers an "Outreach and Education" program. The primary service of the program is to provide "Pleasure Parties," an updated sexual version of the old-fashioned Avon or Mary Kay parties. Pleasure Parties, which are currently offered only in the San Francisco Bay area, may be held in one's home, or in a Good Vibrations store.[10]

The Pleasure Party promises participants the opportunity to explore the largest premium-quality sex toy collection in the world "in your own living room" (www.goodvibes.com). Parties are "graciously hosted by two staff members," who share information and answer questions about the sex toys. Party hosts do not "perform demonstrations." However, participants

are encouraged to touch and examine the sex toys for themselves following the presentations (www.goodvibes.com).

Somewhat stronger sexual fare can be found on Karen Jones's
www.sexforwomen.net. Jones describes herself as an "ecstatically married" Australian journalist who writes and creates Web sites. Her
www.sexforwomen.net concentrates on masturbation, vibrators, orgasms,
g-spots, female ejaculation, anal sex, adult videos, better sex, and centerfolds. "While we receive commissions for promoting their products,"
explains Jones regarding her decision to include advertisements on her
site, "we do not advertise any site that may be offensive or disrespectful to
women" (www.sexforwomen.net/about_us.html).

Among the sex products advertised on Jones's site is the "clit pump," a
medical device (officially called the EROS-CTD Treatment Device) that
was approved by the U.S. Food and Drug Administration in May 2000.
This device was created for the treatment of a female sexual dysfunction,
which Jones claims "affects 50 [percent] of women at some time in their
lives" (www.sexforwomen.net/clit_pumps.html).

The clit pump is the female equivalent of the penis enlarger for men,
which is frequently advertised on the Internet. "You place the suction cup
over your clitoris," Jones describes flippantly, "and the inner labia, creating a seal, then you activate the pump and whammo! Your clit is sucked
into the tube, and the subsequent vacuum basically creates an artificial
female erection. The idea behind the whole thing is an enlarged clit, an
aroused and sensitive clit, and female orgasm becomes as easy as pressing
down the toaster button" (www.sexforwomen.net/clit_pumps.html).

On her Web site, Jones also offers "The best adult videos for women"
that provide "male centerfolds." Jones also links to her erotica mega-site,
*For The Girls*.

Another popular Internet Web site is Toys in Babeland, which started
as a retail store in Seattle and has now expanded to two additional stores
in Soho and the Lower East Side in New York City. The Web site for this
enterprise is www.babeland.com.[11] Claire Cavanah and Rachel Venning
created their first Toys in Babeland store in 1993, because they were "fed
up with the lack of women-friendly sex shops" in Seattle. Cavanah and
Venning remain "Committed to providing information and encouragement to women who want to explore their sexuality," but their specialty
is sex toys. Their stores in Seattle and New York have been described as
"the Williams-Sonoma of the well-stocked boudoir," and "the best place
to buy sex toys" (http://www.babeland.com).

In 2003 Cavanah and Venning published *Sex Toys 101*, which they
describe as "the ultimate guide to choosing and using sex toys." Vibrators

are still the mainstay of this full-color catalog of largely female sex toys, but other objects include an assortment of dildos, strap-on harnesses for dildos, nipple toys (both clamps and suctions), "butt toys" (beads, plugs, anal vibes), lubrications, and studded leather wristbands for bondage and masochistic sex.

All of the Web sites described in this last section clearly reflect the *pleasure-hedonistic* mode of sexual discourse. The emphasis is always on the pleasure provided by sexual activity, from autoerotic sex to various forms of sexual experimentation. A few sites, such as with SIECUS, provide an additional undercurrent of *rational-intellectual* discourse, through which sex is discussed and examined rationally and scientifically, yet with the implicit goal of achieving sexual pleasure.

The Internet has made information about sexual behavior and sexuality more accessible to women than ever before. The information ranges from sexual publications especially directed toward women, sexual educational materials, and information on how women can experience greater sexual pleasure.

## ONLINE SEXUAL DISCOURSE

The Internet provides unprecedented opportunities for interpersonal discourse about sex. A generation ago only the most prescient futurists could have imagined how easy it would be to discuss sexual issues with people of like minds (or opposite minds) anywhere in the world. Internet users, most of whom never see each other in person, can engage in conversations about any and all aspects of sex, make suggestive statements aboout sex, provide details about their sexual experiences, reveal their most hidden sexual fantasies, make suggestive remarks, and if they want to engage in Internet sex.

The Internet provides many different online dating sites. These more or less follow the format of newspaper and magazine personals (women seeking men, men seeking women, men seeking men, etc.). Some sites, such as www.adultfriendfinder.com, which bills itself as "the world's largest sex and swingers personals site," emphasize the sexual dimension of personal relationships.

The Internet also provides the possibilities for personal meetings between people of like minds about sex. Chat-room discourse about sex can cover any version or variety of sex, from conventional heterosexual topics to gay and lesbian sex and sexual fetishes of all kinds. At the dark end of the sexual spectrum, some Internet users who are interested in sex with children can discuss pedophilic sex (Jenkins 2001; Taylor and Quayle 2003).

The title of one recent book on child pornography labels such deviant behavior as "An Internet Crime" (Taylor and Quayle 2003, 2). This is an especially apt characterization because the Internet provides an unprecedented communication medium for adults (usually men) who are sexually attracted to young children and preteens. In his meticulously researched study of Internet child pornography, Jenkins (2001) has accumulated detailed information on how the Internet has changed the world of child pornography. Today, pedophilic Internet users around the world can converse about their obsession with children, often discussing their justifications and rationalizations for engaging in pedophilic activities. These people also often compare their strategies for eluding the authorities. Because many Internet sites are created in countries that tolerate sex with children, pedophiles can now create and abandon sites in the blink of an eye and are generally able to avoid arrest.[12]

But child pornographers constitute only a small portion of Internet users who engage in interpersonal talk about sex. Most sex talk on the Internet, either in chat rooms or blogger sites are relatively benign. On occasion, news reports describe encounters between individuals who have met on the Internet where the end result has been horrible.

The most ominous of these Internet exchanges about sex occur between adult males and pubescent or teenage girls.[13] While many of these conversations lead to nothing more than suggestive wordplay, in some instances the underage girl (or boy) may eventually agree to meet with the male. There is no way to know how many of these Internet encounters lead to sexual contact between adults and minors. The incidents that become public are primarily those that are reported in the press, especially those that have led to violence, abduction and even death. Another source of information on Internet child predators is found on television. The NBC show *Dateline* features "To Catch a Predator," which regularly uses the Internet to entice males to a location where they expect to have sex with an underage girl. But when they arrive they are confronted by Chris Hansen, the NBC reporter. After some embarrassing questions the men are allowed to leave, only to be apprehended by law enforcement officers.

One Web site (http://www.perverted-justice.com) has been expressly designed by a non-law enforcement officer to trap adult males who make contact with teenage girls. This site provides photographs of alleged male predators and presents transcripts of exchanges between men and "teenage girls" (on this site the originator poses as an underage female). The following excerpted dialogue illustrates one such exchange, between

an adult male (Steve) and a girl (*longislandlisa*) who has just informed the
man that she is fourteen years old:

> [Steve]: damn u look alot older in pic
> *longislandlisa*: no way
> [Steve]: hell yes I thought like mid 20
> *longislandlisa*: nobody ever told me that
> [Steve]: well i did now

The exchange goes on to discuss where the girl lives, what school she goes
to, and how it happens that she is not in school. "My mom is gone and
I'm playing hookey." This is followed by questions about the girl's experiences online and in chat rooms. She claims to have met with other men
and then asks if he wants to meet up with her.

> [Steve]: this sounds like a set up
> *longislandlisa*: a set up? huh? I don't get it.
> [Steve]: police.

After his fears about police entrapment have been allayed, Steve questions
the girl about what she might be willing to do if they were to meet.

> *longislandlisa*: i dunno i just want to kind of have some fun while mom is
>    gone
> [Steve]: at your place?
> *longislandlisa*: yeah
> [Steve]: well what will u let me do?
> *longislandlisa*: what do u want to do?

After the girl tells Steve she will not do oral sex, they work out an arrange-
ment for a meeting (http://www.pervertedjustice.com/?archive=sr82194).

While the above conversation is contrived and manipulated by the
site's creator, there is sufficient evidence that similar, real-life conversations occur on a daily basis. The Internet undoubtedly offers many thousands, perhaps millions, of people of all ages and genders the opportunity
to talk about sex in a way that would never have been possible before.

In the world of gay males, for example, the Internet has been an especially effective way of making impersonal contacts with sex partners
(Specter 2005). As one gay male explains, "I'm a fifty year old, overweight,
HIV-positive man. . . . I am balding; I'm not that attractive. But we [I]
can go online any time of the day and I can get a sexual hookup" (Specter
2005, 40). The Web sites that offer opportunities for sexual contacts

between men include: www.craigslist.com, www.m4m4sex.com, www
.manhunt.org, www.hunkhunter.com, www.bigmuscle.com, and many
others (Specter 2005, 42).

## BLOGGING, MYSPACE, YOUTUBE, VIMEO, FACEBOOK, FLICKR

In the spring of 2004, an online gossip column called *Wonkette*, located
in Washington DC, revealed the sexual escapades of a congressional staff
assistant named Jessica Cutler. Cutler, on her personal blog,
*Washingtonienne*, had been describing her very active sexual life, mostly for
the amusement for her girlfriends. When *Wonkette* "outed" Cutler it made
the news, because not only was Cutler working in the office of then-
Republican Senator Mike Dewine from Ohio, but also because some of
the men she was having sex with were apparently high-level governmental
officials (some of them married, and some giving her money for sex).

Jessica Cutler once posted a list of her sex partners along with brief
thumbnail sketches, which were made necessary because her girlfriends
couldn't keep track of them. Cutler wrote on her blog site:

> By popular demand, I have finally created a key to keeping my sex life
> straight. In alpha[betical] order:
>
> FD =The intern in my office whom I want to fuck.
> X = Married man who pays me for sex. Chief of Staff at one of the
>     gov agencies, appointed by Bush.
> T = Lost my virginity to him and fell in love. Dude who has been
>     driving me crazy since 1999. Lives in Springfield, IL. Flies
>     halfway across the country to fuck me, then I don't hear from
>     him for weeks.
> HK = Dude from the Senate office I interned in Jan. thru Feb.
>     Hired me as an intern. Broke up my relationship w/QV (see
>     below).
> QV = Serious, long-term boyfriend whom I lived with since 2001.
>     Disastrous breakup in March, but still seeing each other.
> P = AKA "Threesome Dude." Somebody I would rather forget
>     about.
> YZ = My new office bf with whom I am embroiled in an office sex
>     scandal. The current favorite.
> K = A sugar daddy who wants nothing but anal. Keep trying to end
>     it with him, but the money is too good.
>
> Shit, I'm fucking six guys. Ewe. (http://www.wonkette.com/archives/
> the-lost-washingtonienne-wonkette-exclusive-etc-etc-004162.php)[14]

This posting on Cutler's Web log illustrates one of the most remarkable features of today's Internet world: namely, that many people (especially those under thirty) are willing to reveal almost everything about their personal lives on the Internet. Very often these personal revelations include information on the writer's sexual life (Nussbaum 2007). It does seem that the Internet is an impersonal form of discourse (not face to face) and many users are willing to reveal the most personals details of their lives, including the sexual.

Currently, popular Web sites that facilitate personal disclosures include MySpace, YouTube, Vimeo, Facebook, Flickr and others. The content posted on these sites ranges into all aspects of personal lives, but many provide details about sexual lives.

This chapter, as we acknowledged at the outset, has offered only a sampling of the vast amount of sexual material on the Internet. This is in large part due to the always-expanding, ever-changing nature of the Internet. New Internet technologies are always emerging and each one offers new possibilities for increasing the amount of sexual discourse (Ludlow and Wallace 2007).[15] The Internet more than any other previous technological development has added immensely to the hypersexuality of American society.

# THE HYPERSEXUAL SOCIETY

## WHERE WE ARE AND WHAT LIES AHEAD

It is now time to review what we have seen in the preceding chapters and to consider where American society is headed. The basic thesis of the book is that America is a hypersexual society. We have seen again and again how sexual materials, including erotica and pornography, are found in abundance in nearly every part of American culture. These sexual materials constitute the fundamental part of the hypersexuality. But it is not simply the amount of sexual material, erotica, and pornography in the United States that distinguishes it from many other countries around the world. As we pointed out at the beginning of the book, it is also the vigorous opposition to sexual materials, erotica, and pornography that adds to the high level of sexual discourse in American society.

Many of the preceding chapters have described how authors, artists, publishers, entrepreneurs, filmmakers, entertainers, scholars, therapists, and others have relentlessly pushed the boundaries of sexual openness and have added to the abundance of sexual materials. But in response, many other Americans, ranging from the nineteenth century Anthony Comstock, to the twentieth century's Catholic Church's Legion of Decency, and the twenty-first century antipornography crusaders, have tried again and again to repress sexual materials, erotica, and pornography. While those who want to repress sexual materials have not generally achieved their objectives they have nonetheless contributed to sexual discourse in American society. This is an appropriate place to review how those who try to suppress sexual materials add to hypersexuality.

## How the Antipornography Activists
## Contribute to Hypersexuality

It may seem extreme to use the label *antipornography* activists for all those who oppose the abundance of sexual materials in society. But I would argue that the label is appropriate because many opponents of sexual materials apply the word "pornography" to nearly everything sexual. As I also noted at the beginning of the book, the tendency to use the word pornography indiscriminately and excessively is a major reason we have not tried to produce a precise nominal definition of the term.

So how do the antiporn activists add to hypersexuality? At the most basic level antiporn activists increase awareness of sexual materials among their followers, and even to those who are only casually interested in the antiporn cause. Antiporn activists routinely report on and describe the sexual materials they consider objectionable. Followers may then predictably respond: "My Goodness, have you heard (or "seen" or "read") about this?" The followers may then tell their friends and neighbors about the outrageous things that are going on in the society (sex on television, sex in the movies, sex on the Internet, and so on). The outrage among followers continues to add to sexual discourse.

The informational function of the antiporn movement has had an interesting impact on the research for this book. In accumulating information and examples, I have tried to inform myself about all available examples of sexual material and pornography in American society. I have relied on my own exploration and reading, the research of others, mass media reports and publications, and the Internet. Throughout this process, the publications and Internet sites of those fighting to suppress sexual materials and pornography have been a surprisingly helpful resource for learning about and gaining access to sexually explicit materials. The watchdogs of public morality have often brought to my attention materials that I might otherwise have missed. Two examples will illustrate this point.

The Concerned Women for America is a lobbying organization based in Washington, DC. The political agenda of this organization concentrates on issues associated with the traditional roles of women and marriage. As part of its activities, CWFA monitors all news stories related to pornography, which it then publishes in the "pornography library" on its Web site. The list provides a convenient link to every major-media news story related to pornography (both pro and con). CWFA thus provides a wealth of information about pornography topics. I have gratefully used the information in the pornography library in the writing of this book. But the main purpose of CWFA's pornography library is to provide its members and supporters with material they can read and then discuss with their families and friends. All of which leads to more discourse about pornography in the United States.

A second example is the Parents Television Council (already discussed in Chapters 3 and 8), an organization that concentrates primarily on monitoring television programming (Poniewozik 2005; Thompson 2004). The PTC is headed by L. Brent Bozell, who writes a weekly syndicated entertainment column in which he often describes what he considers egregious examples of blatant and offensive sexuality in the media. While Bozell usually concentrates on television, he sometimes turns his attention to other parts of the entertainment industry. In a reprint of his column on the PTC Web site (http://www.parentstv.org), I first learned about two independently made films that had been introduced at the 2004 Sundance Film Festival. In a column attacking the sexual content of MTV, Bozell veered off to criticize two films that he claimed were aimed at sexualizing children "as young as possible" (http://www.parentstv .org/PTC/publications/lbbcolumns/2005/2004.asp). One of these independently produced films was *The Squid and the Whale*, which won awards at the Sundance, Chicago, and Toronto Film Festivals, along with Academy Award and Golden Globe nominations for 2006. Though it was an R-rated film, *The Squid and the Whale* was considered by most reviewers to be a touchingly poignant drama of a family going through a divorce. But Bozell saw it differently. He especially objected to a scene in which an eleven-year-old boy masturbates in the school library stacks. He also provided detailed accounts of other sexual activities in the boy's family (including the attempt by both the teenage son and his father to seduce the same high school girl). Bozell's primary complaint—and the key point in his column—was that contemporary movies depict children and teenagers as too precocious when it comes to sex.

Another film that earned Bozell's criticism was *Me and You and Everyone We Know*, another independently produced R-rated film that received good reviews and various awards (including the Sundance Special Jury Prize and Cannes Camera d'Or). While the film is primarily a love story, a minor subplot involves two high school girls competing to see who gives the best oral sex. The girls blindfold a male classmate who is then asked to judge their skills

It was Bozell's Web site—and not the mainstream media—that first made me aware of both of these independent films, even before either of them received many of their awards and before they were widely distributed in theaters around the country. While Bozell is dedicated to suppressing sexual material on television (and, by extension, movies), he was instrumental in bringing both of these films to my attention.

Another irony regarding Bozell's attack on these films is that he had apparently not seen either of them himself when he wrote his columns about them. Instead, he based his attack on a review written by Todd McCarthy for the entertainment newspaper *Variety*. McCarthy had complained in his review that independent movies today often depict children and preteens as sexually precocious. While *Variety* readers do not represent the same audience as those who regularly read Bozell's antiporn column, Bozell has extended McCarthy's public reach into the antiporn community and thus has added to the total amount of discourse about sexual matters.

Antiporn activists also increase sexual discourse in society by inciting and encouraging the defenders of sexual materials and pornography to fight back. This counterattack mode of sexual discourse illustrates Foucault's description of the ongoing interplay and tension among the various forms of sexual discourse (*political-legal, rational-intellectual,* and *pleasure-hedonistic*) in society. Each of these discourses, Foucault has observed, is constantly striving for power (to define standards for, to regulate acceptable beliefs and behavior; to critique, restrict and repress opposing viewpoints and behaviors). In striving for power, all discourses provoke the resistance of those with different positions and interests (Foucault 1978, 95). The existence of power relationships at all levels of society, says Foucault, "depends on a multiplicity of points of resistance: these play the role of adversary, target, support, or handle in power relations" (Foucault 1978, 95).

An interesting example of a counterattack, this time coming from an antiporn voice, occurred after *Hustler* magazine published its crude spoof claiming that the Rev. Jerry Falwell, a long-time critic of pornography, had had sex with his mother. The scurrilous and fictitious story in *Hustler* led an aggrieved Falwell to file a libel suit against Flynt and his magazine, which made headlines in newspapers throughout the country. *Hustler,* not surprisingly, played up the case in issue after issue. Flynt also prominently featured the court case in his autobiography (2004), and it was a central dramatic episode in the subsequent movie *The People v. Larry Flynt*. The movie may have provided many Americans with their first awareness of the legal dispute between Flynt and Jerry Falwell. The entire controversy—from the magazine article, to Falwell's lawsuit, to newspaper accounts of the suit, to Flynt's book and the subsequent movie about his life—all generated an enormous amount of public discourse about sexual matters.

In summary, there are two major ways that antiporn forces actually add to sexual discourse in American society. First, antiporn groups and individuals seek out and describe examples of sexual content and pornography in the culture of American society. Their reporting on the topic is then consumed not only by their followers, but also by their critics, as well as others who are relatively neutral on the issue. In this way, they are provoking discussion (Foucault called this "inciting discourse") about sex and pornography. Secondly, the attempts by antiporn forces to repress and censor sexual material and pornography are likely to provoke their opponents to fight back. Recall, for example, how many women, most of whom considered themselves feminists and/or civil libertarians, wrote articles and books to express their opposition to the MacKinnon and Dworkin crusade to outlaw pornography (see Chapter 3).

Following Foucault's analysis, the power struggle between antiporn forces and their various critics always results in more discourse about sexual topics and pornography. The United States is a hypersexual society, not just because sexual materials and pornography pervade all aspects of the society and culture (though that is an important element), it is also a hypersexual society because these countervailing forces both contribute to the total amount of sexual discourse within the society.

Given the longstanding and seemingly intensifying battle between these antiporn forces and pro-porn forces, we can reasonably conclude that sexual discourse in the Unites States will continue to flourish in the years ahead.

What is less clear, and what needs to be considered further is whether sexual materials, erotica, and pornography will continue to be as pervasively present in American society as they are today. Or will they be even more pervasive? Will magazines and books, radio, television, and film, the worlds of sex therapy and academe, and, most importantly, the Internet, provide increasing amounts of sexual content, erotica, and pornography? Or might there be a decline? This is the next issue I would like to address.

## SEXUAL DISCOURSE, EROTICA, AND PORNOGRAPHY IN AMERICA: WHERE ARE WE HEADED?

Will there be even more sexual discourse, erotica, and pornography in the years ahead? Or, will the amount of sexual material in our society diminish? The easy way out would be to say that these parts of the culture will probably remain about the same, but that would keep us from some interesting lines of analysis.

Answering questions about the future is not easy, as many prognosticators have learned. In 1999, when the American stock market was booming, some economists, many business writers, and many day-trading investors predicted that the stock market would continue to climb indefinitely. They based their optimistic position on the emerging technology sector and the fact that many Americans were investing in the market through their 401k accounts and pension plans. In 1999, two respected economic analysts published a book they daringly titled, *Dow 36,000: The New Strategy for Profiting from the Coming Rise in the Stock Market* (Glassman and Hassett 1999). Since the Dow-Jones average was then around eleven thousand, it seemed unlikely that it would soon reach thirty-six thousand, but these experts boldly said otherwise. Soon after the book's publication, the Dow average dropped below ten thousand, and at the time of this writing, it is fluctuating again in the eleven thousand range.[1]

A further cautionary note about predicting the future can be found in Philip Tetlock's book *Expert Political Judgment: How Good Is It? How Can We Know?* (2005). Tetlock, a University of California, Berkeley psychologist, conducted a systematic study of political experts and pundits over a two-decade period, during which he asked them to predict the future with respect to hundreds of political issues. He accumulated predictions regarding 284 political events (examples: Would Canada break up? Would the United States go to war in the Persian Gulf in 1990?). The experts interviewed by Tetlock were people who regularly appeared on television talk shows, were interviewed on radio, wrote newspaper and magazine opinion columns, participated in roundtable discussions, and gave lectures. Tetlock's systematic research produced the surprising conclusion that the experts were no better at predicting the future than any average person who reads the newspaper and generally keeps informed about current events. The experts were wrong about as much as they were right.

The humbling conclusion from these examples is that predicting the future—whether about the stock market, political events, or trends in sexual discourse, erotica, and pornography—must be approached with trepidation. Nonetheless, I will try, if only as a way of initiating and encouraging further discussion.

## PREDICTING THE FUTURE OF SEXUAL DISCOURSE, EROTICA, AND PORNOGRAPHY

Very often people who try to predict the future simply assume that a prevailing trend will continue in the immediate years ahead. But trends may slow down, stop, or even reverse themselves. If we are to predict future trends with respect to sexual discourse, erotica, and pornography in

American society, we cannot simply project into the future what has been happening over the last twenty-five or fifty years. A more prudent approach would be to consider the potential impact of the three societal factors described in Chapter 2 as major influences on access to sexual materials:

1. Economic development and personal affluence,
2. Political democratization and personal liberty,
3. Technological advances and personal accessibility.

Before considering these factors, however, we will first introduce and examine a factor that has been dealt with only incidentally in the preceding chapters: generational differences in attitudes toward and acceptance of sexual materials, erotica, and pornography.

### THE IMPORTANCE OF GENERATIONAL PERSPECTIVES ON SEXUAL MATERIALS AND PORNOGRAPHY

Many older Americans are especially likely to express concern about the amount of sexual material and pornography in American society. Regardless of their religious beliefs or political affiliations, older Americans are much more likely than younger Americans to complain about the amount of sex they see on television (from broadcast programming to cable and satellite TV), the sex and profanity that confronts them at the movies (including the previews of upcoming films), and the sex they find in books and magazines or read about in their daily newspapers. For those who use the Internet, sexual material and pornography often seem to dominate cyberspace.

The resistance of older Americans to the increased hypersexualization of American society is understandable. They grew up in a society in which sexual materials and pornography, while not totally absent, were more undercover and were rarely talked about openly. Now they find themselves bombarded with sexual materials and pornography.

The Henry J. Kaiser Family Foundation, for example, which monitors television programming and attitudes toward it, has reported that people fifty years and older are much less tolerant of condom advertisements than are people younger than fifty. Among the fifty-and-over group, 40 percent report that condom advertisements should not be on television, while in the eighteen to forty-nine age group, by contrast, only 16 percent say that condom advertisements should not be allowed on television (reported in Shehan 2003, 170–71).

Of course, not everyone in the over-fifty crowd is resistant to the amount of sexual material and pornography they encounter in American society. Many older Americans still vacation in Las Vegas and Atlantic City, where they often pay high prices for tickets to shows that feature bare-breasted showgirls and comedians who build their acts around sexual material. On the opposite side of the live entertainment spectrum, Branson, Missouri offers a more "wholesome" form of entertainment and clearly attracts a great many older-generation visitors (Romano 2005).

Based on the evidence at hand, the majority of older Americans are offended by, or resistant to, the amount of sexual material they encounter in American culture. The younger generation holds the key to the future of sexual expression and sexual discourse in American society, and it is to them that we will turn next.

## THE YOUNGER GENERATIONS, SEXUAL MATERIALS, AND PORNOGRAPHY

A familiar platitude holds that the *future rests in the hands of the young*, but even if this statement has become a cliché, it still contains considerable truth. Any realistic projection of the future of sexual materials and pornography in American society demands that we devote our attention to the younger end of the age spectrum: especially preteens, teenagers and the twenty-somethings. Roughly everyone under age thirty today will (unless they have lived very sheltered lives) have been frequently exposed to sex and pornography throughout their lives. Most members of this age group probably consider sexual materials and pornography commonplace; for many it is an acceptable part of the culture (Aratani 2005).

A revealing example can be found in the ongoing debate about sex education in the curricula of public schools. Parents of preteens and teenagers in many communities very often argue about whether sex education should be a part of the curricula of schools and, if so, how it should be taught. The argument usually concerns what children should be taught beyond the basic physiology of sex. One group argues that the schools should go beyond teaching the physiological basics and on to informing children about "safe sex," particularly about contraceptives that will protect them from sexually transmitted diseases and unwanted pregnancies. The opposing group insists that schools should refrain from teaching students about contraception, since doing so delivers the implicit message that premarital sex is acceptable. As an alternative this group usually argues for an emphasis on celibacy before marriage.

Those who favor teaching contraception generally believe that young people are already informed about sex, both by conversations with their parents, ongoing exposure to popular media (television, movies, books, magazines, and the Internet), and interactions with their more knowledgeable peers. To support this position, advocates of contraception point out that over 60 percent of high school seniors (males 60.7 percent; females 62.3 percent) have already had sexual intercourse at least once (Centers for Disease Control 2004). They therefore argue that adolescents need to be given trustworthy information about birth control and protection against sexually transmitted diseases.

But what do we actually know about teenagers' awareness of and receptivity to sex and sexual activity? Evidence on teenage sexual awareness and experience is provided by both scientific research and anecdotal accounts. At the anecdotal level, frequent newspaper and magazine articles provide examples of teenagers who are well-informed about sex and become involved in sexual activity at an early age. Laura Sessions Stepp, a Pulitzer prize-winning author, has described how some middle-school students in Arlington, Virginia (a well-to-do suburb of Washington, DC) engage in oral sex at parties and sometimes at school (Stepp 1999). Young girls may use fellatio as a way to please their boyfriends, often viewing oral sex as an easy way to avoid sexually transmitted diseases and pregnancy.[2]

Karin Painter has assembled other examples of sexual attitudes and behavior among early teenagers in a *USA Today* article, "The Sexual Revolution Hits Junior High" (Painter 2002, 1A). The article's headline proclaims: "The kids are doing more than baring bellies: They're shocking adults with their anything-goes behavior" (Painter 2002, 1A). Painter goes on to assemble information about preteens and teenagers in such widely dispersed communities as affluent neighborhoods of Washington, DC, Omaha, Nebraska, and Bettendorf, Iowa. Painter describes how many middle schoolers claim to be aware of sexual activity among their peers.

Journalist Lori Aranti collected views about sex and sex education from students attending high school in an upscale Maryland community. The students reported that sex is often casually discussed in their everyday conversations with other students. They explained that they are comfortable when they talk about sex because they see it and hear about it constantly on television, on the radio, and on the Internet as well as their instant messaging. A high school sophomore named Laura expressed her views about sex education in the curriculum succinctly and insightfully: "You can take the sex out of the curriculum, but its still going to be in society" (Aratani 2005, A16).[3]

In the realm of social scientific research, exploration into the sex attitudes and activities of teenagers remains as touchy a subject as it was during the time of Kinsey's research. Sharon Thompson is one of the few researchers with the courage to interview teenage girls about their sexual and romantic lives (Thompson 1990, 1995). Among the girls she interviewed, most were willing to talk openly about sex and their personal experiences. Thompson observed that young women have a new openness about discussing their sexual lives, especially among their peers. The sexually active girls reported that with their friends they almost always talked about their "first time" and how they reacted to having sex (Thompson 1990, 1995). Many described it as a relatively unpleasant or neutral experience, though a few described it as enjoyable and exciting.

Doctor Lynn Ponton has talked with hundreds of teenagers in carrying out her research on adolescent sexual activity. While some of the teenagers are confused, uncertain and misinformed about sex, almost all have considerable awareness of sexual activity. Ponton's experience with teenagers has led her to conclude that they are receiving "a highly conflicted message" by the culture. "Teens' views of their sexuality, however, differ from those of adults," she explains. "For teens, the ways of sex are fraught with struggle, but also filled with excitement and pleasure" (Ponton 2000, 258).

All of the studies and examples clearly demonstrate the degree to which young people today, beginning as early as their middle-school years, live in a culture that provides them with continuous information about sex. While the information they get may be inaccurate and misleading, they routinely think and talk about sex, and many engage in some form of sexual activity. Exposure to sexual materials, including pornography, is a regular part of their day-to-day lives. For this reason, teenagers and young adults are much less likely to be offended by or resistant to the sexual content of the culture than are older adults.

Of course, not every young adult is favorably disposed toward sexual materials and pornography. Some young people disapprove of the amount of sexual material and pornography they encounter because of their commitment to feminist, conservative, or religious convictions. These young people are more likely to be in a minority, however.

Young adults, however, may develop reservations and negative attitudes about sexual materials, erotica and pornography after they become parents. Having children tends to make people more conservative about anything that might be harmful to their children. For this reason, young parents, many of whom have previously had liberal attitudes about sex, may join the ranks of those opposed to sex. They may get concerned about children's access to sexual materials and pornography on the radio and television, in music lyrics, and on the Internet (some of these efforts were discussed in Chapter 3).

There is no absolute evidence to demonstrate the relationship between young people's exposure to sexual materials and their attitudes (positive, negative or neutral) about sexual materials. It does appear, however, that extensive exposure to sexual materials and pornography, combined with the secondary effects of interaction with peers, tips the balance in the direction of greater acceptance of (or at least less opposition to) sexual materials and pornography. In the years ahead, it is unlikely that today's young adults, having grown up with Madonna, Britney Spears, Lil' Kim, Howard Stern, Chris Rock, *Sex and the City, Nip/Tuck*, and *The Sopranos*, as well as frequent exposure to PG-13 and R-rated movies, will argue for the suppression of sexual materials and pornography.

From a generational perspective, it seems likely that future opposition to sexual materials and pornography will be limited primarily to the conservative and religious elements of the population. While the next generation of young adults may object to some of the more flagrant displays of sexual material and pornography, their views will probably have moved far beyond what was acceptable to most twentieth-century Americans.

Now we can turn to the social factors that have led to the increase of sexual material and pornography, along with the discourse about them, in the United States. We will begin with the economic development of society and the personal affluence that it has generated.

## ECONOMIC DEVELOPMENT AND PERSONAL AFFLUENCE

As was demonstrated in Chapter 2, pornography in early Western societies was reserved primarily for the wealthy males of the society. It was only in the latter half of the twentieth century that Americans at almost all economic levels could begin to afford sexual and pornographic materials. And while the 1960s and 1970s were the breakthrough years in the widespread affordability of sexual materials, it was only in the last decades of the twentieth century that economic constraints became even less important for Americans who wanted to purchase sexually explicit materials and pornographic materials.

In the twenty-first century, sexual material and pornography have become economically accessible for hundreds of millions of Americans. Today, almost everyone who wants to see or read about sex of whatever type, and to whatever extreme, can afford to do so. They can see sexually explicit movies in theaters, rent or purchase videos and DVDs, buy books, or borrow them from their local libraries, or purchase magazines with photos and articles about sex.

For those with computers and Internet connections, including almost all young and middle-age Americans, pornography and other sexual materials are now available in abundance. The cost, while not trivial to some Americans, is nonetheless affordable to most.

What does this increased affordability suggest about the future of sexual materials and pornography in American society? The general trend is for the standard of living of Americans to move in an upward direction. Even among those Americans who continue to live at or below the poverty level and many others who are "just getting by," television (at least in its broadcast form) is frequently considered a necessity. Tens of millions of other Americans can afford cable or satellite television, computers with Internet capabilities, tickets for movies, rental fees for videos and DVDs, and the cost of magazines and books. In all these media of communication, sexual materials and pornography are plentiful.

Adam Smith observed centuries ago, "the invisible hand" of the buying public will inevitably shape the economy. And so it is with the sex and pornography economy. Only if Americans start to reject sexual materials and pornography at the cash register, will the sex and pornography industry begin to decline.

Today, however, millions of Americans do read sexually suggestive and sexually explicit magazines, romance novels and other sexually explicit literature. They watch R- and X-rated movies, and rent and buy pornographic videos and DVDs. They have access to the Internet, which provides them with easy access to pornographic photos and videos. Since the marketplace tells us that the public enthusiasm for sexual materials and pornography seems to be flourishing, it is likely to continue. The synergy between the continuing affluence of Americans and an accommodating entrepreneurial economic system will almost certainly lead to an increase in sexual materials in the Untied States.

### POLITICAL DEMOCRATIZATION AND PERSONAL LIBERTY

Authoritarian political regimes often repress sexual and pornographic materials. The examples are numerous, but the Soviet Union under communism and Afghanistan under the Taliban are among the best documented. In both cases, sexual materials and pornography were more or less successfully repressed while the regime was in power. As soon as the authoritarian government was removed from power, however, sexual and pornographic materials were soon found in the marketplace. The trend is unmistakable: as nations have moved toward greater democratization, their citizens have been given more personal liberty, and as part of that personal liberty, they have had greater access to sexual materials and pornography. It is relevant to note that the official foreign policy of the

United States in the first years of the twenty-first century has been to increase democracy in nations around the world.

In the United States today, personal liberty is a widely revered positive value—at least in principle. Those who call themselves "libertarians" are most intensely focused on personal freedom and object most strenuously when the government intrudes on the personal lives of citizens.

Others in the political spectrum are more ambivalent about personal freedom. Conservatives generally respect an individual's personal freedom, with the exception of some extremely personal choices, such as abortion, suicide, same-sex marriage, and viewing pornography. When it comes to the right to produce, distribute, and purchase sexually explicit materials and pornography, conservatives are frequently among the advocates of various forms of repression and censorship.

Liberals and progressives, at the opposite end of the political spectrum, also claim to respect personal freedom. Once again, however, their support for complete individual freedom is constrained by competing values, particularly with regard to their outspoken opposition to sexist and racist actions or speech. Even in the case of pornography, liberals sometimes advocate limited forms of censorship and repression, as has been evidenced in the support of some liberals for feminists MacKinnon and Dworkin's attempts to stop the publication of pornographic materials.

Regardless of their political, moral or religious convictions, Americans who favor repression have generally failed in their attempts to prevent widespread public access to sexual and pornographic materials. Courts at all levels have consistently ruled that sexually explicit written or visual materials are legally permissible, unless they can be proven to be obscene (a legal distinction that still escapes the comprehension of many literate people).

From the political/legal perspective, almost anything can be published or printed in books, magazines, or on film today. Video and adult bookstores may still be challenged and harassed by local politicians or antipornography activists, but many persist. According to current legal interpretations, sexual and pornographic materials must not offend community standards—though this principle is only enforced in isolated incidents and in particular communities. In most places in the United States, adult bookstores and Mom & Pop video stores (to the degree that either can survive economically) continue to provide erotica and pornography. While the average American shopping mall continues to provide a variety of sexual material and even some pornography (as we saw in the first chapter).

More importantly, the Internet and cable/satellite remain relatively unrestricted by governmental action. Americans live in a society that ensures they will be able to read, see, and hear nearly anything they wish, including sexual and pornographic material (but not child pornography). The Internet under current legal conditions remains especially immune from censorship.

Americans today have very few restrictions on their personal freedom when it comes to sexual material and pornography. The major battles of censorship and repression were fought in the last century and provided individual Americans with a constitutional right to read, see, and hear almost anything they desire, including sexual, erotic, or pornographic materials.

It is unlikely that future attempts at governmental censorship or repression will be successful in turning around the prevailing court decisions. Since there appear to be few current legal impediments to the availability of sexual and pornographic materials, it is reasonable to assume that sexual and pornographic materials will continue to be widely available in American society in the years ahead. In order to achieve greater sexual repression, political leaders would need to craft legislation that avoids Supreme Court nullification, and few such congressional efforts appear to be in the offing.

## TECHNOLOGY AND PERSONAL ACCESS

Technology continues to play an important part in how Americans access sexual and pornographic material. While the ability of early twentieth-century technological developments (such as radio, movies, and television) to deliver sexual content was largely restricted by legal censorship and other social factors, more recent technological innovations have been much quicker to realize the potential they have to deliver sexual and pornographic materials. The rapid progression from the silicon chip to personal computers and the Internet has provided Americans with unlimited sexual access. The Internet has been further augmented by satellite and cable television and other emerging media technologies.[4]

Technology, by its very nature, will almost certainly increase in its effectiveness over time, providing more personal accessibility in the years ahead. While the specifics are not predictable, new technologies will inevitably make sexual materials and pornography ever-more available—and affordable—to Americans.

## CAN THE ANTIPORNOGRAPHY GROUPS TURN THE TIDE?

Chapter 3 identified the major groups and individuals that are currently trying to censor or restrain the availability of sexual and pornographic materials in American society. Among the most prominent groups are: The American Family Association, headed by the Rev. Donald Wildmon; Focus on the Family, for which David L. Weiss is the major spokesperson; Morality in Media, created by the late Father Morton A. Hill; Citizens for Community Values, started by Dr. Jerry Kirk; and Parents Television Council, headed by Dr. L. Brent Bozell III.

These organizations have two lines of attack. First, as we noted earlier in this chapter, by informing their members about offensive materials, they may generate public outrage and activism. If enough people write letters to the various news media, complain to members of Congress, or raise objections to the FCC they may bring about changes, especially in the radio and television fields.

The second line of attack involves putting pressure directly on distributors, sponsors, or advertisers through organized boycotts of programs and products. Bozell claims that the PTC has driven fifty sponsors away from cable television's *Nip/Tuck* and *The Shield*. To the extent that PTC and other organizations can dry up advertising revenues, the lifeblood of television, they can have a significant impact on programming. Of course, if programs with sexual content continue to draw large audiences, many brands and products will continue to sponsor them, even if part of the population is offended.

A possible third area of influence can come from the ability of antiporn forces to generate greater awareness, and objections to sexual materials, among the public at large (not just among loyal supporters). Occasionally an egregious incident (Janet Jackson's revealed breast at the Super Bowl, or an Internet case of child sexual abuse) will arouse larger numbers of people, but these are often passing concerns among the general public.

To what degree will the political, social, and religious groups involved in the antiporn movement be able to turn the tide and limit the future availability of sexual material and pornography in American society? To date, these organizations have enjoyed their greatest successes against the most public and vulnerable of media: broadcast radio and television programming delivered on publicly owned airwaves. There appears to be little that can be done, however, about the amount of sexual material in movies, magazines, and books, as well as on the Internet. Attending movies, renting and purchasing videos/DVDs, buying magazines, and accessing specific Internet sites are strictly voluntary activities. Since none of these media are dependent (as are broadcast radio and television) on a publicly supported infrastructure or licensing, they are virtually immune from federal regulation (except in extreme cases, such as child pornography). For this reason, court rulings have repeatedly favored the freedom of Americans to choose what they do or do not want to see.

In spite of their high-profile success (particularly in recent FCC fines of and restrictions on broadcast radio), antiporn activists and supporters represent a comparatively small part of the population. The movement draws its greatest public support from fundamentalist Christians, political conservatives (on social issues), and older citizens. More moderate religionists or those with no formal religious affiliation, political liberals and moderates, and younger Americans are much more likely to be tolerant of the availability of sexually explicit materials and pornography in society.

Today's America is a hypersexual society, and the factors that have contributed to its current condition (a high level of economic affluence, increasingly liberal judicial rulings, and ongoing advances in media technology) remain firmly in place. There is little reason to believe that sexual materials will be any less available in American society, or that discourse about sexuality, will be any less prominent in the foreseeable future.

# NOTES

1. The process of creating ever-more dazzling and appealing consumer settings is what Ritzer has called "enchanting a disenchanted world" (Ritzer 2005). This process is not limited to everyday items of consumption but extends as well to the world of erotica and pornography. As just one example, early pornographic stag films, which were produced in the first half of the twentieth century, were crudely made, grainy, often with barely discernible images. Today's pornography films, while not necessarily cinematographic works of art, are generally slickly filmed and cleverly marketed; the porn film is increasingly "enchanted."

2. A few planned shopping centers were created in the decades before World War II, but the first modern shopping mall was created in Edina, Minnesota, in 1956. It was Victor Gruen who conceived of the "introverted" mall, which was distinctive because the entrances and windows of the stores faced inward to an enclosed mall rather than outward toward the parking areas (Gladwell 2004).

3. Despite the general acceptance of Victoria's Secret window displays, occasionally their decorators overstep the bounds of acceptance. In 2005, the Victoria's Secret store in a Northern Virginia shopping mall created some shopper outrage, which led to newspaper and television stories. The window display went "over the top" with female mannequins that were barely dressed and in provocative poses (Dwyer 2005). The ensuing *discourse* about this display is an early illustration of how those who are offended by sexual displays and materials often add to the attention directed toward them. The next chapter will elaborate on how opponents of sexual material, erotica, and pornography add to the level of discourse about subjects they oppose.

4. A more extreme interpretation of how many American women, especially young women, have accepted the idea of sexually displaying their bodies can be found in Ariel Levy's *Female Chauvinist Pigs: Women and the Rise of Raunch Culture* (Levy 2006).

5. Exotic shoes are a version of what Marilyn Monroe once famously called, "Come f . . . me" shoes.

6. *Hustler* magazine routinely encloses DVDs featuring hard-core sex.

7. This title is not to be confused with Janet Hobhouse's book of the same name (Hobhouse 1988).

8. For a sociological analysis of Hooters, see Meika Loe's article describing the intersection of power, gender, and sexuality in the world of "Bazooms" (an obvious code name for Hooters) (Loe 1996). A less-scholarly exposé of Hooters is April Pederson's book *What About Hooters?* (Pederson 1998).

9. Even the highly touted cleanup of Times Square in New York City was largely accomplished by changes in the zoning laws. Even though Times Square has been cleaned up, pornography shops and strip clubs have simply moved a few blocks away from Times Square where they thrive today (Richburg 2008).

10. In a public appearance in New York City, Baudrillard was asked to sum up his view of himself and his life's work. He answered cryptically, "What I am, I don't know. . . . I am a simulacrum of myself" (MacFarquhar 2005, 64).

11. Baudrillard's most recent book, *The Conspiracy of Art* (2005), even argues that art, which by its very nature is an image or representation of reality, is not reality, or as he puts it, is not "truth" (MacFarquhar 2005).

12. Thompson (1994) has reached a conclusion similar to ours about erotica and pornography in his book *Soft Core: Moral Crusades against Pornography in Britain and the United States.*

## CHAPTER 2

1. For a recent journalistic book with the title *Sex Sells*, see Streitmatter 2004.

2. While the "Women of Russia" have a certain pornographic cachet on the Internet, many of the models on these Web sites come from other Eastern European countries, especially Hungary (Milter and Slade 2005).

3. In 1992, the *Naked Maja* by Goya was the cause of a contretemps at Pennsylvania State University, when a female instructor objected to a reproduction of this painting hanging on a classroom wall. The picture was removed from the classroom and banned from all other classrooms at Penn State (Strossen 1995).

4. Foucault makes a similar point when he notes that elite males have been most likely to have sexual access to boys.

5. Even in the twenty-first century, legislatures and courts in a number of states are still debating whether or not two consenting adults may engage in sodomy, which includes anal and oral sex either by persons of the same or the opposite sex.

6. It should be noted, however, that the first book Gutenberg printed with his new invention was a Christian Bible.

## CHAPTER 3

1. When Attorney General Ashcroft resigned, the new attorney general quietly had the draperies removed from in front of the statuary (Eggen 2005). On the occasion of Ashcroft's resignation, President Bush praised him for his

success in fighting Internet pornography (http://nytimes.com/2004/11/10/politics/10cabinet), although most observers could not discern any decrease in Internet pornography during the Ashcroft years.

2. A vestige of the Comstock crusade to suppress sex still survived as late as 1946 when seventy-year-old John Sumner, Comstock's successor as the head of the New York Society for the Suppression of Vice, stopped the sale of Edmund Wilson's *Memoirs of Hecate County*. Wilson was America's most-renowned literary critic at the time (Meyers 1995).

3. Because of Joyce's writing style, it is difficult to capture in a few brief excerpts the sexuality of his *Ulysses*, but anyone who has read the novel will not forget Molly Bloom's orgasmic soliloquy in the final pages of the book (Max 2006).

4. In an earlier era (1955), Senator Estes Kefauver held Senate hearings to investigate whether or not pornography contributed to juvenile delinquency (Slade 2000a, 150). No apparent causal link was found.

5. Today, 7-Eleven and many other convenience, magazine, and book stores sell *Playboy, Penthouse, Hustler*, and various other sexually oriented magazines.

6. In her personal life, Dworkin had an unorthodox relationship with her long-time partner John Stoltenberg, who is also an outspoken critic of pornography. Both Dworkin and Stoltenberg are primarily oriented toward same-sex relationships.

7. Father Hill served on the 1970 Presidential Commission on Pornography.

8. Rice Hughes made a brief appearance on a January 2006 ABC evening news show, speaking in support of the Child Protection Act, the legislation designed to protect children from seeing pornography on the Internet.

## CHAPTER 4

1. Millet's American publisher is Grove Press, which, since the 1950s has had a history of publishing sexually explicit books. Grove Press will be described in more detail later in the chapter.

2. In April 2006, Hefner reached his 80th birthday, an event that was noted in many major American publications (Gentile 2006).

3. The film *The People vs. Larry Flynt*, starring Woody Harrelson, concentrates on the story of Flynt's crusade for freedom of the press.

4. Goldstein was assisted by Penn Jillette of the Penn and Teller magician act. Jillette's financial help allowed Goldstein to escape from homelessness and land a job at New York City Bagel selling bagels to retail outlets (Paumgarten 2005). More recently, Goldstein was reported to be out of work again.

5. Through the 1930s and into the 1940s many of *Esquire*'s cartoons were blatantly sexist, and some were crudely racist.

6. Helmut Newton was a pioneer in sexual fashion photography, and throughout his career, his photographs mixed edgy sex with fashion (Newton 2002). Newton died in an automobile accident in Los Angeles in 2004.

7. As but one example, in the January 2008 issue, Judith Thurman begins with a full-page photograph of the female photographer Lee Miller in the

nude. This classic photo was taken by Man Ray.

8. Two recent examples: A story by Singer (2008) described a cross-dressing beauty contest in an Omaha, Nebraska, gay-male bar, a second article is about the female photographer Lee Miller by Thurman (2008), which features a full-page nude photograph of Miller. The photo was taken by Man Ray, her lover at the time.

9. D. H. Lawrence once offered a surprisingly negative assessment of pornography, despite the fact that many people considered his writing pornographic. Lawrence, somewhat cryptically said: "you can recognize [pornography] by the insult it offers, invariably, to sex, and to the human spirit" (Hyde 1965, 20).

10. This book was seized by the Philadelphia police and the bookseller was charged with selling obscene books. The charges were later dropped, but the accompanying publicity greatly increased the sales of Robbins's book.

11. This assessment is in no way meant to minimize the importance of many of Roth's other novels, including the highly acclaimed Zuckerman books: *Zuckerman Unbound* (1981) and *Zuckerman Bound* (1985).

12. Dailey's productivity is somewhat tarnished by the fact that in 1997 she admitted plagiarizing from another very successful romance novelist, Nora Roberts (Regis 2003, 161).

13. Comic books of the standard 8 1/2 x 11 format date back to 1938 when two high school students sold the idea for Superman to DC Comics for one hundred and thirty dollars. Along with superheroes, comics have also been inclined toward the humorous (*Archie* and *Donald Duck*, for example).

## CHAPTER 5

1. Even though Kinsey contributed greatly to the organization and popularity of the marriage course, within two years he was forced to withdraw from teaching his unit on sex. His teaching material in the course and the interviews with students about their sexual lives (as well as his counseling on sexual matters) had made Kinsey a lightening rod for opposition. Some objections came from his fellow professors, but the most vocal opposition came from the community of Bloomington where clergymen led the assault.

2. As a contemporary footnote to the cultural or subcultural pattern of non-gay men having sex with other men (or young boys), recent journalistic accounts report on similar patterns among some Latin-American and African-American men (Denizet-Lewis 2003; Paternostro 1998). Paternostro first learned that Latina women, both in the United States and in a number of Latin American countries, were contracting AIDS from their husbands. On further exploration, she discovered that these husbands were often having sex with other men as a demonstration of their manliness (*machismo*). Denizet-Lewis describes how, in some parts of African-American male subculture, the concept of "living on the Down Low" has come into vogue. Down Low refers to the semi-secret lifestyle of heterosexual black men, most of whom do not consider themselves gay or even bisexual, who have sex

with other men. This form of sex represents a kind of "hypermasculine" behavior for some African-American men in major American cities.

3. For example, this study raised serious questions about the long-accepted Kinsey conclusion that 10 percent of the population is gay. The percentage found in the Laumann study, based on random-sampling procedures, and also supported by similar scientific studies in Europe, shows that the number is closer to 5 percent (Laumann et al. 1994, 287ff.). The authors of this study also bravely predicted, on the basis of their empirical evidence of sexual networks, that in the United States, AIDS would not have a high prevalence in the general heterosexual population. That prediction has proven to be true (Centers for Disease Control and Prevention 2005).

4. From the first decade of the twentieth century until the 1960s, crudely made films showing naked women, sometimes engaged in sex with men, were illegally produced. These were called stag films, because they were typically shown at men's clubs, fraternity parties, and "smokers" (an informal social meeting of men, where smoking was allowed). See Chapter 7 for a fuller discussion of stag films.

5. Williams gives credit to Constance Penley, who had already been "teaching pornography as simply another film genre" at UC Santa Barbara (Williams 2004b, 13).

6. The story lines of many Tijuana Bibles (discussed in Chapter 4) have the same emphasis on women who are sexually unsatisfied while their male partners are physically unsatisfying or sexually spent (Adelman 1997).

7. Slade is currently working on a history of stag films, which will cover their worldwide production and distribution.

8. Bettie Page's fame has been given new life in a recently released film titled *Bettie Page: Dark Angel* (Cult Epics) starring a young look-alike actress Paige Richards (*Femme Fatale*, September/October 2004, 64).

## CHAPTER 6

1. Freud unabashedly claimed sole paternity for his theory. He once told an American audience, "psychoanalysis is my creation; for ten years I was the only one occupied with it" (Brill 1938a, 933).

2. Masters and Johnson added to the linkage, and notoriety, when Masters divorced his wife of many years and married Virginia Johnson. By the time of Masters' death at age eighty-five he had also divorced Virginia Johnson (Bernstein 2001).

3. Masters and Johnson divided the physiological sexual responses of males and females into stages "excitement," "plateau," and "orgasm," and then meticulously diagrammed the typical differences between males and females. Their diagrams have appeared in textbooks ever since.

4. The linkage between sex surrogates and AIDS/HIV is extremely tenuous, since sex with surrogates is a highly controlled, almost scripted, sexual encounter. But Masters and Johnson, along with Kolodny, seem to have been influenced by the near-panic about any kind of impersonal sex that

gripped most Americans in the 1980s and 1990s.

5. Almost all of the faculty members of the Institute for Advanced Study of Human Sexuality received their doctorates from that very same institution. This makes it an inordinately inbred institution of higher learning.

6. Some of the older pornography movies similarly used the ploy of having a medical doctor (or perhaps an actor playing one) introducing sex scenes. In the past this was done with an eye toward neutralizing the censors.

## CHAPTER 7

1. It is reported that Linda Lovelace, in the year or so before her death, enjoyed going to memorabilia shows and signing autographs, and that she was once again seeking work in the pornography business.

2. In a current ranking of the top fifty porn stars by the porn industry Lovelace ranks #5, behind Ron Jeremy, Jenna Jameson, John Holmes, and Traci Lords (www.excaliburfilms.com/avn/Linda_Lovelace), but it is doubtful that any of these actors have the public recognition of Linda Lovelace. And, astoundingly, her reputation rests on only one film.

3. Slade also lists *Behind the Green Door* as a film that illustrated "porn chic," but it is unlikely that this film had anywhere near the notoriety or name recognition of *Deep Throat*.

4. The 2005 revelation that Mark Felt, a man who had been second in command at the Federal Bureau of Investigation at the time, was the real "Deep Throat," gave new life to discourse about Lovelace's famous pornographic film.

5. With an NC-17 rating, seventeen year olds and younger are not supposed to see the film (a fuller explanation and discussion of the current movie rating system appears below).

6. O'Toole (1998, 62) describes the venues where stag films were shown as "men's clubs, private societies, brothels and 'smoking rooms.'" He was probably describing places that were more typical of Europe, but it is obvious that these were exclusively places where men congregated.

7. *Behind the Green Door* starred one of the most enduring porn stars, Marilyn Chambers, who later married Chuck Traynor the former husband of Linda Lovelace. Chambers is often noted for the fact that she was once, early in her career, the model for Ivory soap ads (the Ivory slogan was 99 and 44/100ths percent pure).

8. John Waters films have generally been more outrageous than strictly pornographic. His 1972 *Pink Flamingos* starring the obese drag queen named Divine, as an example, involved sex with a live chicken (later served up as dinner), Divine defecating in public, Divine giving oral sex to her son as a birthday present, and in the ultimate film gross-out, Divine eating dog feces (http://en.wikipedia.org/wiki/Pink_Flamingos).

9. The linkage between film names (*Deep Inside Jenna* and *Deep Throat*) is an example of what postmodernist scholars call *intertextuality*—a focus on the relationship between one text and another (Ritzer 1997). Other examples of intertextuality are found in many of the names of porn films described later

in the chapter.

10. The 2004 movie *The Aviator*, directed by Martin Scorsese and starring Leonardo DiCaprio as Howard Hughes gives a glimpse of some parts of Hughes's life.

11. On a couple of occasions Meyer did work with major Hollywood studios. With 20th Century Fox he made *Beyond the Valley of the Dolls*, which satirized an earlier film based on Jacqueline Susan's trashy novel, *Valley of the Dolls*.

12. Russ Meyer movies have been variously labeled over the years as exploitation films, nudie cuties, tits and ass pics, and cult porn films. These labels are all at least mildly pejorative. Yet, Meyers's movies have achieved some artistic and critical acclaim. Many film critics have praised the technical filmmaking and film-editing skills of Meyer. Several of Meyer's films are in the permanent collection of the Museum of Modern Art. Numerous reviewers have, at one time or another, found artistic value in his movies (Bernstein 2004, B4).

13. This *Time* story also reports that the movie "The Brown Bunny" features a scene in which actress Chloe Sevigny performs fellatio on Vincent Gallo. Though there is some uncertainty about whether the Gallo penis is the real thing.

14. The Lusty Lady theaters have an interesting management feature. The theaters are described as cooperatives, which means that all the employees, including the strippers, are part owners of the establishment.

## CHAPTER 8

1. Howard Stern, in a pique because he had been fined by the FCC, used his Web site to organize a complaint against Oprah Winfrey. Oprah had broadcast a program about teenage sex that Stern believed was just as sexually explicit as the material on his show. The FCC dutifully turned its attention to Oprah's show.

2. Hope built his career on the persona of a leering, woman chaser, who chased, but rarely caught the woman. His personal life was more interesting and complex. He had the longest-lasting marriage in Hollywood (sixty-nine years), a fact that is often noted in newspaper and magazine stories, but in his lesser-known personal life he had several serious romantic/sexual affairs and an uncounted number of one-night stands (Marx 1993).

3. The title, *Miss America*, is inexplicable since it has nothing to do with the contents of the book. Stern appears in drag on the dust jacket and inside the cover/flyleaf. He facetiously claims in the acknowledgments to have won the Miss America title in 1996.

4. While Stern may be right about radio, *Saturday Night Live* gets credit for being the first network television show to use the words penis and vagina (Shales and Miller 2002, 95).

5. A recent Obie and Anthony broadcast featured "Homeless Charlie" describing at length how he would like to have sex with Condoleeza Rice

and Laura Bush. This prompted outrage, and much sexual discourse, on the Internet (e.g., The Drudge Report) and television (e.g., The O'Reilly Factor).

6. In an earlier era (1930s and 1940s), even the Broadway show tunes of composer Cole Porter were censored for their suggestive lyrics and double entendres. In a Porter song called "Nobody's Chasing Me" the female singer laments her situation, with the lyric "The gander's chasing the goosey, But nobody's goosing me, Nobody, Nobody's chasing me." The censors in Boston insisted that "nobody's goosing me" be deleted from the song (McBrien 1998, 323).

7. Lil' Kim was out of business for a while. On March 17, 2005, she was convicted of perjury and conspiracy by a New York jury for lying to a grand jury about who was in her entourage at the time of a shooting in front of radio station Hot 97. She did serve ten months in a Pennsylvania corrections facility, after which she resumed her recording career.

8. Years after the series ended, the cast members of *Married with Children* appeared on television for a reunion discussion of the show. All the actors concurred that strangers on the street still called out to them with the names of their characters. Christina Applegate, who played Kelly, reported that her most frequent fan request continued to be "Kelly, show us your tits."

9. The current-day soap operas, most of which have survived for decades are *All My Children*, *The Bold and the Beautiful*, *As the World Turns*, *Days of Our Lives*, *General Hospital*, *One Life to Live*, and *The Young and the Restless*. A recent entry in the soap-opera derby, and one that reflects the hypersexual tenor of the times, is *Passions*.

10. Sexual content, as measured by the Kaiser Family Foundation studies, is divided into two major categories: talk and behavior. Talk includes comments on one's own or another person's sexual interests, talk about sexual intercourse that has already occurred, talk about sex-related crimes, talk about soliciting or encouraging sex, and expert advice or technical information about sex. Sex behavior includes physical flirting, passionate kissing, intimate touching, sexual intercourse strongly implied, sexual intercourse depicted, and other sexual behavior (such as oral sex and voyeurism) (Kunkel et al. 2003, 19–26).

11. Reality shows in this study are a "diverse mix that includes game shows, documentaries, and public affairs shows, along with shows such as *American Idol* or *Extreme Makeover: Home Edition*" (Kaiser Family Foundation Report, Executive Summary, 2005, 6).

12. For all the hundreds of ways the f-word is used or has been used, see Jesse Sheidlower's book *The F Word* (1995).

13. In the interest of historical accuracy, the fake orgasm entered public discourse in a limited, and a much less humorous, way when Susan Lydon wrote an article called "The Politics of Orgasm" for *Ramparts* magazine in 1970. Lydon argued that many women who had been informed about female orgasms by Freud and other twentieth-century writers, believed they

should experience vaginal orgasms, not clitoral, during sexual intercourse. Therefore, many women who wanted to appear "good in bed," often faked their orgasms.

14. Comedienne Sue Costello has a bit in her act about the fake orgasm when she asks, Is there ever a time when it is appropriate for a woman to fake an orgasm? "Yes, when she's late for a shoe sale."

15. After the television series ended, rumors persisted that the original foursome would make a movie with the same name. The film has now been made and was released in the spring of 2008.

16. In one scene, the teacher asks Eric for the definition of sexual harassment. He answers, "when you're having sex with your lady friend and some other guy comes up and tickles your balls from behind." Kids may "say the darnedest things," but this is not one of them.

17. Saget had a long run on the sitcom *Full House* where he played the wholesome father of three daughters after the death of the girls' mother. The Olsen twins (Mary Kate and Ashley) shared the role of the youngest daughter.

### CHAPTER 9

1. Although the judge awarded Kremen 65 million dollars, the defendant Cohen didn't come up with the money. Kremen did get a seven-bedroom mansion in affluent Rancho Santa Fe, California (O'Brien 2004).

2. Another example of a clever and anticipatory pornography Web site was created by Dan Parisi in 1997. He laid claim to www.whitehouse.com, the familiar name of the president's home. Parisi promptly turned it into a pornography site. Between 1997 and 2004, 85 million Internet users visited this site. No one knows how much money Parisi has made from this Internet site, but Parisi paid ten thousand dollars for the site in 1997 and today is asking more than 1 million dollars for it (Milbank 2004; news@whitehouse.com).

3. Almost no pornographic Web sites are directed specifically toward women. Some women claim to be interested in the heterosexual male-directed sites, even though these usually feature females only. Lesbians, of course, might find some of these sites interesting, but very few appear to be aimed at lesbian audiences. The few sites that do feature men are obviously aimed at gay males, not heterosexual women.

4. The masculine pronoun is used here and in other places in this discussion to reflect the fact that most pornography users are male.

5. While the following descriptions are exactly as they appear on the Web site (www.amateurindex.com) the names, which may in any case be fictitious, have been scrambled. The number of **** before a name indicates the level of sexual appeal as judged by the creator of the index.

6. Suspension of rationality is a key feature of pornography. Viewers and readers of pornography must be willing to imagine that the sex being portrayed could actually happen in real life—perhaps even to them.

7. As a cautionary note, it is possible to fabricate Internet images, and some images may not be of actual celebrities.

8. The author of this book cannot resist reporting that he and his wife, quite by coincidence, were staying at a Seattle hotel in which furry conferees were meeting. Coming across some of the attendees in the lobby, my wife innocently complimented one of the young men, saying, "I like your tail."

9. The Web sites we will be describing next are primarily directed toward women. Certainly the Internet has many comparable sites that offer information, advice, and products aimed at men and their sexuality (e.g., the already mentioned promotion of Viagra and penis enlargement products). Our focus on female-oriented Web sites here provides some gender balance.

10. Parties organized around the sale of sexual products (sexy underwear, massage oils, and so on), have been around for a couple of decades. These were usually designed for couples and were mildly risqué, but not explicitly sexual.

11. A similar retail outlet in Manhattan is Eve's Garden, which features the slogan, "We Grow Pleasurable things for women."

12. In February 2007, authorities in Austria discovered and exposed a child pornography Web site originating in Russia. This site had been visited by 2,360 people from 77 countries.

13. Adult males may also make contact with young males on the Internet. These too may lead to personal tragedies, or sexual abuse.

14. Cutler used the publicity she received to get a novel published. This novel was a barely disguised version of her real life (Cutler 2005).

15. Ludlow and Wallace describe one of the latest Internet developments, the online games that involve a massive number of people participating in virtual environments. One dimension of this virtual world is cybersex—"sometimes called tinysex, netsex, or just plain cyber" (Ludlow and Wallace 2007, 128).

## CHAPTER 10

1. The Glassman and Hassett book now sells for forty-nine cents at amazon.com.

2. Stepp has also written about another sexual fad among some high school females: bisexuality. Some girls, according to Stepp, consider dabbling in bisexuality as a chic behavior (Stepp 2004). This, too, indicates a high level of sexual sophistication among teenagers.

3. A recently published book has described the sex lives of students at an upscale prep school, which was made famous when a fifteen-year-old girl was videotaped giving oral sex to members of the boys' lacrosse team. According to the authors, this event was a reflection of the sexual lives of the students (Jones and Miley 2007).

4. Cell phone technology is, at the moment, one of the most important means for communication. Cell phones today can connect with the Internet where they provide access to all forms of sexual material, including pornography.

# REFERENCES

Achenbach, Joel. 2006. "Dropping the F-Bomb." *The Washington Post*, June 25, p. B1.

Adelman, Bob, with Art Spiegelman and Richard Merkin. 1997. *Tijuana Bibles: Art and Wit in America's Forbidden Funnies, 1930s–1950s.* New York: Simon & Schuster.

Ahrens, Frank. 2004. "Radio Giant in Record Indecency Settlement." *The Washington Post*, June 9, pp. A1, A7.

Ahrens, Frank. 2005a. "House Raises Penalties for Airing Indecency." *The Washington Post*, February 17, pp. E1, E12.

Ahrens, Frank. 2005b. "Senator Bids to Extend Indecency Rules to Cable." *The Washington Post*, March 2, pp. E1, E3.

Althof, Stanley E. 2000. "Erectile Dysfunction: Psychotherapy with Men and Couples." In *Principles and Practice of Sex Therapy*, 3rd ed., edited by Sandra R. Leiblum and Raymond C. Rosen, 242–75. New York: Guilford Press.

Anonymous. 2003. *The Bride Stripped Bare.* New York: HarperCollins.

Aratani, Lori. 2005. "Teens' Take: Sex Is All Around Them." *The Washington Post*, June 20, pp. A1, A16.

Assiter, Alison, and Carol Avedon. 1993. *Bad Girls and Dirty Pictures: The Challenge to Reclaim Feminism.* Boulder, CO: Pluto Press.

Associated Press. 2001. "Swedish-Made Niagara: The '*Drink?* of Love,' the New American *Passion?*" *Nordstjernan*, April 19, pp. 1, 3.

Atlas, James. 1999. "The Loose Canon: Annals of Academia." *The New Yorker*, March 29, pp. 60–65.

Avedon, Carol. 1994. *Nudes, Prudes and Attitudes: Pornography and Censorship.* Cheltenham, UK: New Clarion Press.

Baird, Robert M., and Stuart E. Rosenbaum, eds. 1991. *Pornography: Private Right or Public Menace?* Buffalo, NY: Prometheus Books.

Baker, Peter. 2006. "Bush Signs Legislation on Broadcast Decency." *The Washington Post*, June 10, p. A6.

Barker-Benfield, G. J. 1976. *The Horrors of the Half-Known Life: Male Attitudes toward Women and Sexuality in Nineteenth-Century America.* New York: Harper & Row.

Barron, Martin, and Michael Kimmel. 2000. "Sexual Violence in Three Pornographic Media: Toward a Sociological Explanation." *The Journal of Sex Research* 37:161–68.

Bartlett, Carol. 2001. "Romance Readers' Advisory." Anne Arundel County Public Library. Annapolis, MD.

Bateson, Gregory. 1972. *Steps to an Ecology of the Mind*. New York: Aronson.

Baudrillard, Jean. 1983/1990. *Fatal Strategies*. New York: Semiotext(e).

Baudrillard, Jean. 1992/1994. *The Illusion of the End*. Palo Alto, CA: Stanford University Press.

Baudrillard, Jean. 2005. *The Conspiracy of Art*. New York: Semiotext/art.

Beisel, Nicola. 1997. *Imperiled Innocents: Anthony Comstock and Family Reproduction in Victorian America*. Princeton, NJ: Princeton University Press.

Bellah, Robert N., Richard Madsen, William M. Sullivan, Ann Swidler, and Steven M. Tipton. 1985. *Habits of the Heart: Individualism and Commitment in American Life*. Chicago: University of Chicago Press.

Berendt, John. 1995. "High Heel Neil." *The New Yorker* (January 16): 38–45.

Berger, Ronald J., Patricia Searles, and Charles E. Cottle. 1991. *Feminism and Pornography*. New York: Praeger.

Berman, Jennifer, Laura Berman, and Elisabeth Bumiller. 2001. *For Women Only: A Revolutionary Guide to Reclaiming Your Sex Life*. New York: Henry Holt.

Bernstein, Adam. 2001 "William Masters, 85, Dies; Pioneering Sex Researcher." *The Washington Post*, February 19, p. B6.

Bernstein, Adam. 2004. "Russ Meyer, Producer of Cult Porno Films, Dies at 82." *The Washington Post*, September 23, p. B4.

Binik, Yitzchak M., Sophie Bergeron, and Samir Khalifé. 2000. "Dyspareunia and Vaginismus: So-Called Sexual Pain." In *Principles and Practice of Sex Therapy*, 3rd ed., edited by Sandra R. Leiblum and Raymond C. Rosen, 154–80. New York: Guilford Press.

Bogart, Leo. 2005. *Over the Edge: How the Pursuit of Youth by Marketers and the Media Changed American Culture*. Chicago: Ivan R. Dee.

Bosworth, Patricia. 2005. "The X-Rated Emperor." *Vanity Fair* (February): 148–61.

Boyd, Brian. 1991. *Vladimir Nabokov: The American Years*. Princeton, NJ: Princeton University Press.

Bozell, L. Brent, III. 2004. "'Nip/Tuck' Knows No Bounds." August 19. Available at http://www.parentstv.org/ptc/shows/main.asp?shwid=1726 (accessed June 4, 2008).

Breger, Louis. 2000. *Freud: Darkness in the Midst of Vision*. New York: John Wiley & Sons.

Briggs, Joe Bob. 2002. "Linda Lovelace Gets Some Peace at Last." April 24. Available at http://www.joebobbriggs.com/drivein/2002/lindalovelace.html (accessed June 4, 2008).

Briggs, Joe Bob. 2003. "Kroger Babb's Roadshow." *Reason* (November): 30–38.

Brill, A. A., ed. and trans. 1938a. *The Basic Writings of Sigmund Freud*. New York: Random House.

Brill, A. A. 1938b. Introduction to *The Basic Writings of Sigmund Freud*, edited and translated by A. A. Brill, 3–32. New York: Random House.

Brite, Popry Z. 2004. *Love in Vein II*. Edison, NJ: Castle Books.

Britton, Patti. 2005. *The Art of Sex Coaching*. New York: W. W. Norton & Company.

Broun, Heywood, and Margaret Leech. 1927. *Anthony Comstock: Roundsman of the Lord*. New York: Albert & Charles Boni.

Brown, Helen Gurley. 1962. *Sex and the Single Girl*. New York: Bernard Geis Associates.

Brown, Helen Gurley. 1982. *Having It All*. New York: Simon & Schuster.

Brown, Helen Gurley. 2000. *I'm Wild Again: Snippets from My Life and a Few Brazen Thoughts*. New York: St. Martin's Press.

Brown, Tina. 2005. "'Deep Throat': When Naughty Was Nice." *The Washington Post*, February 10, p. C9.

Bruce, Lenny. 1992. *How to Talk Dirty and Influence People*. New York: Fireside.

Bulman, Robert C. 2005. *Hollywood Goes to High School*. New York: Worth.

Burnham, John C. 1972. "American Historians and the Subject of Sex," *Societas* 2 (Autumn): 307–16.

Burroughs, William. 1959. *Naked Lunch*. New York: Grove Press.

Califida, Pat. 1994. *Public Sex: The Culture of Radical Sex*. Pittsburgh: Cleis Press.

Callahan, Michael. 2006. "Peyton Place's Real Victim." *Vanity Fair* (March): 331–39.

Cameron, Ardis. 1999. "Open Secrets: Rereading *Peyton Place*." In *Peyton Place* by Grace Metalious, xii–xxx. Boston: Northeastern University Press.

Carlson, Peter. 2003. "From Here to 'Absurdity: One Strange Trip." *The Washington Post*, November 4, pp. C1, C9.

Carlson, Peter. 2004. "2004's Sassy, Trashy, Gassy, Flashy Glossies." *The Washington Post*, December, 21, pp. C1, C4.

Carlson, Peter. 2007. "How to Put Your Country on the Map: In Her Breast Interest." *The Washington Post*, September 4, p. C8.

Centers for Disease Control and Prevention. 2004. *Surveillance Summaries, MMWR, 2004*, p. 53.

Centers for Disease Control and Prevention. 2005. *HIV/AIDS Surveillance Report, 2004*. Vol. 16. Atlanta: U.S. Department of Health and Human Services, Centers for Disease Control and Prevention.

Christensen, Harold T. 1962. "Value-Behavior Discrepancies Regarding Premarital Coitus in Three Western Cultures." *American Sociological Review* 27:66–74.

Chunovic, Louis. 2000. *One Foot on The Floor: The Curious Evolution of Sex on Television from I Love Lucy to South Park*. New York: TV Books.

Clark, Megan. 2005. *Rescue Me: An Erotic Novel*. New York: Kensington Books.

Clarke, John R. 2003. *Roman Sex: 100 BC–AD 250*. New York: Harry N. Abrams.

Cleland, John. 1963. *Memoirs of a Woman of Pleasure (Fanny Hill)*. New York: Putnam.

Collins, Ronald K. L., and David M. Skover. 2002. *The Trials of Lenny Bruce: the Rise and Fall of an American Icon*. Naperville, IL: Sourcebooks.

Conrad, Peter, and James W. Schneider. 1980. *Deviance and Medicalization: From Badness to Sickness*. St. Louis: Mosby.

Cooperman, Alan. 2004. "Kinsey Movie Frustrates Christians." *The Washington Post*, November 24, p. A11.

Coote, Stephen. 2001. *Samuel Pepys: A Life*. New York: St. Martin's Press.

Cullen, Lisa Takeuchi. 2006. "Sex in the Syllabus." *Time* (April 3): 80–81.

Cutler, Jessica. 2005. *The Washingtonienne: A Novel*. New York: Hyperion Press.

DeJean, Joan. 1993. "The Politics of Pornography: *L'Ecole des Filles*." In *The Invention of Pornography: Obscenity and the Origins of Modernity, 1500–1800*, edited by Lynn Hunt, 109–24. New York: Zone Books.

D'Emilio, John, and Estelle B. Freedman. 1988. *Intimate Matters: A History of Sexuality in America*. New York: Harper & Rowe.

Denby, David. 2004a. "They Like to Watch." *The New Yorker* (February 9): 74–76.

Denby, David. 2004b. "Sex Appeal: Alfred C. Kinsey Reconsidered." *The New Yorker* (November 29): 171–73.

Denby, David. 2008. "Rock of Ages: Movies about Getting Old and Playing Music." *The New Yorker* (January 7): 80–81.

Denizet-Lewis, Benoit. 2004. "Double Lives on the Down Low." In *The Best American Sex Writing, 2004*, edited by Daniel O'Connor, 43–67. New York: Avalon. Originally published in *New York Times Magazine* (August 3, 2003).

Dines, Gail. 1998. "Living in Two Worlds: An Activist in the Academy." In *Pornography: The Production and Consumption of Inequality*, by Gail Dines, Robert Jensen, and Ann Russo, 163–66. New York: Routledge.

Dines, Gail, Robert Jensen, and Ann Russo. 1998. *Pornography: The Production and Consumption of Inequality*. New York: Routledge.

Dodson, Betty. 1996. *Sex for One: The Joy of Selfloving*. New York: Crown Publishing Group. Originally titled *Liberating Masturbation*.

Dodson, Betty. 2002. *Orgasm for Two: The Joy of Partnersex*. New York: Crown Publishing Group.

Donnerstein, Edward, Daniel Linz, and Steven Penrod. 1987. *The Question of Pornography: Research Findings and Policy Implications*. New York: The Free Press.

Dworkin, Andrea. 1980. *Pornography: Men Possessing Women*. New York: Putnam's.

Dworkin, Andrea. 1987. *Ice and Fire*. New York: Weidenfield and Nicholson.

Dworkin, Andrea. 1995. *Contemporary Authors Autobiography Series*. Vol. 21. Farmingtion Hills, MN: Gale Research.

Dworkin, Andrea. 2002. *Heartbreak: The Political Memoir of a Militant Feminist*. New York: Basic Books.

Dwyer, Timothy. 2005. "Skimpy Underwear: Ample Commentary at Tyson's Corner." *The Washington Post*, October 5, pp. B1, B5.

Earle, Ralph H., and Marcus R. Earle. 1995. *Sex Addiction: Case Studies and Management*. New York: Brunner/Mazel.

Eggan, Dan. 2005. "Sculpted Bodies and a Strip Act at Justice Dept." *The Washington Post*, June 25, p. A2.

Ehrmann, Winston W. 1959. *Premarital Dating Behavior*. New York: Holt, Rinehart and Winston.

Elias, James, Veronica Diehl Elias, Vern L. Bullough, Gwen Brewer, Jeffrey J. Douglas, and Will Jarvi. 1999. *Porn 101: Eroticism, Pornography, and the First Amendment*. Amherst, NY: Prometheus Books.

Elmer-Dewitt, Philip. 1995. "On a Screen Near You: Cyberporn." *Time* (July 3): 45.

Erickson, Miltion H. 1967. "Pediatric Hypnotherapy." In *Advanced Techniques of Hypnosis and Therapy: Selected Papers of M. H. Erickson*, by J. Hayley, 420–21. New York: Grune & Stratton.

Evans-Prichard, E. E. 1970. "Sexual Inversion among the Azande." *The American Anthropologist* 72:1428–34.

Faceliere, R. 1962. *Love in Ancient Greece*. Translated by James Cleugh. New York: Crown Books.

Faludi, Susan. 1995. "The Money Shot." *The New Yorker* (October 30): 64–87.

Faludi, Susan. 1999. *Stiffed: The Betrayal of the American Man*. New York: HarperCollins.

Farhi, Paul. 2004. "We've Built Shock into the Culture." *The Washington Post*, February 15, p. B3.

Farr, Kathryn. 2005. *Sex Trafficking: The Global Market in Women and Children*. New York: Worth.

Feifer, Jason. 2004. "Is There a Sexologist in the House?" *The Washington Post*, June 15, p. HE05.

Femme Fatale. 2004. "Fatale Favorite: Bettie Page." *Femme Fatale* (September/October): 64.

Ferguson, Robert. 1991. *Henry Miller: A Life*. New York: W. W. Norton & Company.

Ferocius. 2000. "The College of Erotic Sciences." San Francisco: Last Gasp of San Francisco.

Finan, Christopher M. 2004. "Catherine A. MacKinnon: The Rise of a Feminist Censor, 1983–1993." Available at http://www.mediacoalition.org/reports/mackinnon (accessed June 4, 2008).

Flynt, Larry. 2004. *Sex, Lies and Politics: The Naked Truth*. New York: Kensington Books.

Ford, Clellan S., and Frank A. Beach. 1951. *Patterns of Sexual Behavior*. New York: Harper & Row.

Foucault, Michel. 1978. *The History of Sexuality. Vol. 1, An Introduction*. New York: Pantheon Books.

Foucault, Michel. 1984/1985. *The History of Sexuality. Vol. 2, The Use of Pleasure*. New York: Pantheon Books.

Freedman, Estelle. 1982. "Sexuality in Nineteen-Century America: Behavior, Ideology and Politics." *Reviews in American History* 10 (December): 196–215.

Frey, Jennifer. 2001. "What's Tingly and Easy to Swallow." *The Washington Post*, May 7, pp. C1, C4.

Frey, Jennifer. 2004. "Clear Channel Fined $495,000, Dumps Stern." *The Washington Post*, April 9, pp. C1, C8.

Friedman, David M. 2001. *A Mind of Its Own: A Cultural History of the Penis*. New York: The Free Press.

Gates, Katherine. 2000. *Deviant Desires: Incredibly Strange Sex*. New York: Juno Books.

Gentile, Gary. 2006. "Mr. Playboy at 80: No Regrets." *The Washington Post*, April 9, p. D4.

Gertzmann, Jay A. 1999. *Bookleggers and Smuthounds: The Trade in Erotica, 1920–1940*. Philadelphia: University of Pennsylvania Press.

Gibson, Pamela Church, and Roma Gibson, eds. 1993. *Dirty Looks: Women, Pornography and Power*. London: British Film Institute.

Gill, Brendan. 1975. *Here at The New Yorker*. London: Michael Joseph.

Gittler, Ian. 1999. *Porn Star*. New York: Simon & Schuster.

Gladwell, Malcolm. 2004. "The Terrazzo Jungle." *The New Yorker* (March 15): 120–27.

Glassman, James, and Kevin A. Hassett. 1999. *Dow 36,000: The New Strategy for Profiting from the Coming Rise in the Stock Market*. New York: Times Business.

Goldman, Albert. 1974. *Ladies and Gentlemen: Lenny Bruce!!* New York: Balantine Books.

Goldschmidt, Paul W. 1999. *Pornography and Democratization: Legislating Obscenity in Post-Communist Russia*. Boulder, CO: Westview Press.

Gordon, Lyndall. 2005. *Vindication: A Life of Mary Wollstonecraft*. New York: HarperCollins.

Gover, Robert. 1989. *One Hundred Dollar Misunderstanding*. New York: Grove Press.

Green, Russell G., and Edward Donnerstein, eds. 1998. *Human Aggression: Theories, Research, and Implications for Social Policy*. New York: Academic Press.

Green, Shelley, and Douglas Flemons. 2004. *Quickies: The Handbook of Brief Sex Therapy*. New York: W. W. Norton & Company.

Grindstaff, Laura. 2002. *The Money Shot: Trash, Class, and the Making of TV Talk Shows*. Chicago: University of Chicago Press.

Groneman, Carol. 2000. *Nymphomania: A History*. New York: W. W. Norton & Company.

Gurley, George. 2001. "The Pleasures of Fur." *Vanity Fair* (March): 174–88, 193–96.

Haley, J. 1967. *Advanced Techniques of Hypnosis and Therapy: Selected Papers of M. H. Erickson*. New York: Grune & Stratton.

Hallett, Judith P., and Marilyn B. Skinner, eds. 1997. *Roman Sexualities*. Princeton, NJ: Princeton University Press.

Hamalian, Leo. 1974. "Nobody Knows My Names: Samuel Roth and the Underside of Modern Letters." *Journal of Modern Literature* 3, no. 4 (April): 889–921.

Harris, Frank. 1922. *My Life and Loves*. New York: Grove Press, 1963. Originally published in private edition in Paris.

Henry, Madeleine M. 1992. "The Edible Woman: Athenaeus's Concept of the Pornographic." In *Pornography and Representation in Greece and Rome*, edited by Amy Richlin, 250–68. New York: Oxford University Press.

Hobhouse, Janet. 1988. *The Bride Stripped Bare: The Artist and the Female Nude in the Twentieth Century*. New York: Weidenfield and Nicolson.

Holliday, Jim. 1999. "A History of Modern Pornographic Film and Video." In *Porn 101: Eroticism, Pornography, and the First Amendment*, edited by James Elias, Veronica Diehl Elias, Vern L. Bullough, Gwen Brewer, Jeffrey J. Douglas, and Will Jarvis, 341–51. Amherst, NY: Prometheus Books.

Horn, Maurice. 1985. *Sex in the Comics*. New York: Chelsea House.

Horowitz, Helen Lefkowitz. 2000. "Victoria Woodhull, Anthony Comstock, and Conflict over Sex in the United States in the 1870s." *The Journal of American History* 87, no. 2 (September): 403–34.

Hughes, Donna Rice, with Pamela T. Campbell. 1998. *Kids Online: Protecting Your Children in Cyberspace*. Grand Rapids, MI: Revell.

Humphries, Laud. 1975. *Tearoom Trade: Impersonal Sex in Public Places*. Chicago: Aldine Press.

Hunt, Lynn, ed. 1993a. *The Invention of Pornography: Obscenity and the Origins of Modernity, 1500–1800*. New York: Zone Books.

Hunt, Lynn. 1993b. "Introduction: Obscenity and the Origins of Modernity, 1500–1800." In *The Invention of Pornography: Obscenity and the Origins of Modernity, 1500–1800*, edited by Lynn Hunt, 9–45. New York: Zone Books.

Hunt, Lynn. 1993c. "Pornography and the French Revolution." In *The Invention of Pornography: Obscenity and the Origins of Modernity, 1500–1800*, edited by Lynn Hunt, 301–39. New York: Zone Books.

Hyde, H. Montgomery. 1965. *A History of Pornography*. New York: Farrar, Straus, and Giroux.

Itzin, Catherine, ed. 1992a. *Pornography: Women, Violence, and Civil Liberties*. Oxford: Oxford University Press.

Itzin, Catherine. 1992b. "Pornography and the Social Construction of Sexual Inequality." In *Pornography: Women, Violence, and Civil Liberties*, edited by Catherine Itzin. Oxford: Oxford University Press.

Jackson, Don. 1961. "Interactional Psychotherapy." In *Contemporary Psychotherapists*, edited by M. Stein, 256–71. New York: Free Press of Glencoe.

Jenkins, Philip. 2001. *Beyond Tolerance: Child Pornography on the Internet*. New York: New York University Press.

Jensen, Robert. 1998. "Introduction: Pornographic Dodges and Distortions." In *Pornography: The Production and Consumption of Inequality*, edited by Gail Dines, Robert Jensen, and Ann Russo, 1–7. New York: Routledge.

Jones, Abigail, and Marissa Miley. 2007. *Restless Virgins: Sex and Survival at a New England Prep School*. New York: William Morrow/HarperCollins.

Jones, E. Michael. 2000. *Libido Dominandi: Sexual Liberation and Political Control*. South Bend, IN: St. Augustine's Press.

Jones, James Howard. 1997a. *Alfred Kinsey: A Public/Private Life*. New York: W. W. Norton & Company.

Jones, James Howard. 1997b. "Annals of Sexology: Dr. Yes." *The New Yorker* (August 25 and September 1): 98–113.

Juffer, Jane. 1998. *At Home with Pornography: Women, Sex, and Everyday Life*. New York: New York University Press.

Kafka, Martin P. 2000. "The Paraphilia-Related Disorders: Nonparaphilic Hypersexuality and Sexual Compulsivity/Addiction." In *Principles and Practice of Sex Therapy*, 3rd ed., edited by Sandra R. Leiblum and Raymond C. Rosen, 471–503. New York: Guilford Press.

Kaiser Family Foundation Report. 2005. Executive Summary, *Sex on TV 4*. Menlo Park, CA: The Henry J. Kaiser Family Foundation. Available at http://www.kff.org/entmedia/entmedia110905pkg.cfm (accessed June 4, 2008).

Kaplan, Helen Singer. 1974. *The New Sex Therapy*. New York: Brunner/Mazel.

Kaplan, Helen Singer. 1975. *The Illustrated Manuel of Sex Therapy*. New York: Quadrangle Books.

Kaplan, Helen Singer. 1979. *Disorders of Sexual Desire*. New York: Brunner/Mazel.

Kaplan, Helen Singer. 1986. *Sexual Aversions, Sexual Phobias, and Panic Disorders*. New York: Brunner/Mazel.

Kaplan, Helen Singer. 1995. *The Sexual Desire Disorders: Dysfunctional Regulation of Sexual Motivation*. New York: Routledge.

Katz, Jonathon. 1976. *Gay American History: Lesbians and Gay Men In the U.S.A.* New York: Thomas Crowell.

Kearney, Patrick J. 1982. *A History of Erotic Literature*. London: Macmillan.

Kendrick, Walter. 1987. *The Secret Museum: Pornography in Modern Culture*. New York: Viking.

Kinsey, Alfred C., Wardell B. Pomeroy, and Clyde E. Martin. 1948. *Sexual Behavior in the Human Male*. Philadelphia: Saunders.

Kinsey, Alfred C., Wardell B. Pomeroy, Clyde E. Martin, and Paul H. Gebhard. 1953. *Sexual Behavior in the Human Female*. Philadelphia: Saunders.

Kipnis, Laura. 1996. *Bound and Gagged: Pornography and the Politics of Fantasy in America*. New York: Grove Press.

Kipnis, Laura. 2003. *Against Love: A Polemic*. New York: Pantheon.

Kipnis, Laura. 2006. *The Female Thing: Dirt, Sex, Envy, Vulnerability*. New York: Pantheon.

Kirch, Jonathon. 1997. *The Harlot by the Side of the Road: Forbidden Tales of the Bible*. New York: Ballantine Books.

Kunkel, Dale, Erica Biely, Keren Eyal, Kirstie Cope-Farrar, and Edward Donnerstein. 2003. *Sex on TV 3*. Santa Barbara, CA: The Henry J. Kaiser Family Foundation.

Kunkel, Thomas. 1995. *Genius in Disguise: Harold Ross of The New Yorker*. New York: Random House.

Kurtz, Howard. 1995. "Morality Guru Takes on Talk TV." *The Washington Post*, October 26, pp. C1, C8.

Kurtz, Howard. 2003. "Bikini Island: Geographic Goes a Bit Off Track." *The Washington Post*, January 25, pp. C1, C4.

Kurtz, Howard, and Frank Ahrends. 2004. "Sirus Lands a Big Dog: Howard Stern." *The Washington Post*, October, 7, pp. A1, A12.

Lane, Frederick S., III. 2000. *Obscene Profits: The Entrepreneurs of Pornography in the Cyber Age*. New York: Routledge.

Laumann, Edward O., John H. Gagnon, and Robert T. Michael. 1994. "A Political History of the National Sex Survey of Adults." *Family Planning Perspectives* 34:34–38.

Laumann, Edward O., John H. Gagnon, Robert T. Michael, and Stuart Michaels. 1994. *The Social Organization of Sexuality: Sexual Practices in the United States*. Chicago: University of Chicago Press.

Lederer, Laura, ed. 1980. *Take Back the Night: Women on Pornography*. New York: William Morrow.

Lederer, Laura, and Richard Delgado, eds. 1995. *The Price We Pay: The Case against Racist Speech, Hate Propaganda and Pornography*. New York: Hill and Wang.

Lefkowitz Horowitz, Helen. 2002. *Rereading Sex: Battles Over Sexual Knowledge and Suppression in Nineteenth-Century America*. New York: Knopf.

Lehrman, Nat. 1970. *Masters and Johnson Explained*. Chicago: Playboy Press.

Leiblum, Sandra Risa, and Raymond C. Rosen, eds. 2000. *Principles and Practice of Sex Therapy*, 3rd ed. New York: Guilford Press.

Let's Live. 2001. *Let's Live* Magazine. (May). Santa Monica, CA: William Madonna Group Publishers.

Levy, Ariel. 2004. "Dispatches from Girls Gone Wild." *Slate* (March 22). Available at http://www.slate.com/id/2097485/entry/2097496/ (accessed June 4, 2008).

Levy, Ariel. 2005. "Raunchiness Is Powerful? C'mon, Girls," *The Washington Post*, September 18, p. B5.

Levy, Ariel. 2006. *Female Chauvinist Pigs: Women and the Rise of Raunch Culture*. New York: Simon & Schuster.

Lloyd, Joan Elizabeth. 2003. *Never Enough*. New York: Kensington Books.

Loe, Meika. 1996. "Working for Men—At the Intersection of Power, Gender, and Sexuality." *Sociological Inquiry* 66:399–421.

Loe, Meika. 2004. *The Rise of Viagra: How a Little Blue Pill Changed Sex in America*. New York: New York University Press.

Lords, Traci. 2003. *Traci Lords: Underneath It All*. New York: HarperCollins.

Lovelace, Linda. 1974a. *Inside Linda Lovelace*. London: Heinrich Hanau.

Lovelace, Linda. 1974b. *The Intimate Diary of Linda Lovelace*. St. Louis: Pinnacle Paperbacks.

Lovelace, Linda, with Mike McGrady. 1980. *Ordeal*. New York: Bell Publishing, 1983. Originally published by The Citadel Press, a Division of Lyle Stuart.

Lovelace, Linda, with Mike McGrady. 1986. *Out of Bondage*. Secaucus, NJ: Lyle Stuart.

Ludlow, Peter, and Mark Wallace. 2007. *The Second Life Herald: The Virtual Tabloid that Witnessed the Dawn of the Metaverse.* Cambridge, MA: MIT Press.

MacFarquhar, Louise. 2005. "Men of Letters, Baudrillard on Tour." *The New Yorker* (November 28): 62, 64.

MacKinnon, Catharine. 1993. *Only Words.* Cambridge, MA: Harvard University Press.

Malamuth, Neil M., and Edward Donnerstein, eds. 1984. *Pornography and Sexual Aggression.* New York: Academic Press.

Marritt, Rich. 2005. *Secrets of a Gay Marine Porn Star: A Memoir.* New York: Kensington Books.

Marx, Arthur. 1993. *The Secret Life of Bob Hope.* New York: Barricade Books.

Masters, William H., and Virginia E. Johnson. 1966. *Human Sexual Response.* Boston: Little, Brown.

Masters, William H., and Virginia E. Johnson. 1970. *Human Sexual Inadequacy.* Boston: Little, Brown.

Masters, William H., Virginia E. Johnson, and Robert C. Kolodny. 1985. *Human Sexuality.* 2nd ed. Boston: Little Brown.

Masters, William H., Virginia E. Johnson, and Robert C. Kolodny. 1994. *Heterosexuality.* New York: HarperCollins.

Max, D. T. 2006. "The Injustice Collector." *The New Yorker* (June 19): 34–43.

Maynard, Joyce. 1998. *At Home in the World.* New York: Picador USA.

McBrien, William. 1998. *Cole Porter: A Biography.* New York: Alfred A. Knopf.

McClintock, Anne. 1993. "Maid to Order: Commercial S/M and Gender Power." In *Dirty Looks: Women Pornography, and Power*, edited by Pamela Church Gibson and Roma Gibson, 207–31. London: British Film Institute.

McElroy, Wendy. 1995. *XXX: A Woman's Right to Pornography.* New York: St. Martin's Press.

Merkin, Daphne. 1996. "The Unlikely Obsession." *The New Yorker* (February 26): 98–115.

Merkin, Daphne. 1997. "The Skin Game." *The New Yorker* (October 13): 97–98.

Metalious, Grace. 1956. *Peyton Place.* New York: Julian Messner. Reprinted 1999 by Northeastern University Press.

Metcalf, Allan. 2002. *Predicting New Words: The Secrets of Their Success.* Boston: Houghton Mifflin Company.

Meyers, Jeffrey. 1995. *Edmund Wilson: A Biography.* New York: Houghton Mifflin Company.

Milbank, Dana. 2004. "Curtain Goes Up on Glass-House Attack." *The Washington Post*, February 15, p. A4.

Miller, James. 1993. *The Passion of Michel Foucault.* New York: Anchor Books.

Miller, Jason L. 2005. "X-X-X-it Stage Left: ICANN Offers Safer Porn Domain." webpronews.com, June 2. Available at http://www.webpronews.com/topnews/2005/06/02/xxxit-stage-left-icann-offers-safer-porn-domai (accessed June 4, 2008).

Millet, Catherine. 2002. *The Sexual Life of Catherine M.* Translated by Adriana Hunter. New York: Grove Press.

Milter, Katalin Szoverfy, and Joseph W. Slade. 2005. "Global Traffic in Pornography: The Hungarian Example." In *International Exposure: Perspectives on Modern Pornography, 1800–2000*, edited by Liza Z. Sigel, 173–204. New Brunswick, NJ: Rutgers University Press.

Montgomery, David, and Frank Ahrens. 2004. "Howard Stern Booted in Clear Channel Indecency Crackdown." *The Washington Post*, February 26, pp. C1, C7.

Moretti, Daniel S. 1984. *Obscenity and Pornography: The Law Under the First Amendment.* New York: Oceana Publications.

Morgan, Robin. 1978. *Going Too Far: The Personal Chronicle of A Feminist.* New York: Vintage Books.

Mundy, Liza. 2003. "Do You Know Where Your Children Are?" *The Washington Post Magazine* (November 16): 12–16, 25–30.

Museum of Sex. 2002. *NYCSEX: How New York City Transformed Sex in America.* London: Scala Publishers.

Musgrove, Mike. 2005a. "Code-Abiding Porn to Get .xxx Domain." *The Washington Post*, June 3, p. D5.

Musgrove, Mike. 2005b. "Mini-Porn Could Be Mega-Business." *The Washington Post*, November 15, pp. D1, D4.

Nabokov, Vladimir. 1955. *Lolita.* Paris: Olympia Press.

Nachman, Gerald. 1998. *Raised on Radio.* New York: Pantheon Books.

Nathan, Sharon G. 1995. "Sexual Addiction: A Sex Therapist's Struggles with an Unfamiliar Clinical Entity." In *Case Studies in Sex Therapy*, edited by Raymond C. Rosen and Sandra R. Lieblum, 350–67. New York: Guilford Press.

National Public Radio. 2004. "Adult Entertainment Stores Join Supersizing Trend." Morning Edition. August 10.

Nedjma, C. J. Hunter. 2004. *The Almond: The Sexual Awakening of a Muslim Woman.* New York: Grove Press.

Newton, Helmut. 2002. *Autobiography.* New York: Nan A. Talese.

Noe. 1998. "Doctor I'm Too Big." New York: Nantier, Beall, Minoustchine.

Noire. 2005. *Candy Licker: An Urban Erotic Tale.* New York: One World Ballantine Books.

Norman, Marc. 2007. *What Happens Next: A History of American Screenwriting.* New York: Harmony Books.

Nussbaum, Emily. 2007. "Say Everything." *New York* (February 12): 24–28, 102–3.

O'Brien, Chris. 2003. "The Prisoner of Sex.com." In *The Best American Sex Writing 2004*, edited by Daniel O'Connor, 13–20. New York: Thunder Mouth Press, 2004. Originally in *Wired* (August).

Oldenburg, Don. 2004. "Screen Sizzlers: Video Gaming Industry's Hottest New Titles Aim at Generation XXX." *The Washington Post*, October 20, pp. C1, C10.

O'Toole, Laurence. 1998. *Pornocopia: Porn, Sex, Technology and Desire.* London: Serpent's Tail.

Painter, Kim. 2002. "The Sexual Revolution Hits Junior High." *USA Today*, March 15, pp. 1A, 2A.

Palac, Lisa. 1998. *The Edge of the Bed: How Dirty Pictures Changed My Life*. Boston: Little Brown.

Palmer, Marina. 2005. *Kiss and Tango: Looking for Love in Buenos Aires*. New York: William Morrow/HarperCollins.

Parker, Holt N. 1992. "Love's Body Anatomized: The Ancient Erotic Handbooks and the Rhetoric of Sexuality." In *Pornography and Representation in Greece and Rome*, edited by Amy Richlin, 90–111. New York: Oxford University Press.

Parvaz, D. 2003. "Nudity, Sex Articles in Abercrombie & Fitch." *Seattle Post Intelligencer*, December 3. Available at http:/seattlepi.nwsource.com/lifestyle/150769_abercrombie.html (accessed June 4, 2008).

Paternostro, Silvana. 1998. *In the Land of God and Man: Confronting Our Sexual Culture*. New York: Dutton.

Paumgarten, Nick. 2005. "Bah Humbug Dept. Pluck You." *The New Yorker* (January 3): 23.

Pederson, April S. 1998. *What About Hooters*. New York: New Park Press.

Penley, Constance. 1988. *Feminism and Film Theory*. New York: Routledge.

Penley, Constance. 1997. *NASA/Trek: Popular Science and Sex in America*. New York: Verso.

Penley, Constance. 2004. "Crackers and Whackers: The White Trashing of Porn." In *Porn Studies*, edited by Linda Williams, 309–31. Durham, NC: Duke University Press.

Pomeroy, Wardell B. 1972. *Dr. Kinsey and the Institute for Sex Research*. New York: Harper & Row.

Poniewozik, James. 2005. "The Decency Police." *Time* (March 25): 24–31.

Ponton, Lynn. 2000. *The Sex Lives of Teenagers: Revealing the Secret World of Adolescent Boys and Girls*. New York: Penguin Putnam.

Pridal, Cathryn G., and Joseph LoPiccolo. 2000. "Multielement Treatment of Desire Disorders: Integration of Cognitive, Behavioral, and Systemic Therapy." In *Principles and Practice of Sex Therapy*, 3rd ed., edited by Sandra R. Leiblum and Raymond C. Rosen, 57–81. New York: Guilford Press.

Princess Superstar. 2001. "Bad Babysitter." *Princess Superstar Is*. Berlin: Rapster Records.

Quennell, Peter, ed. 1980. *Vladimir Nabokov: A Tribute*. New York: William Morrow & Company.

Radosh, Daniel. 2004. "The Culture Wars: Why Know?" *The New Yorker* (December 6): 46, 48.

Rechy, John. 1963. *City of the Night*. New York: Grove Press.

Regis, Pamela. 2003. *A Natural History of the Romance Novel*. Philadelphia: University of Pennsylvania Press.

Regis, Pamela. 2004. "Romance: Bestselling Popular Novelists Keep It All in the Family." *The Washington Post*, October 24, p. 13.

Reichert, Tom. 2003. *The Erotic History of Advertising*. New York: Prometheus Books.

Reichert, Tom, and Jacqueline Lambiase, eds. 2003. *Sex in Advertising: Perspectives on the Erotic Appeal*. Mahwah, NJ: Lawrence Erlbaum.

Reinholz, Mary. 2004. "Ex-Porn King Trades Sex for Salami at 2nd Ave. Deli." *The Villager* 74, no. 20 (September 15–21). Available at http://www.thevillager.com/villager_72/expornkingtradessex.html (accessed June 4, 2008).

Reisman, Judith A. 2000. *Kinsey: Crimes and Consequences: The Red Queen and the Grand Scheme*. Crestwood, KY: Institute for Media Education.

Reisman, Judith A. 2005. *Kinsey's Attic: The Shocking Story of How One Man's Sexual Pathology Changed the World*. Nashville, TN: Cumberland House.

Reisman, Judith A., Edward W. Eichel, J. Gordon Muir, John H. Court, and J. H. Court. 1990. *Kinsey, Sex and Fraud: The Indoctrination of a People*. Lafayette, LA: Huntington House.

Reiss, Ira L. 1960. *Premarital Sexual Standards in America*. New York: Free Press.

Reiss, Ira L. 1967. *The Social Context of Premarital Sexual Permissiveness*. New York: Holt, Rinehart and Winston.

Reiss, Ira L., and Harriet Reiss. 1990. *The End of Shame: Shaping Our Next Sexual Revolution*. New York: Prometheus Books.

Reuters. 2004. "TV Ads for Sex Supplement Challenged." *The Washington Post*, September 23, p. A30.

Richburg, Keith B. 2008. "The New 42nd Street, Near a Nude 8th Avenue." *The Washington Post*, January 29, p. A09.

Richlin, Amy, ed. 1992a. *Pornography and Representation in Greece and Rome*. New York: Oxford University Press.

Richlin, Amy. 1992b. Introduction to *Pornography and Representation in Greece and Rome*, edited by Amy Richlin, xi–xxiii. New York: Oxford University Press.

Ritzer, George. 1997. *Postmodern Social Theory*. New York: McGraw-Hill.

Ritzer, George. 2005. *Enchanting a Disenchanting World: Revolutionizing the Means of Consumption*. 2nd ed. Thousand Oaks, CA: Pine Forge Press.

Robbins, Harold. 1948. *Never Love a Stranger*. New York: Knopf.

Roberts, Roxanne. 2002. "Goya's Women, Enduring and Endearing." *The Washington Post*, March 11, p. C3.

Robins, J. Max. 1994. "Talkshow Producers Find Dial-a-Dilemma." *Variety*, April 11–17, pp. 45–46.

Romano, Lois. 2005. "Branson, Mo., Looks Beyond RVs and Buffets." *The Washington Post*, August 8, p. A3.

Rosen, Raymond C. 2000. "Medical and Psychological Interventions for Erectile Dysfunction: Toward a Combined Treatment Approach." In *Principles and Practice of Sex Therapy*, 3rd ed., edited by Sandra R. Leiblum and Raymond C. Rosen, 276–304. New York: Guilford Press.

Roth, Philip. 1959. *Goodbye, Columbus and Five Short Stories*. Boston: Houghton Mifflin.

Roth, Philip. 1970. *Portnoy's Complaint*. New York: Random House.

Roth, Philip. 1981. *Zuckerman Unbound*. New York: Farrar, Straus, and Giroux.

Roth, Philip. 1985. *Zuckerman Bound: A Trilogy and Epilogue*. New York: Farrar, Straus, and Giroux.

Roysner, Mark, Carlos L. Morales, and Michael Barrett. 1999. "Bibliography of the Major First Amendment Cases and the Current State of Obscenity Law in America." In *Porn 101: Eroticism, Pornography, and the First Amendment*, edited by James Elias, Veronica Diehl Elias, Vern L. Bullough, Gwen Brewer, Jeffrey J. Douglas, and Will Jarvis, 595–616. Amherst, NY: Prometheus Books.

Russell, Diana E. H. 1993. *Making Violence Sexy: Feminist Views on Pornography*. New York: Teachers College Press.

Russo, Ann. 1998. "Feminists Confront Pornography's Subordinating Practices." In *Pornography: The Production and Consumption of Inequality*, edited by Gail Dines, Robert Jensen, and Ann Russo, 9–35. New York: Routledge.

Sachs, Oliver. 2006. "A Neurologist's Notebook: Stereo Sue." *The New Yorker* (April 19): 64–73.

Safire, William. 2001. *Let a Simile Be Your Umbrella*. New York: Crown Books.

Sales, Nancy Jo. 2001. "Hugh Hefner's Roaring 70s." *Vanity Fair* (March): 236–45, 277–83.

Schaefer, Eric. 1999. *Bold! Daring! Shocking! True!: A History of Exploitation Films, 1919–1959*. Durham, NC: Duke University Press.

Scheuer, Steven H. 1985. *Movies on TV*. New York: Bantam Books.

Schlosser, Eric. 2003. *Reefer Madness: Sex, Drugs, and Cheap Labor in the American Black Market*. New York: Houghton Mifflin Company.

Schnarch, David. 2000. "Desire Problems: A Systemic Approach." In *Principles and Practice of Sex Therapy*, 3rd ed., edited by Sandra R. Leiblum and Raymond C. Rosen, 17–56. New York: Guilford Press.

Scott, Valerie X. 1971. *Surrogate Wife*. New York: Dell Press.

Seabrook, John. 2000. *Nobrow: The Culture of Marketing and the Marketing of Culture*. New York: Alfred A. Knopf.

Shales, Tom, and James Andrew Miller. 2002. *Live from New York: An Uncensored History of Saturday Night Live*. Boston: Little Brown and Company.

Shehan, Constance L. 2003. *Marriages and Families*. 2nd ed. Boston: Allyn and Bacon.

Sheidlower, Jesse, ed. 1995. *The F Word*. New York: Random House.

Sheiner, Marcy. 2002. *Ripe Fruit: Erotica for Well-Seasoned Lovers*. San Francisco: Clies Press.

Sheiner, Marcy. 2005. *Best of the Best: Women's Erotica*. San Francisco: Clies Press.

Skinner, Marilyn B. 1997. *Best of the Best: Women's Erotica*. San Francisco: Clies Press

Skinner, Marilyn B. 1997. "Introduction: *Quod Multo Fit aliter in Graecia . . . .*" In *Roman Sexualities*, edited by Judith P.Hallett and Marilyn B. Skinner, 3–25. Princeton, NJ: Princeton University Press.

Slade, Joseph W. 1999. "Inventing a Sexual Discourse: A Rhetorical Analysis of Adult Video Box Covers." In *Sexual Rhetoric: Media Perspectives on Sexuality, Gender, and Identity*, edited by Meta G. Carstarphen and Susan Zavoina, 239–54. Westport, CT: Greenwood Press.

Slade, Joseph W. 2000a. *Pornography in America: A Reference Handbook*. Santa Barbara, CA: ABC-CLIO, Inc.

Slade, Joseph W. 2000b. *Pornography and Sexual Representation: A Reference Guide*. 3 Vols. Westport, CT: Greenwood Publishing Group.

Slade, Joseph W. 2005. Personal communication. October 9. 2005.

Small, Beatrice. 2001a. *The Duchess*. New York: Ballantine Books.

Small, Beatrice. 2001b. *Intrigued*. New York: Kensington Books.

Smalley, Suzanne. 2003. "This Guy's Gone Wild." *Newsweek* (September 29): 35.

Soap Opera Weekly. 2004. *Soap Opera Weekly*. October 5, p. 8.

Southern, Terry, and Mason Hoffenberg. 1958. *Candy*. New York: Grove Press.

Specter, Michael. 2005. "Higher Risk: Crystal Meth, the Internet, and Dangerous Choices about AIDS." *The New Yorker* (May 23): 38–45.

Sprinkle, Annie. 1998. *Annie Sprinkle: Post-Porn Modernist: My 25 Years as a Multimedia Whore*. San Francisco: Cleis Press.

Squires, Carol. 1999. *Overexposed: Essays on Contemporary Photography*. New York: New Press.

Steinem, Gloria. 1980. "Erotica and Pornography: A Clear and Present Difference." In *Take Back the Night: Women on Pornography*, edited by Laura Lederer, 35–39. New York: William Morrow.

Stephens, Michael. 2003. "Richie Cunningham, Meet Linda Lovelace!" *Popmatters* (January 29). Available at http://www.popmatters.com/columns/stephens/030129.shtml (accessed June 4, 2008).

Stepp, Laura Sessions. 1999. "Parents Are Alarmed by an Unsettling New Fad in Middle Schools: Oral Sex." *The Washington Post*, July 8, p. A1.

Stepp, Laura Sessions. 2004. "For Some Teenage Girls, Sexual Preference Is a Shifting Concept." *The Washington Post*, January 25, pp. C1,C4.

Stern, Howard. 1993. *Private Parts*. New York: Simon & Schuster.

Stern, Howard. 1995. *Miss America*. New York: ReganBooks.

Strauss, Neil, and Jenna Jameson. 2004. *How to Make Love Like a Porn Star: A Cautionary Tale*. New York: Regan Books.

Streitmatter, Rodger. 2004. *Sex Sells! The Media's Journey from Repression to Suppression*. Cambridge, MA: Westview Press.

Strossen, Nadine. 1995. *Defending Pornography: Free Speech, Sex, and the Fight for Women's Rights*. New York: Scribner's.

Stuever, Hank. 2005. "Boy's Brother Details Sleepover at Neverland." *The Washington Post*, March 8, pp. C1, C7.

Talese, Gay. 1980. *Thy Neighbor's Wife*. New York: Doubleday.

Taschen, Benedikt. 1994. *Feu D'amour: Seductive Smoke*. Koln: Verlag GmbH.

Taylor, Max, and Ethel Quayle. 2003. *Child Pornography: An Internet Crime*. New York: Brunner-Routledge.

Tetlock, Philip. 2005. *Expert Political Judgment: How Good Is It? How Can We Know?* Princeton, NJ: Princeton University Press.

Theroux, Paul. 1998. "Nurse Wolf." *The New Yorker* (June 15): 51–63.

Thompson, Bob. 2004. "Fighting Indecency, One Bleep at a Time." *The Washington Post*, December 9, pp. C1, C8.

Thompson, Sharon. 1990. "Putting a Big Thing into a Little Hole: Teenage Girls' Accounts of Sexual Initiation." *Journal of Sex Research* 27:341–61.

Thompson, Sharon. 1995. *Going All the Way: Teenage Girls' Tales of Sex, Romance, and Pregnancy*. New York: Hill and Wang.

Thomson, Desson. 2004. "'Dreamers': It Now Takes Three to Tango in Paris." *The Washington Post*, February 13, pp. C1, C7.

Time. 2004. "Full Disclosure: More Actors Share Their (Private) Parts." *Time*, August 30, p. 71.

Toepfer, Karl. 1991. *Theater, Aristocracy and Pornocracy: The Orgy of Calculus*. New York: Performing Arts Journal Publications.

Torrey, E. Fuller. 1992. *Freudian Fraud: The Malignant Effect of Freud's Theory on American Thought and Culture*. San Francisco: HarperCollins.

Toth, Emily. 1981. *Inside Payton Place: The Life of Grace Metalious*. Garden City: Doubleday.

Updike, John. 2004. *Villages*. New York: Knopf.

U.S. News and World Report. 1992. *U.S. News and World Report* (June 8).

Vanity Fair. 2006. Cover. *Vanity Fair* (March).

Verstraete, Bert C. 1999. "Classical Roman Perspective on the Erotic, Obscenity, and Pornography." In *Porn 101: Eroticism, Pornography, and the First Amendment*, edited by James Elias, Veronica Diehl Elias, Vern L. Bullough, Gwen Brewer, Jeffrey J. Douglas, and Will Jarvis, 535–44. Amherst, NY: Prometheus Books.

Wagner, Jim. 2005. ".xxx Domain Gets ICANN Nod." internetnews.com, June 2. Available at http://www.internetnews.com/xSP/article.php/3509511/xxx+Domain+Gets+ICANN+Nod.htm (accessed June 4, 2008).

Washington Post, The. 2002. *The Washington Post*. April 23, p. B6.

Watson, Steven. 2003. *Factory Made: Warhol and the Sixties*. New York: Pantheon Books.

Waxman, Sharon. 1999. "The Playboy after Dark." *The Washington Post*, October 10, pp. F1, F4.

Weeks, Jeffrey. 1985. *Sexuality and Its Discontents: Meanings, Myths and Modern Sexualities*. London: Routledge & Kegan Paul.

Weeks, Linton. 2001a. "Books That May Make Parents Blush," *The Washington Post*, March 11, pp. A1, A16.

Weeks, Linton. 2001b. "Publishing—No Clothbound Editions." *The Washington Post*, October 6, p. C3.

Weinstein, James. 1999. Appendix to *Hate Speech, Pornography, and the Radical Attack on Free Speech Doctrine*, by James Weinstein, 205–8. Boulder, CO: Westview Press.

Weldon, Fay. 2004. "Carnal Knowledge." *The Washington Post, Book World*, October 24, p. 3.

Westheimer, Ruth K. 2005. *Sex for Dummies*. Jersey City, NJ: Wiley.

Williams, Linda. 1989. *Hard Core: Power, Pleasure, and the "Frenzy of the Visible."* Berkeley: University of California Press.

Williams, Linda. 1999. *Hard Core: Power, Pleasure, and the "Frenzy of the Visible"* Expanded paperback edition. Berkeley: University of California Press.

Williams, Linda, ed. 2004a. *Porn Studies.* Durham, NC: Duke University Press.

Williams, Linda. 2004b. "Porn Studies: Proliferating Pornographies On/Scene: An Introduction." In *Porn Studies*, edited by Linda Williams, 1–23. Durham, NC: Duke University Press.

Wilson, Andrew. 2007. *Harold Robbins: The Man Who Invented Sex.* London: Bloomsbury.

Wiltz, Teresa. 2003. "'The Real Cancun': Sun, Fun and Tons of Hidden Cameras." *The Washington Post*, April 25, pp. C1, C5.

Wincze, John P. 1995. "Marital Discord and Sexual Dysfunction Associated with a Male Partner's 'Sexual Addiction.'" In *Case Studies in Sex Therapy*, edited by Raymond C. Rosen and Sandra R. Lieblum, 380–92. New York: Guilford Press.

Woody, Jane DiVita. 1992. *Treating Sexual Distress.* Newbury Park, CA: Sage.

Wray, Matt, and Annalee Newitz, eds. 1996. *White Trash: Race and Gender in America.* New York: Routledge.

Wright, Bradford W. 2001. *Comic Book Nation: The Transformation of Youth Culture in America.* Baltimore: Johns Hopkins University Press.

Zawadzinski, John. 2005. "From Smut to Schmears: Al Goldstein's New Venture." *The Washington Post*, January 25.

## WEB SITES

http://www.addicted-to-romance.com
http://www.afa.net
http://www.anythingthatmoves.com/ish19/therapist
http://www.artsreformation.com
http://www.avacadell.com
http://www.babeland.com
http://www.bermancenter.com
http://www.blondflasher.com
http://www.boobfind.com.nakedmaid service
http://www.bookmark.weht.net/weht/traci_lords
http://www.briansdriveintheatre.com
http://www.ccv.org
http://www.cooltech.iafrica.com
http://www.csmonitor.com
http://www.deviantdesires.com
http://www.dpf.com
http://www.drjoekaplan.com
http://www.drjudithreisman.org
http://www.dvd-1.aldokkan.com

http://www.ellorascave.com/ebooks_explicit.htm/erotica
http://www.enough.org
http://www.en.wikipedia.org/wuju/Abercrombie_&_Fitch
http://www.ercollections.com
http://www.excaliburfilms.com/avn/linda_lovelace
http://www.explicit (R)
http://www.family.org
http://www.fangwolf.com
http://www.filmratings.com
http://www.goodvibes.com
http://www.groveatlantic.com
http://www.hootersofamerica.com
http://www.howtohavegoodsex.com
http://www.hypnovision.com
http://www.imbd.com/name/mnooo1769/bio
http://www.indiana.edu/"kinsey"
http://www.joaniblank.com
http://www.joaniblank.com/sexuality
http://www.lastgasp.com
http://www.marketwrapunwrapped.com
http://www.media-awareness/english/parents/music/inappropriate/
    explict_lyrics.cfm
http://www.mediacoalition.org
http://www.monkey.homip.net/clearing
http://www.moralityinmedia.org
http://www.nakednovelist.com
http://www.nbmpub.com
http://www.news@whitehouse.com
http://www.nostatusquo.com
http://www.nostatusquo.com/ACLU/dworkin/AutobiographyII
http://www.oralcaress/therapy.com
http://www.parentstv.org
http://www.penthouse.com/exclusives/editorial/0107_lovelace
http://www.perverted-justice.com
http://www.preview_online.com/july august/feature
http://www.protectkids.com
http://www.rogerebert.com
http://www.romantictimes.com
http://www.rottentomatoes.com
http://www.salon.com/feature/1998/07cov_02feature3
http://www.sexforwomen.net/about_us
http://www.sexforwomen.net/clit_pumps
http://www.sexpert.com
http://www.sextherapyinphiladelphia.com
http://www.sexuality.org/vena99

http://www.sexysmokers.com
http://www.sfgate.com
http://www.siecus.org/policy/index
http://www.splosh.com
http://www.sportsillustrated.cnn.com
http://www.surragatepartners.org
http://www.swingers.com
http://www.theromancereader.com
http://www.turnerlearning.comnewsrrom/ontheroad/westheimer
http://www.vkn.com/newsletters/july2003/holmes
http://www.wethighheels.com

# INDEX

Seinfeld, 174
*700 Club, The*, 58
7-Eleven stores, 51, 221n5
Sevigny, Chloe, 225n13
*Sex and the City*, 74, 173, 174,
    175–77, 213
*Sex and the Single Girl*, 39, 74
sex clubs, 24
sex coaches, 120
sex.com, 181–82
*Sex for Dummies*, 127
*Sex for One: The Joy of Selfloving*, 196
*Sex Forever*, 178
sex hygiene films, 144
*Sex in the Desert*, 178
Sex Information and Education
    Council of the United States
    (SIECUS), 195, 198
*Sex Life of a Cop*, 68, 69
sex pioneers, 38, 39, 115
*Sex Positions*, 126
sex therapy, 22
sex therapy critics, 123
*Sex Toys 101*, 197
Sexology Society of America, 129
sex-surrogate therapy, 118
sexual addiction, 121, 122
*Sexual Behavior of the Human Female*,
    90
*Sexual Behavior of the Human Male*, 90
sexual discourse, 1, 12, 14–15, 17,
    20–25, 36, 39, 42, 43, 70, 71, 72,
    77–78, 89, 92, 102, 116, 117, 119,
    120, 122, 125, 127, 130, 136, 150,
    155, 171, 176, 195, 198, 202, 203,
    204, 206, 207, 208, 210, 226n5
sexual fetish Web sites, 190–95
sexual intercourse, 85
*Sexual Life of Catherine M., The*, 5, 65
*Sexuality and Its Discontents*, 25
sexual nymphet, 82
sexual representation, 107
*Sexual Revolution, The*, 19
sexual violence, 49
Shales, Tom, 226n4

*Shame Agent*, 33
Shaw, George Bernard, 44
Shawn, William, 76
Shehan, Constance L., 209
Sheidlower, Jesse, 227n12
Sheiner, Marcy, 5
Sheridan, Nicolette, 58
*Shield, The*, 217
shock jocks, 37
shopping malls, 1
SIECUS. *See* Sex Information and
    Education Council of the United
    States
Silverman, Sarah, 178
Simon and Schuster, 82
*Simple Life, The*, 172
Sinclair Institute, 128
Singer, Mark, 221n6
Siriono of South America, 97
Skinner, Marilyn B., 93
Slade, Joseph W., 34, 35, 106, 107,
    112, 136, 138, 140, 220n2, 221n4
Small, Beatrice, 83, 84
Smalley, Suzanne, 154
Smith, Linnea, 78
Smith College, 53
smoking women fetish, 192
smut, 44
smut peddler, 72
*Soap Opera Weekly*, 169
*Social Organization of Sexuality, The*,
    101
"social purity" movement, 45
social scientists' sex research, 97–101
social values debate, 17
*Soft Core: Moral Crusades Against
    Pornography in Britain and the
    United States*, 220n12
Somers, Suzanne, 167
*Sopranos, The*, 173, 177, 213
Southern, Terry, 80
Southland Corporation, 51
Soviet Union, 26
Specter, Michael, 24, 200
Spiderman, 6

DATE DUE